MAO TSE-TUNG

MAO TSE-TUNG

ROBERT PAYNE

WEYBRIGHT AND TALLEY

NEW YORK

PHOTO CREDITS

Page 1 EASTFOTO: *Page* 2 EMIL SCHULTHESS *from* BLACK STAR: *Page* 3 *middle,* WIDE WORLD PHOTOS; *bottom,* MARC RIBOUD *from* MAGNUM PHOTOS: *Page* 4 EARL LEAF *from* RAPHO GUILLUMETTE PICTURES: *Page* 5 WIDE WORLD PHOTOS: *Page* 8 HARRISON FORMAN *from* PIX: *Page* 9 HARRISON FORMAN *from* PIX: *Pages* 12 & 13 EASTFOTO: *Page* 13 CAMERA PRESS *from* PIX: *Page* 16 EARL LEAF *from* RAPHO GUILLUMETTE PICTURES.

Published in the United States by
WEYBRIGHT AND TALLEY, INC.
3 East 54th Street
New York, New York 10022

Published simultaneously in Canada by
CLARKE, IRWIN & COMPANY LIMITED,
Toronto and Vancouver

Library of Congress Catalog Card No. 68-17753

PRINTED IN THE UNITED STATES OF AMERICA

CONTENTS

MAO TSE-TUNG

THE FORERUNNERS

FROM THE EARLIEST times, China has been plagued with peasant revolts. Small groups of disaffected peasants, hiding in the forests or the marshes, have sometimes extended their power until the emperor has been toppled from his throne. The pattern of the peasant revolt seems to have been established before history came to be written, for traces of these revolts can be found in the very earliest documents; and many of the poems of the classical *Book of Songs* hint at peasant defeats and peasant victories. In the long history of China the war between the peasants and the central government has been continuous; and it is still going on.

It could hardly be otherwise, given the nature of the Chinese peasantry and the feudal ownership of land. The Chinese peasant lives on the margin of existence: there are only a few regions where he can hope to make a profit from the Chinese earth. Floods, drought, epidemics, and invasions have added to his insecurity. To survive, the peasants have always banded themselves together in mutual assistance societies; inevitably these societies acquire their own passwords, their own grand masters, their own

1

dogmas. The Chinese secret societies nearly always began as perfectly harmless mutual assistance societies. In time, as they grew more powerful, they threatened the throne.

We know very little about the operations of the secret societies, whose histories were rarely recorded, but we know enough to realize that they formed over many centuries a shadow government which ruled as effectively as the legal government. These societies had their high officials, their tax-gatherers, their stores of arms: they infiltrated into the government, appointed local governors, recruited their own armies. The peasants obeyed them more readily than they obeyed the commands issuing from the capital, for the capital was far away, but the secret societies were very close to them. The feudal lords were themselves sometimes members of these societies, thus complicating the issue. For the most part the secret societies reflected the ideas of the peasants, who were naturally rebellious, for they had nothing to lose.

When the Chinese Communists established themselves in Yenan in the remote borderlands of northwest China, they were following the established practice of Chinese rebels. By carving out a principality for themselves beyond the reach of the central government, and using it as a base, they were merely following a practice hallowed by long usage. Though they claimed to be Marxists, their methods of thought and propaganda were not markedly different from those of the secret societies. Long before the Communist armies conquered China, they had sapped the strength of the Kuomintang by the same methods employed by the secret societies in their wars against the reigning dynasties.

The White Lotus Society

The oldest and most deeply rooted of the secret societies is the White Lotus Society, which still survives, though it no longer wields its former vast and shadowy influence.

Originally it came into existence when a small group of devoted men gathered around the Buddhist monk, Hua Yin, at a place called Lushan, south of the Yangtse. Hua Yin died in A.D. 416, and the first meeting of the society seems to have taken place around A.D. 380. There were only eighteen devotees. They studied, prayed, and meditated together, learning from the monk the doctrines of Amitabha pietism, taking as their symbol the white lotus, which rises to the surface of the water when the sun appears, and sinks down at night. The lotus with its roots in the mud and its petals opening upon the world is of course a characteristic Buddhist symbol, and these young men were indistinguishable from thousands of other devotees of Buddhism except that they were unusually ascetic, wore gray gowns, walked barefoot, and as a sign of their new-found faith sometimes wore a white lotus looped over one ear.

With the death of Hua Yin, the White Lotus Society gradually lost its purely religious character. By 1133 it had emerged as a powerful secret society dedicated to the overthrow of the Sung emperors, and when the Mongols rode into China in triumph the secret society made peace with the invaders until it became evident that the Mongols were determined to uproot Chinese customs and to destroy the secret societies. The struggle against the Mongols was led by the monk Chu Yuan-chang, who rallied all the members of the White Lotus Society against the enemy. By 1368 the Mongol power was overthrown, and the monk became the Emperor Hung Wu, the founding emperor of the Ming dynasty.

The revolt against the Mongols was a peasant revolt, led by peasants. Chu Yuan-chang was the son of poor peasants in the province of Anhwei. He was seventeen when an epidemic carried off his entire family and he entered a monastery. He was twenty-five when he led his first raiding parties against the towns, forbidding his soldiers to loot, with the result that he was hailed as a liberator and soon a vast army was flocking to his banners. In 1356 he conquered Nanking. During the following years he occupied all the region south of the Yangtse. When his armies were approaching Peking, the Mongol Emperor fled to Mongolia. Some years later the White Lotus Society, which had brought the Emperor to power, was proscribed. Yet it continued to exist, especially in the south.

The Ming dynasty lasted for nearly three hundred years,

dying of old age and corruption. The Manchus poured over the frontier. During the early years of Manchu domination the White Lotus Society was quiescent. There were revolts led by the White Lotus Society in 1760. The Emperor Ch'ien Lung issued an imperial rescript commanding that all leading members of the society be apprehended and beheaded; less important members were to be punished with a hundred blows of a heavy bamboo, crippling them for life. The revolts continued, clouding the last years of the Emperor's life. By 1807 large areas of south China had fallen into the hands of the White Lotus Society: the new Emperor ordered mass executions in the towns and villages which had sworn allegiance to the society. Accordingly the White Lotus Society sentenced the new Emperor to death. In 1812, when the Emperor was entering the Forbidden City in a palanquin, a Manchu cook savagely attacked him. The Emperor was wounded, and three guards were cut down before help arrived. By the Emperor's decree the cook was punished by being made to watch the beheading of his sons, who were innocent. Afterward the cook was given "the torture of the thousand knives," which leads to a slow death. He was a member of the White Lotus Society.

Two years later the society attacked again. Three hundred men disguised as farmers carrying baskets filled with persimmons appeared at the gate of the Forbidden City. Instead of the white lotus, they wore white chicken feathers looped over their ears. Previously they had concealed weapons in the eunuchs' quarters within the Forbidden City, for they had willing helpers inside the purple walls. At a given signal they attacked, forced their way through the gates, took possession of their weapons, and for the rest of the morning and most of the afternoon they fought off the imperial guards. Once more the dynasty had escaped by a hair-breadth. It was learned later that all preparations had been made to fire the Forbidden City, but a single eunuch defected. All the conspirators were tortured to death.

After this the White Lotuses went underground. They changed their names, proliferated into various sects, and while opposing the reigning emperor they also threw their weight against the foreigners who were beginning to descend upon China like a cloud of locusts. They became the White Clouds, White Fans, White Eyebrows, followers of the Society of the Eight Diagrams and of the Divine Mother. In 1900 they assumed the name of the Society of the Righteous Fists, which we know as the Boxers. Dr. Sun Yat-sen was a member of the White Lotus Society, and it is believed that his battle flag, with a white sun on a blue field, derives from the white lotus rising out of the blue water. The flag is now used by the Nationalist Chinese.

The Taiping Rebellion

For at least eight hundred years the White Lotus Society was a revolutionary power, making and unmaking emperors, extending its mysterious authority over entire provinces, deriving its strength from the peasantry organized in permanent opposition to the central government. Dangerous and all pervasive, it was all the more powerful for being invisible. The local leader might be a monk, a humble farmer, or the feudal lord of immense estates. These men did not always start rebellions, but whenever rebellions broke out they hurried to fan the flames. When the Taiping Rebellion broke out in the Yangtse Valley in the middle years of the last century, they were among the first to come to the aid of the rebels and must bear some responsibility for the endless massacres that occurred. There are Chinese authorities who believe that forty million perished before the uprising was put down.

In all Chinese history nothing is so strange as the sudden, disastrous emergence of the Taiping princes to power. An obscure peasant from Kwangtung, who believed devoutly in Christianity and who called himself "the younger brother of God" and "the Prince of Heaven," led a national movement against the Manchus, ruled central China as emperor for many years, and went down to defeat, leaving no traces of the Christian and theocratic empire he had brought into being.

Tall, thin, with a slight stammer, unusually large almond eyes, and delicate small ears, Hung Hsiu-ch'uan in his youth was probably the last person anyone would have believed to be a future emperor of China and a consummate revolutionary. He was

handsome, moody, and intractable. He belonged to the Hakka
race, which had come down from the north to the coastal regions
of Kwangtung and had never become assimilated to the native
population. Born near Canton, in a small village, he had set himself when very young to become a scholar: he would take the
imperial examinations and so rise to high position in the Manchu
government.

He failed in the examination when he was sixteen. He believed that his failure was at least partly due to his ancestry:
seven generations previously there had been members of his family
fighting against the Manchus. He brooded over his failure, and
attempted the examination again three years later. He failed
again. Altogether he failed four times, and each time he suffered
a kind of nervous breakdown. The third failure, in 1837, appears
to be the one which affected him most. He lay prostrate in bed
with a high fever, and during the fever he experienced the visions
which were to change the course of Chinese history.

These visions began simply enough. First he saw a dragon,
a cock, and a tiger; then there came a great multitude of men
playing musical instruments who approached with a beautiful
sedan chair, on which he was transported to the neighborhood of
a heavenly mansion. For a while he rested among green fields;
then an old woman came to bathe him in a stream. Shortly
afterward an old man came with a knife: the visionary's heart
and entrails were removed and replaced with new ones. Soon he
was led to the heavenly mansion, where he was received by an
old man who is described as "most ancient, wearing a gold beard
and a long black robe." This was God, who said, "All human
beings in the world are produced and sustained by me. They eat
my food and wear my clothing, but not a single one among them
has the heart to remember and venerate me: they worship
demons, they rebel against me, and they arouse my anger." Then
God offered him a sword, a gold signet ring, and a yellow fruit.
Finally, God took him to a high mountain from which he could
look down on all the kingdoms of the world. Here Hung Hsiu-
ch'uan received the command to destroy utterly all those who
opposed God's will, for God could no longer endure the sight

of the depravity and sin which existed in the world. When he woke up from the fever, Hung Hsiu-ch'uan went running madly around the room in his sickness, shouting in his Hakka dialect: "Tsan ah! Tsan ah! Slay the demons! There is one and there is another. Many cannot withstand one single blow of my sword."

At that moment he was clearly mad; but he recovered quickly. He worried about the meaning of the vision and began to wonder whether, after all, it might not have been a direct message from God. He remembered nine small pamphlets given to him by Liang A-fah, a missionary belonging to the London Missionary Society. These pamphlets, issued under the title Good Words Exhorting the Age, constituted an almost incredible olla podrida. Here were religious discourses, sermons, paraphrases, a fragment of Liang A-fah's autobiography, and translations of some of the more imaginative chapters of the Bible. The whole of the first chapter of Genesis was included; so was the nineteenth psalm; so were the first and fifty-eighth chapters of Isaiah and the fifth chapter of Ephesians, and long passages from Revelation. In particular, Revelation seems to have affected Hung Hsiu-ch'uan. Had he not seen the demons becoming birds and lions? The apocalypse was at hand, and he was the cherished evangel.

After his fourth failure, Hung Hsiu-ch'uan wandered away among the hills of Kwangsi, selling pens. He had wanted to be a scholar. Instead, he was a poor beggar who had suffered a vision. Gradually, he drew about him a small but devoted band of followers who believed in him implicitly. There were famines in Kwangsi, and with them came a sudden outbreak of idol-destroying. Hung Hsiu-ch'uan urged upon his followers the destruction of all Buddhist and Taoist idols. Curiously, he omitted to urge them to destroy the Confucian tablets, perhaps because he remained half a Confucian to the end. Soon, joining forces with the White Lotus Society, he established himself in the marshy and hilly regions where the three provinces of Kwangtung, Kwangsi, and Hunan meet. Like all rebels against the government, he found safety in the border regions. It was here that he inaugurated the society, called the Shang Ti Hui, or the "Society of the Highest God."

He was biding his time. He spoke of his vision to everyone
who cared to listen, already calling himself "the younger brother
of God." It is probable that he was completely unaware that God
had said in the vision what Hung Hsiu-ch'uan himself desired to
say: had not God worn the black robe of the poor scholars of
the time? God demanded vengeance of the world. His words
expressed the vengeance which Hung Hsiu-ch'uan himself desired
to exact from the world, for his own failure in the examinations;
and God's final words, with their nihilist violence, echoed across
the centuries the terrible tablet which the mad General Chang
Hsien-chung ordered to be engraved in Chengtu during the Ming
Dynasty, after he had slaughtered thirty million inhabitants of
Szechuan—slaughtering so well that eighty years later Father de
Mailla declared that in spite of every care and privilege Szechuan
had not recovered from the catastrophe. The message on the
tablet read:

> Heaven brings forth innumerable things to support man.
> Man has not one thing with which to recompense Heaven.
> Kill. Kill. Kill. Kill. Kill. Kill. Kill. Kill. Kill.

But, though the movement which Hung Hsiu-ch'uan began gave
signs, in its origins, of a nihilist violence, its development showed
that he possessed a quite extraordinary insight into Chinese politics, and that he understood the social problems which weighed
upon China.

In the border regions he published his divine commission:
"We command the services of all, and we take everything. All
who resist us are rebels and idolatrous demons, and we shall kill
them without sparing. But whoever acknowledges the Prince of
Heaven and exerts himself in our service shall have a full reward."
He called himself "the Prince of Heaven," and he published five
new gospels, including a Book of Celestial Decrees and The Revelations of the Heavenly Father.

The strange epic had hardly begun. Hung Hsiu-ch'uan had
assumed a title, but he possessed no empire over which to rule.
Now, with the help of an early convert named Feng Yun-shan,
who received the title "Prince of the South," Hung set about

conquering China. Under his command he had hardly more than three thousand men and women armed with spears and pitchforks, distinguished by the bright red cloth turbans which held up their long hair.

The war, which was later to lead the rebels almost to the gates of Peking, began in 1848. Hung Hsiu-ch'uan's peasant columns descended from the hills, seized small villages, converted the villagers, and then withdrew to the hills. There were a few hastily fought battles with imperial garrisons. The guerrillas, who called themselves "the little children of God," already possessed a sense of purpose, and they were ruled by a hard taskmaster, who invoked the Mosaic law to punish them whenever they disobeyed his commands. The small battles were easily won. The popular faith in the Prince of Heaven deepened, for was he not God indeed? And would they not go immediately to Heaven when they were killed in battle? Seeing his happy bands of guerrillas at work, the Prince of Heaven could reflect that only a small knife was needed to open China.

A peasant uprising in the winter of 1850 against the tax-gatherers led to a sudden increase in the size of his armies, for though the rebellion in Kwangsi was suppressed, the survivors flocked to his banners. He now felt himself strong enough to attack walled towns. Six months later, on August 27, 1851, the market town of Yunganchow was captured, and there, in the market place, wearing the imperial robe with the five-clawed dragons embroidered upon it, Hung Hsiu-ch'uan announced the creation of a new dynasty, to be called *Taiping Tienkuo*, or "the Heavenly Kingdom of Great Peace." He gave himself the dynastic title *Tien Teh*, or "Heavenly Virtue." Here, too, he made an appeal for universal brotherhood and wrote a poem called "The Awakening of the World," in which he announced the social purpose of the revolution. "We are the light, and should fight against darkness," it says. "We desire to build the fallen society so that the world shall become just, the strong shall not oppress the weak, the wise exploit the ignorant, or the brave impose upon the timid." At last he was welding his own visions of kingship with a far more powerful force—the peasant revolt.

From this moment there begins the story of the Prince of Heaven who hoped to impose Communism on China.

The victory at Yunganchow was followed by reverses. By creating a new dynasty, Hung Hsiu-ch'uan had raised the standard of open rebellion. He was openly building up his armies and buying arms. The government in Peking was alarmed and sent the Emperor's chief minister, Saishangah, with thirty thousand imperial troops, to reduce the town. Yunganchow was surrounded and an attempt was made to starve it into submission. The imperial armies arrived in December, and it was not until April that a small band of Hung Hsiu-ch'uan's followers, numbering no more than three or four thousand, escaped through the enemy lines. They moved westward, in the direction of Hunan, and somewhere along the borders of Hunan the dispirited group of survivors of the new dynasty encountered one of the most mysterious men in Chinese history. His name was Chu Kiu-t'ao, he was a Hunanese and a military genius of the highest order, and almost everything else about him is unknown, except that he too had failed in the provincial examinations and like Hung Hsiu-ch'uan was descended from a clan which had fought for the Ming dynasty against the Manchus, and he was consumed with the desire to overthrow the foreigners who ruled in Peking. Unlike Hung Hsiu-ch'uan, he was not moved by visionary dreams. For years he had secluded himself in a monastery, where he studied military tactics. He had met Hung Hsiu-ch'uan somewhere in Kwangtung in 1844. They had kept up a correspondence, and they seem to have sworn blood brotherhood at some stage in their acquaintance. From this point onward, until he disappeared into obscurity, the Hunanese took command of the Taiping armies, and welded them together into a force so powerful that in time the Prince of Heaven was able to say that he had thirty million soldiers and could if he desired have conquered the world.

To Chu Kiu-t'ao goes the credit for introducing organization where none existed before. Until this time the army consisted of volunteers; he introduced conscription. He gave the Taipings their military system of squadrons, companies, battalions, and divisions; he made a professional army out of the guerrillas. He introduced

the strictest discipline. No one in the army was allowed to re-
quisition food; everything must be paid for. Rape was punished
with death. The soldiers were ordered to carry their own cooking
utensils, oils, and salt, and they were not permitted to enter any
dwelling place unless invited. All had to attend morning and
evening prayers. The smoking of opium in the army was absolutely forbidden. He gave women a privileged position in the
army, and he arranged for the families of soldiers in service to
be supported from a common treasury. All these regulations were
enforced. He was also responsible for the introduction of a form
of Communism in the army. He based his entire administrative
system on a unit of twenty-five households, the largest unit, comprising 12,500 households, being known as a *chun*, or army. He
arranged for each communal unit of twenty-five households to
possess its own treasury and its own church. The fields were to
be tilled in common. Food, clothing, and money were to be used
in common, and the surplus of the harvest reverted to the communal treasury. He advocated that the private ownership of land
be abolished, and he began very early to organize a system of
promotion in the army based on the recommendations of soldiers
who acted as guarantors of those who were promoted. In the
proclamations of the time there can be detected a hard residue,
which clearly comes from Chu Kiu-t'ao, embedded in the soft
visionary declamations of the Prince of Heaven.

But most of this lay in the future. Chu Kiu-t'ao was busy
organizing his army and leading it along the Hsiang River toward
Changsha, hammering out of an army equipped with bows and
arrows, sabers, and pitchforks, an incredibly hard-hitting force.
All the towns and villages along the Hsiang River were occupied,
the Taoist and Buddhist idols overthrown. Because his soldiers
neither pillaged nor plundered, and because they sided with the
peasants against the landlords, the army gained in numbers; and
they were fifty thousand when they reached the gates of Changsha
on September 18, five months after the escape from Yunganchow.
Here they halted. They intended to besiege the city, but the
resistance of the garrison was far greater than they had expected,
and in November they were compelled to raise the seige.

Though Changsha held out, the Yangtse Valley offered softer material for the Taipings. In January 1853, Hankow, Wu-chang, and Hanyang were in their hands. Almost immediately they fitted out war vessels and sailed down the Yangtse River. In the beginning of March they were outside Nanking, and ten days later they were butchering twenty thousand Manchus who had remained in the city. In May a column led by Li Hsin-cheng, a Taiping general who had once been a charcoal-seller, came almost in sight of Peking, and they might have conquered the capital if the Mongol general, Sankolinsin (known to British soldiers as "Sam Collinson"), had not fought them off. The Taiping armies turned south. They marched through Fukien, Szechuan, and Kwangtung; and Yeh Ming-shen, the fiery Hunan-ese viceroy who was later to be captured by the British and sent into exile in Calcutta, turned away from the contem-plation of a coastal war with the British to observe: "Our whole country swarms with rebels. Our funds are nearly at an end, and our troops are few. The commander of the imperial forces thinks he can put out a bonfire with a thimbleful of water. I fear that we shall have hereafter some serious affairs, and the great body of the people will rise up against us and our own followers will leave us."

Meanwhile, foreign opinion concerning the Taipings was divided. "I hope Tien Teh will be successful," wrote an official of a Shanghai company to Humphrey Marshall, the American commissioner. "We cannot be worse off, and he is said to be a liberal man." Bishop George Smith, speaking in Trinity Church, Shanghai, delighted in the new outbreak of Christianity. "Dynas-ties and thrones are crumbling in the dust," he said, his eyes on the tottering Peacock Throne in Peking.

Other missionaries deplored the eighty-eight consecrated wives and unnumbered concubines of the Prince of Heaven. All were perhaps secretly afraid of him and the strange power he exerted over the faithful.

The Taipings had spread like wildfire over South China, they had threatened Peking, they were introducing reforms on an unprecedented scale, and to none of them would it have occurred that their fate depended upon the decisions of a Kentucky lawyer, who had been chosen for the post of American commissioner in Shanghai only after it had been formally offered to three others and declined. Humphrey Marshall graduated from West Point, served two terms in Congress, and at the outbreak of the Civil War he was to become a brigadier general in the Confederate Army. He knew no Chinese, and he was pitifully vain, dictatorial, and ignorant. He arrived in China in January 1853. By April he had come to the conclusion that the Taiping rebels would overthrow the existing dynasty, but in the next month, having heard that Sir George Bonham had attended the Prince of Heaven at his court, he suddenly reversed his position. He became suspicious of the British minister, and especially of the minister's interpreter, and he began to believe that the British desired to exercise a protectorate over the Taipings. When he heard that the Manchus had received an offer of protection from the Czar, he reported to the Secretary of State his fears for the future. The letter is important, for it bears heavily on events which happened a hundred years later.

> Her [Russia's] assistance would probably end in passing China under a Russian protectorate, and in the extension of Russian limits to the Hoangho, or the mouth of the Yangtse; or, it may be, when circumstances and policy shall favor the scheme, in the partition of China between Great Britain and Russia. The interference of the Czar would readily suppress the rebellion, by driving the rebels from the great highways of commerce, and from the occupation of the towns on the seaboard. Whatever might be the ultimate compensation demanded by Russia for this timely service, China could not resist its collection.
>
> I think that almost any sacrifice should be made by the United States to keep Russia from spreading her Pacific boundary, and to avoid her coming directly to interference in Chinese domestic affairs; for China is like a lamb before the shearers, as easy a conquest as were the provinces of India. Wherever the avarice or ambition of Russia or Great Britain shall tempt them to make the prizes, the fate of Asia will be sealed, and the future Chinese

relations with the United States may be considered as closed for
ages, unless now the United States shall foil the untoward result
by adopting a sound policy.

It is my opinion that the highest interests of the United
States are involved in sustaining China—maintaining order here,
and gradually engrafting on this worn-out stock the healthy
principles which give life and health to governments, rather than
to see China become the theatre of widespread anarchy, and
ultimately the prey of European ambition.*

The letter is illuminating, for Marshall represented a hard
core of merchant opinion in Shanghai. The rumor concerning the
the Czar was false; he never referred to it again, but he never
changed his opinion about the necessity of "maintaining order."
There was widespread sympathy for the Taipings in America.
His government ordered him to make contact with them. He
refused. Hardly conscious of the effect of his actions, he was
setting down the policy which was to lead eventually to the
débacle of 1949.

Meanwhile the Prince of Heaven ruled from the Heavenly
City, wielding his imperial powers with considerably more understanding of the problems of the Chinese people than the Manchus
in the north. He instituted equality of the sexes, inveighed against
slavery and concubinage, and forbade foot-binding and the wearing of the queue. Even more important, in the third year of his
assumption of power, he introduced agrarian reforms, dividing
the land into nine classes, graded according to the fertility of the
soil; for example, one *mou* of the highest class of land was
equivalent to three *mou* of the lowest. Land was to be allotted
according to the number of mouths in the family, though some
preference was given to men over sixteen and under fifty, largely

---

* The full text of the letter is given in Tyler Dennet, *Americans in Eastern
Asia* (New York, 1941), pp. 214–15. Fear of the British was strong at this
time. Nikolai Muraviev, the governor general of eastern Siberia, wrote in
1850, when a young and short-lived Chinese emperor was coming to the
throne: "The British will use this change to seize control of not only the
trade but also the policies of China." But it shoud be added that Muraviev
only rarely represented public Russian opinion, and the anarchist Bakunin
described him as the one Russian in high position "who can and must fully
and without the least reservation be considered one of us."

because these were the men who formed the army. He proposed the complete redistribution of the land and stated his program most succinctly when he declared: "All shall eat food, all shall have clothes, money shall be shared, and in all things there shall be equality: no man shall be without food or warmth."

These social and agrarian reforms sprang from the movement he led. They were deeply religious, but they corresponded to the age-old desires of the peasantry. They destroyed the land titles, exactly as the Chinese Communists were to destroy land titles later, and nearly all the reforms first instituted by the Taipings were followed by the Chinese Communists, almost to the letter. There is no evidence that the reforms were instituted as the result of any knowledge of foreign social doctrine, and though the Communist Manifesto appeared during the rule of the Taipings, it was not translated into Chinese until thirty years later. And it was not only the peasantry which demanded these reforms: the merchants and the gentry had their own grievances against the Manchus, and so, too, had the educated classes, the scholars who were at the mercy of the Manchu academies.

For more than a decade the Prince of Heaven ruled over the Yangtse Valley. Feng Yun-shan, the Prince of the South, died fighting in 1852. Chu Kiu-t'ao, the Prince of the West, mysteriously disappeared, and his place as the chief military strategist was taken by General Li Hsin-cheng, now elevated to the title of Chung Wang or "Faithful Prince." But not everything went well with the Taipings. Those who had taken part in the long march from Yunganchow to Nanking received preference, and discrimination began to undermine the morale of the army. Discipline began to fail. In the upper hierarchies a strange violence broke out. Yang Hsiu-ch'ing, the Prince of the East, had claimed to be the holy spirit and on one occasion exercised the privilege of scourging the Prince of Heaven on the strength of a revelation received, but he fell into disfavor and was executed. Worse still, the puritanical laws of the Taipings were being exchanged for license. The foreigners watched. In 1860 they decided to strike. Curiously, the foreigners did not strike their first blows at the Taipings. They struck at Peking, captured Taku, destroyed the

Emperor's Summer Palace, demanded an indemnity of eight million taels for their trouble in destroying so much splendor, and
only later launched a campaign against the Taipings. First an
American, Frederick Townsend Ward, and later an Englishman,
General Gordon, helped the Manchus to recover their lost territory; and there was formed an Ever Victorious Army under
foreign leadership to fight against the Long-Haired Army of the
Taipings. Both sides fought mercilessly; the Manchus fought
treacherously.

On December 4, 1863, four surviving Taiping princes under
a safe conduct from General Gordon surrendered Soochow. They
came with their long hair falling down their backs, in yellow
robes and wearing royal crowns. They sued for terms: they proposed that they should receive commissions in the imperial army
and that their followers should be enrolled among the imperial
troops, and that part of the city should be assigned to them for
a place d'armes. Instead, they were summarily executed, and some
time later General Gordon resigned his commission on the
grounds that their execution was an act of unpardonable treachery.

There followed eighteen months of sporadic fighting, but by
now the tide was turning. On June 1, 1865, the great Hunanese
scholar-soldier Tseng Kuo-fan completed the close investment of
Nanking, and within a month the strange genius Hung Hsiu-
ch'uan had committed suicide by poison, his body being buried
behind his palace by one of his wives. On July 19 the city fell.
The Chung Wang escaped on horseback, carrying in his arms
the son of the Taiping Emperor, but both were captured and
executed, though the death of the Chung Wang was delayed a
week to enable him to complete the writing of his memoirs. All
the defenders of the city were put to death, and all the members
of the Prince of Heaven's family were dismembered. There were
left only the armies of Prince Shih Ta-k'ai, known as the Helping
Prince: they were pursued into the remote gorges of the Tatu
River on the frontiers of Tibet and cut down by the armies of
Tseng Kuo-fan. Eighty years later the Chinese Communists, during their own Long March, came upon the weapons of these
rebels against the Manchu empire. Some of their spears could

still be sharpened: they picked up these relics of an ancient war and used them in their own battles.

The Taiping empire fell, but the causes which brought it into being remained. The strength of the Taipings lay in the visions of the Cantonese, Hung Hsiu-ch'uan, and the administrative genius of the mysterious Hunanese, Chu Kiu-t'ao, and their social policy which obeyed a classic canon derived from the Confucian *Book of Rites.* "All the families in every place will be equally provided for, while every individual will be well fed and well clothed," wrote the Prince of Heaven; and the social form attempted by the Taipings approached a primitive communism. They destroyed private property. They regarded themselves as people with the mission to share the world's wealth equally among the world's inhabitants, and they used the phrase, "The wealth must be shared," a phrase which the Chinese Communists were to employ later when they came to name their party *Kung-ch'an-tang,* or "the Sharing Wealth party." The remarkable similarities between the programs of the Taipings and the Chinese Communists should not be underestimated: both drew their strength from the same common cause.

In *China's Destiny,* Chiang Kai-shek dismissed the Taipings as ignorant and stupid men entirely outside the current of Chinese history. Sun Yat-sen, with more reason, claimed that the Kuomintang had come into existence to complete what the Taipings had only begun.

The Reformers: Yen Fu and K'ang Yu-wei

Yen Fu and K'ang Yu-wei never held guns, but they, too, changed the course of Chinese history. Coming before the revolution—their most imposing work was accomplished under the Manchus—they subtly changed the atmosphere of the time. The defeat of the Taipings had confirmed the Manchu empress in her contempt for social change, but vast social and intellectual changes were occurring nevertheless.

A young naval cadet called Yen Fu returned from the Naval College at Greenwich with a rough draft of a translation of

Darwin's *Origin of Species* in his pocket, completed the translation in Peking, and had it published. The Empress Dowager read the book, admired the classical perfection of his prose, and shook her head uncomprehendingly. Of course, it was nonsense to say that men were descended from apes, but if it was clearly indicated that this was a foreign belief, it only made the foreigners appear more stupid in Chinese eyes.

More and more translations by Yen Fu appeared. He translated Huxley's *Evolution and Ethics*, Adam Smith's *Wealth of Nations*, Herbert Spencer's *The Principles of Sociology*, Montesquieu's *De l'Esprit des Lois*, which became almost a handbook for the students of Peking at the beginning of the century. More important, he translated John Stuart Mill's *On Liberty*, though necessarily he gave the book a more innocuous title. In all he translated more than 112 books from five languages, even from languages of which he was entirely ignorant. He was still translating vigorously when he died in 1920, having spent the last thirty years of his life translating one book after another. He was not a good translator. He was often inaccurate. He had a habit of adding commentaries, and he delighted in showing similarites between foreign opinion and Confucian doctrine, even when, as often occurred, there were no similarities at all.

His innate Confucianism had important consequences. The philosophy and the social sciences of the West penetrated China in Confucian clothing. A few of his books were banned by imperial edict: most of them were in wide circulation throughout even the most troubled times of the Empress Dowager's reign. Reading these authors in translation, Chinese scholars could feel that they were reading some lost classics which might have appeared at the time of Confucius, so antiquated was the style, so solemn the presentation of the perennial problems of government. Confucius, that vast image which the Chinese have erected as a mirror of themselves, seemed indeed to be leading the West into the Chinese fold.

Yen Fu translated the documents, but K'ang Yu-wei, a Cantonese who came like Hung Hsiu-ch'uan from a village near Canton, put them to use. Like the Prince of Heaven, he suffered an apocalyptic vision of the whole world at peace. Standing on the Bund in Shanghai, it occurred to him quite suddenly that all the vast resources of modern industry, steamships, the telegraph, the postal service, even the destructiveness of modern weapons, were moving the world toward a stage where a single empire or a single world state became inevitable. He had read Yen Fu's translations. He knew something about the mechanics of Western thought. He also knew Confucius, and he knew the theory, expressed in the Confucian *Book of Rites*, of the three stages of peace and contentment.

He was so impressed with his vision that he returned to Canton and surrounded himself with young students with the express purpose of discovering whether his dream was valid. With a vast knowledge of Confucianism and Buddhism, and deep learning of the Sung and Ming philosophies, he examined the histories of the East and the West, coming to the conclusion that the most dangerous disease of all was nationalism, and that the most dreadful torments awaited the world if this disease was allowed to remain unchecked. He admired the West for its industry, its parliaments, its inventiveness, its unquenchable desire to tame the elements; he particularly admired the institution of the ballot box. He turned to the chapter called "The Evolution of Rites," in the *Book of Rites*. There you could read that the world would pass through the stage of disorder and confusion, followed by a stage of "small tranquility," until finally there came the stage of "great unity":

> When the great *Tao* was practiced, the world was common to all men: men of talents, virtue, and ability were selected; sincerity was emphasized, and friendship was cultivated. Therefore, men do not love only their own parents, nor did they treat as children only their own sons. Provision was secured for the aged until their death, employment was given to the able-bodied, and means were provided for the upbringing of the young. Kindness and compassion were shown to widows, orphans, childless men, and those who were disabled by disease, so that all had the wherewithal for support. Men had their proper work, women had their homes. They hated to see the wealth of natural resources unde-

veloped, but when they developed these resources, they did not put them to their own use. They hated not to work, but when they worked, it was for the common profit. This was known as the Great Unity (Ta Tung).

It was a dream which was to haunt the Chinese, who stated and restated it in a thousand poems. It was the significance of K'ang Yu-wei that he interpreted the dream in modern terms and was the first to envisage Confucius as a social reformer.

For K'ang Yu-wei the famous phrase Ta Tung had vast social implications, but to the end of his days he remained the dreamer, living in proud isolation in a foreign settlement in Shanghai, annotating the classics, seeing the world still in terms of the fantasy of his dream. It was left to Mao Tse-tung to employ the ancient Confucian phrase for a practical purpose, and he was probably the first to see how the phrase could be harnessed to the Chinese revolution. Years later, when he came to power in Peking, he was to use the phrase again, but this time it meant the dictatorship of the proletariat over the whole earth: so subtly had a Confucian text received a Marxist-Leninist interpretation.

Though K'ang Yu-wei was a powerful and imposing figure, and was the first to claim the authority of Confucius for a world state, Mao Tse-tung was almost certainly right when he said later that K'ang Yu-wei did not, and could not under existing conditions, discover the road which led to the "Great Unity." K'ang Yu-wei's judgment was often confused. He envisaged companionate marriage, the partners being allowed to associate for a year before deciding to marry; he favored a constitutional monarchy, and he believed that the state should own all the means of production; and there were too many contradictions in his plans to make them practicable. He desired a world in which monkeys and parrots were taught to speak, and oxen, chickens, geese, and fish, instead of being killed, would be allowed to multiply.

Under the impulse of Yen Fu's translations and K'ang Yu-wei's interpretations, and with the help of the young Emperor Kuang Hsu, who had recently come to the throne, a vast program of reform was instituted. K'ang Yu-wei was appointed chief of the Tsungli Yamen, or Foreign Office. The young Emperor, handsome, brilliant, delighting in everything that appertained to the West, with a passion for maps and Swiss watches, became the willing prisoner of the reformers. In the space of a hundred days, from June to September 1898, he issued twenty-seven imperial rescripts, all of them concerned with essential reforms. The whole of society was to be reorganized from top to bottom. The army, the postal services, the banks, the railroads were to be reorganized; and K'ang Yu-wei began to believe that he would see the day of Ta Tung, when the state disappears and there occurs a universal equality and both money and private property are abolished, the day when there is no punishment because there is no crime and armies are no longer needed.

Driven by the vision of Ta Tung, he overreached himself and drew up reforms so far-reaching that they attracted the hostility of the noblemen at the court, who recounted the proposed reforms in great detail to the Empress. She was not driven by visions. She was in semiretirement, and now she suddenly showed her strength by arresting the Emperor, who spent the last ten years of his life on an island in one of the lakes within the high walls of the Forbidden City. The reformers were publicly cursed, and orders were given for their execution. Some were strangled; others, like K'ang Yu-wei and Hsiung Hsi-ling, escaped to Japan. For the second time in fifty years the Manchus had prevented necessary change.

Sun Yat-sen

Sun Yat-sen bridges the gap between the Taiping rebels and the Chinese Communists, for he was born in the year which saw the defeat of the last remnant of the Taiping armies and he died as the Chinese Communists were slowly mounting to power. This young doctor, who had received his early education under the British in Honolulu, had studied the Taiping rebellion at its source—in the villages of Kwangtung. Inspired by it, he had smashed idols and at one time declared that Christianity was the sole solution for China's problems. Thirteen times he led or ordered revolutionary expeditions against the Manchus from bases

in Hong Kong and French Indochina. All failed. But he fought
so bitterly that when, in 1911, the Manchu dynasty tottered under
the weight of its own contradictions, he had become for most
Chinese south of the Yangtse River the indispensable president
of the new republic.

The revolution of October 1911 changed the current of Chinese history, releasing the forces submerged under the dictatorship
of the Manchus, but it was a rebellion without deep purpose,
having its source in the same contradictions which plagued the
Manchus. A thousand disparate elements were involved. The
Szechuanese rebelled because a railway was being built between
Chengtu and Chungking. The Hunanese revolted against a preda-
tory governor, and the Kwangtungese revolted against land taxes.
It was a curiously anarchic rebellion, carried out under the banner
of "Down with the Manchus," but without any positive element
of social revolution. As soon as he realized that he would be
called to the presidency of the new republic, Sun Yat-sen appealed
to the Western powers for help; but their replies were uncon-
vincing. Strangely enough—for his sources of information were
limited—Lenin alone among Westerners seems to have realized
that almost legendary authority which Sun Yat-sen was later to
exert. Early in 1912, in an article called *Democracy and Narodism
in China*, he wrote:

> A militant, sincere spirit of democracy pervades Sun Yat-sen's
> thoughts. He shows no trace of a nonpolitical spirit or of indiffer-
> ence toward political liberty, or any admission of the idea that
> Chinese autocracy is compatible with Chinese social reform; and
> he directly presents the problem of the conditions of the masses,
> and of the mass struggle, with warm feeling toward the toilers
> and the exploited, and belief in the justice of their cause and in
> their strength.
>
> What we have before us is a really great ideology of a really
> great people, which is able not only to bemoan its age-long
> slavery, not only to dream of liberty and equality but is able also
> to fight the age-long oppressors of China.*

* Lenin, *Selected Works*, IV, 306.

Lenin's admiration of Sun Yat-sen remained, but by the time the article was printed, Sun Yat-sen no longer possessed the power, the inclination, or the social knowledge to direct a successful revolution.

At his death in 1925, Sun Yat-sen left behind him a dangerous legacy. The famous *Three Principles of the People*, written hurriedly in 1924 in Canton, elaborated a wholly unreal system of government. The mild-mannered doctor showed, as he grew older, a strangely authoritarian temper. Continual defeats and perpetual frustrations led him to harden his views of the Chinese people. In 1905 the oath of the revolutionary party he led contained the words "The spirit and the binding principles of our various aims are Liberty, Equality, and Universal Love." Nineteen years later he wrote in the *Three Principles*:

> There is one thing of the greatest importance to a political party, that is, that the members of the party should possess spiritual unity. In order that all members may be united spiritually, the first thing is to sacrifice freedom, the second is to offer abilities. If the individual can offer his abilities, then the whole party will possess ability.

The wheel had turned full circle: the revolutionary who had once fallen in love with love, with egalitarianism, and with freedom had become transformed into the hardened ruler who desired nothing so much as a dictatorship. The freedom of the individual had no place in the *Three Principles of the People*. For him, individual freedom was irrelevant, for were not the Chinese like "shifting sand," too individualistic for the safety of any government? When the Kuomintang came into power under Chiang Kai-shek, it was inevitable that the new government should have all the appearance of a dictatorship. Chiang Kai-shek was merely carrying out the wishes of Sun Yat-sen. One wish, however, he never carried out. The third of the three principles was called simply "livelihood." By this Sun Yat-sen meant that in exchange for their liberties the people should be provided with sufficient food, clothing, and sustenance; and these the Kuomintang dictatorship was incapable of providing.

When Mao Tse-tung came to power in 1949 he especially singled out the Taiping Emperor, Yen Fu, K'ang Yu-wei, and Sun Yat-sen as "the four men who sought the truth from the West." They had opened the way. Each had attempted a revolution. Each had failed. Mao studied their failures, and contrived to bring about a fifth revolution, which succeeded where all the others failed. He succeeded largely because he had learned from them.

THE YOUNG REBEL

THE HSIANG RIVER cuts through the heart of Hunan like a sword. White-sailed sampans laden with rice float down the deep blue river; ring-necked cormorants fish in midstream; red cliffs hang over the sandy beaches, and silver lakes among forests of reeds lie in the north. The inhabitants of Hunan are generally hand-somer than those of neighboring provinces, with red cheeks and clean, open faces, broad foreheads and striking dark eyes; many of them show signs of tribal blood derived from the Miaos who live in the shelter of the lakes. They are a hot-tempered people, but their temper generates heat slowly, like the red peppers they are continually chewing, and they are hardly aware of their own capacity to hurl themselves into violent fits of anger. They claim that the best soldiers and the best scholars come from Hunan: and they regard themselves quite dispassionately as a race apart.

Mao was born in the village of Shao Shan, thirty miles from Hsiang T'an, on December 26, 1893. At the time of his birth, his father had acquired some wealth by trading in rice. His name was Mao Jen-sheng, which can be translated as "Hair

Increase Gentlemanliness." Mao Tse-tung means "Hair Moisten
East." The names of his brothers, Tse-hung and Tse-t'an mean
"Moisten Red" and "Moisten Dawn." But nothing could have
been further from the father's mind than any suggestion of
prophecy. He was a hard-bitten peasant with a taste for the Confucian classics, and a friend who knew Mao in his youth remembers the old father grumbling by the stove in winter and hurling
Confucian maxims at his unwilling listeners, or poring over his
accounts, a thin, sharp-faced, bigoted man with a drooping mustache who had fought for the Manchus and respected the Empress
Dowager and treated his servants and farm laborers with contempt. He had few friends and took little interest in his family.
Some secret anxiety gnawed in him; he was always restless, ill at
ease, the hot temper never very far from the surface. By contrast,
the mother was plump and placid, with a handsome round face,
not unlike the faces which are found in the north of China and
called "pear-shaped." She was deeply religious, a Buddhist, and
therefore averse to any form of killing. For a long period of his
childhood and his early youth Mao Tse-tung attended the Buddhist ceremonies with his mother, sang Buddhist hymns, and
believed that nothing was more criminal than the killing of living
things, and nothing more necessary for salvation than the giving
of rice offerings to the poor. The father kept meticulous accounts
of the rice, bursting into a temper whenever he found that some
had been given away; and these inexplicable bursts of temper,
arising sometimes from no known cause, threw the whole family
into hysterical recriminations. After one of these outbursts, the
boy ran away and hid in the woods for three days, returning
only because it had occurred to him that his mother would have
no one to defend her.

Except for the terrifying presence of the father, whose anger
could rarely be placated, life in the village of Shao Shan was
pleasant enough. The house was well but sparsely furnished, and
kept spotlessly clean by the mother, who employed no servants.
It was a house like all the other houses, with a room of thatched
rice straw, with red peppers hanging from the roof beams and
a high-walled courtyard. In front of the house was a lake used

by the villagers for laundering clothes, and the village boys bathed
in it.

The boy was physically frail—this may have been the reason
for his father's dislike of him—but he grew rapidly: at the age
of ten he had his first serious fight and pummeled a boy who
was slightly larger, only to receive the plaintive remonstrances of
his mother, who still hoped he might enter the Buddhist priesthood, or perhaps, by becoming a merchant, support a monastery.
By the age of seven he was already working in the fields, helping
to plant rice seeds, or sitting on a wicker platform to frighten the
birds away. He was reading avidly. He intensely disliked working
in the fields when there were so many books to read, and all the
time he was having endless secret discussions with the laborers
his father employed, and he would listen to their complaints and
advise them on how to deal with his father. In China, where
family problems are fought out with an intensity usually unknown
in the West, there was nothing in the least extraordinary in
Mao's relentless fight against his father from the age of five or
six. The fight was fought with all the weapons at the boy's command, and it never ceased while he remained in the village.

He told Edgar Snow that his father was walking down a
road one day, intending to collect some money, when he was
surprised by a tiger. Reflecting on the incident, it occurred to
him that he might have offended the gods and that his miraculous
escape had been ordained by Buddha as a means of bringing him
to the Buddhist religion. It is a good story, but unfortunately
there were no tigers in Hunan at that time, though a few existed
in Manchuria and the mountains of southeast Kiangsi. Strangely
enough, a very similar story is told by the "Christian General"
Feng Yu-hsiang in his autobiography, where an enormous yellow
snake, twenty feet long, slowly entering the house and quietly
coiling up near the wall, takes the place of Mao Jen-sheng's tiger.

What is certain is that the father mellowed as he grew older.
Though there were sudden flashes of the old temper, a kind of
weariness settled on him, and he could be seen burning incense
and bowing mechanically before the bronze Buddha which stood
on a blackwood table in a place of honor, an old and gaunt man,

ready even at such moments to curse the first person who came into his field of vision, but generally quiet, resigned to living in a rebellious household.

By this time a technique for dealing with his tantrums had been elaborated. If necessary, his rage could be brought on deliberately, to forestall the greater rage that might come later; his Confucian texts could be answered with even more pertinent texts, and if he threatened to strike anyone, he would be reminded of the most classical of all Confucian texts: "Not a hair of the head must be touched." Around the old soldier, the boy played with a deliberate cunning. It is as though he had been trained from birth to sabotage quietly and effectively the pretensions of a nineteeth-century soldier with a propensity for Confucian maxims; and the figure of the old father merges imperceptibly into the figure of Mao's future adversary.

In all this Mao was not alone. Though born much later, his two brothers and his sister were useful weapons in the continual struggle with the father. Mao was very close to them. Like most elder brothers in China, he assumed the role of teacher: from the beginning there was the element of the pedagogue in him. As he grew older and more skeptical of the Buddhist religion, his mother began to believe that if he was not made for the priesthood, at least he would become a teacher.

In those days little news came to the villages of Hunan except by word of mouth. There were no newspapers. The imperial rescripts were posted in the village and read aloud by the village schoolmaster, but usually they were concerned only with taxes, conscription, and the special ceremonies to be performed on the birthdays of the Empress Dowager. When Mao was eleven, on October 10, 1904, the birthday of the Empress Dowager was celebrated with the usual offerings of incense, the usual flowery speeches calling upon heaven to preserve the Empress for ten thousand years. On the same day, columns of soldiers passed through Hsiang T'an on the way to Changsha. It was whispered that Hwang Hsing, a young Hunanese revolutionary, had attacked the yamen in Changsha at the head of some peasant guerrillas. He had fought his way into the interior of the yamen,

had been captured, thrown into a dungeon, and then by some
miracle he had escaped in disguise—no one knew where. Martial
law was proclaimed. Through all the villages soldiers came in the
hope of discovering Hwang Hsing's hiding-place. It was learned
that a reward of ten thousand silver taels had been placed on his
head. For the first time Mao came in contact with the thought
of insurrection. He was not particularly impressed. Changsha was
a long way away. Besides, he possessed something of the peasant
contempt for disorder, and his loyalty to the monarchy was
undimmed.

Hwang Hsing escaped to Tokyo, fleeing down the Hsiang
River and then taking a boat from Hong Kong to Japan, only
to return the following February. The second insurrection failed.
The third was more successful, for by this time Hwang Hsing
possessed the help of the *Tung Men Hui*, the revolutionary organization he had founded together with Sun Yat-sen. He had
intended to capture the city again on the anniversary of the
previous uprising, but the outbreak was delayed until October 19
because some of the ammunition failed to arrive in time. This
time the insurrection was more carefully planned. Three columns
were formed, amounting to about thirty thousand men, a force
which included the coal miners of Pinghsiang, the garrison of
Lilin, and the secret societies of Liuyang. It was the largest force
ever brought together for the purposes of insurrection since the
Taiping rebellion. The Viceroy saw the danger and ordered the
combined forces of the four provinces of Hunan, Kiangsi, Hupeh,
and Szechuan to put down the rebels. Faced with these overwhelming forces, the revolutionaries were compelled to withdraw;
and Sun Yat-sen, from his small rooming-house in Tokyo, observed
sadly that the insurrection had been premature, there were no
clear communications, and the attack was unauthorized.

Following a pattern which was to be repeated many times
during the following years, the rebellion was crushed ruthlessly,
and Hwang fled, joining Sun Yat-sen, Wang Ching-wei, and Hu
Han-min later in Annam, where they prepared a fourth insurrection
from bases within French Indochina. With these revolutionary
figures Mao was to become intimate in later years, and the three

revolutionary centers, Pinghsiang, Lilin, and Liuyang, were to supply guerrilla forces for his own revolutionary army.

For Mao, the year 1906 was full of strange events. There had been a severe famine during the year, especially affecting Changsha, and now for the first time he was faced with the problems of poverty and insurrection. In the early autumn, peasants had assaulted the yamen and demanded that the rice granaries be opened. They were reprimanded for their audacity and ordered to be punished. The peasant leaders were executed, and the whole province was in ferment. Everything in which Mao believed was now put to the test. His Buddhism, his belief in the monarchical system, his family's comparative wealth based on rice, even his growing delight in learning—all these were assailed by the fact that innocent peasants were executed in broad daylight, officially, with all the sanctions of the monarchy. What could he believe in? He discussed the murders endlessly with the students in the small schoolhouse, and only his position as the elder son of one of the richer rice merchants in the village saved him from being labeled a rebel.

There were insurrections nearer home. The centuries-old secret society called the *Ko Lao Hui*, or "Society of Elder Brothers," had ramifications throughout Hunan, and all the small peasants in the village belonged to it. The society had originally been organized to protect the peasants from the landlords, with elaborate rituals and a mysterious oath of brotherhood, but it had developed anti-Manchu leanings, and in Kwangtung it was sufficiently powerful to threaten an attack on Canton in 1860, "in order to preserve the honor of our country and to prevent our city from falling into the hands of the enemy," at a time when Peking was captured by British, American, French, and Russian forces. In Hunan the society was scarcely less powerful than in Kwangtung. In Shao Shan it was in conflict with the landlords, who called to their assistance their own secret society. The small local rebellion was put down, and the leaders fled to a nearby mountain where they held out for some months before being caught and publicly executed.

In a single year, at the sensitive age of thirteen, Mao had

been brought into contact with two insurrections, a riot of famine-starved peasants, and a small uprising in his own village.

Meanwhile, his studies progressed. He read the Trimetrical Classic, which all children were taught to read in their first school year, and went on to the Confucian Analects and the Four Classics; and these extraordinary books, written with a careful humanism, had a far deeper influence on him than he was ever to admit. If he objected to the Confucian concept of filial piety for good reasons, certain Confucian terms and many of the characteristic Confucian methods remained with him. "I hated Confucius from the age of eight," he told a friend. "There was a Confucian temple in the village, and I wanted nothing more than to burn it to the ground. At first it was because I hated the teacher, and because my father quoted Confucius against me; only much later did I reason out my hatred." He seems to have been protesting too much. He was not alone in his detestation of Confucius, which was sweeping over the whole of China: Sun Yat-sen at an equally tender age had suffered from the same virus. There remained with him the Confucian concept of political power and political energy, the idea of the Great Unity (Ta Tung), and a host of Confucian apothegms, which he employed then, as he does now, with surprising accuracy and wit.

He was friendly with one of the village teachers, who began to lend him books. He was under ten when he first began to read the great Chinese novels, The Dream of the Red Chamber, The Journey to the West, All Men Are Brothers, and The Three Kingdoms. There was nothing particularly unusual in this. Most sensitive Chinese schoolboys read these books at an early age, sharpening their minds on the fantastic subtlety and complexity of these enormously long books, written in such a way that it is almost impossible not to surrender to the world they create. He was particularly impressed with All Men Are Brothers after the insurrection of the Ko Lao Hui, for the novel told the story of bandits who took refuge in the hills.

One other writer, the celebrated Han Yu, influenced him deeply at the time when he was growing skeptical of Buddhism. His mother's explanations of Buddhism were subtly satisfying.

The Buddhist heaven, to be reached only when the last of the
sinners has entered into Buddhahood, possessed an essential the-
ological charm, and he delighted in the incantations and prayers
in the evening. Buddhism was almost the official religion of
Hunan, but he suspected an error somewhere, something unex-
plained, some lapse of logic or rhetoric. Where was it? He found
it in the essay Han Yu wrote to the Emperor Hsien Tsung on
the subject of Buddha's finger bone, which the Emperor, in an
imperial rescript, had ordered to be brought ceremoniously to the
capital. Han Yu laughed the project to scorn. He pointed out
that Buddha had disobeyed two of the cardinal Confucian duties:
he had rejected the throne, and he had fled secretly from his
father's palace; he possessed neither a sense of duty nor filial
piety. The reasonable behavior toward the finger would be to
treat it as an honored guest, invite it to a banquet, let the
dancing girls dance before it, bestow gifts on it, and then escort
it to the frontiers of the empire: it should be treated as one
treats any barbarian visitor from abroad. Or else it should be
destroyed. He wrote:

> I request that the proper officials may be entrusted with the
> relic and it shall be hurled into water or consumed by fire:
> that the error may be destroyed root and branch: that in all the
> earth the threads of doubt may be avoided; and that the people
> under Heaven may rise ten thousand times ten thousand times
> above their own mortality. Is not this excellent? Is not this in-
> spiring!

For his effrontery Han Yu was summarily banished to the
wilds of Kwangtung, at that time considered to be an immense
miasmic swamp. His adventures were not over. An enormous
crocodile infested one of the rivers. Han Yu, as a celebrated
scholar, was asked to use his influence with the crocodile. He
obeyed the request, proceeded to the river, recited an ode to the
crocodile and threw the ode into the river together with a propi-
tiatory pig. The crocodile was never seen again.

Han Yu's furious wit was close to Mao's heart. He modeled
his style on the old Confucian who opposed Taoism and Bud-

dhism and employed magic against the magicians and, bitterly but in the most rhythmic prose, mocked the most sacred cults. The soaring innuendoes, the savage humor, the pomposity which is half mockery and half delight in an exalted poetic prose, the vigor and deliberation of the attack—all of these made Mao confess to being a disciple of Han Yu. It delighted him that Han Yu should resolve the problem by simply destroying the finger. He did not, however, approve of all the writings of Han Yu. In particular, he disapproved of a famous essay in which Han Yu defends the actions of Prince Po Yi, who lived at the time of confusion between the Yin and Chou dynasties a thousand years B.C., and who decided to live a life of contemplative solitude beside a white lake, while the wars were fought all around him. "I decided that such an attitude was essentially non-Marxist," Mao said later. But he remembered the story of the crocodile when he nicknamed Chiang Kai-shek "the crocodile of the Kwangtung River."

At an age when he was beginning to see himself as a future teacher with years of quiet study in front of him, Mao suddenly discovered that he was expected to spend his whole time either in the fields or poring over the account books of his father. For some time his father had encouraged him to keep the accounts. Mao Jen-sheng had suffered losses owing to his inaccuracy with the abacus. The boy could do better. As the eldest son—there were by now two younger brothers and a sister—Mao was expected to take over the family business; and it is possible that he would have remained a rice broker all his life if he had not been encouraged by one of his schoolteachers to go to the middle school at Hsiang-hsiang, which lay some fifteen miles upriver.

At first his father refused to let him go. Mao rebelled. He reminded his father that the proper vocation of a Chinese was to follow in the path of Confucius; he would become a scholar, enter the imperial government, and perhaps—for all positions were open to scholars—receive high office and bring fame to his parents and his native village. The parents of great scholars received almost the same veneration as the scholars themselves, but Mao Jen-sheng seems to have been concerned only with the possibility that his son might provide a stable income. In September 1907, at the age of fourteen, carrying only some books and a few ragged clothes in two pieces of luggage, which hung from a carrying-pole slung over his shoulders, Mao arrived at the school. He was friendless except for some peasant cultivators, relatives of his mother, who lived outside the town.

Again and again, in his conversations and in his writings, Mao has spoken of the horror of that first day in school. In Shao Shan he was known, and generally liked; here he was unknown, and despised. His father had given him money for his school fees, but no other money was forthcoming. Most of the other students were comparatively rich; they could afford good clothes, good food, and sometimes good servants. Laughing, one of the students offered Mao employment as a servant. For a few pieces of cash delivered monthly, he would be expected to perform a few menial services. He indignantly refused.

Poverty-stricken, given the worst food and the worst sleeping quarters, hating the other students, who referred to him as "the dirty little peasant from Shao Shan," Mao had only one resource, his excellence at his work. He studied hard, melted down old candles to fashion new ones, hid at night over his books while the other students were asleep, and was soon at the head of his class, only to discover that he was now even more despised for being diligent. He had half-hated the classics at Shao Shan; now he spent nearly all his waking hours in a prolonged study of the Four Classics, egged on by his teacher, who admired the prose style based on Han Yu's essays, and the bitter romanticism of the boy's themes. At the same time he was coming to know more and more about the Reform movement, and he was a fervent admirer of K'ang Yu-wei.

It was during this time that he met a young student called Hsiao Chu-chang, who, though two years younger, fell under his spell and became one of his closest friends, encouraging Mao when he was depressed, listening to him open-mouthed in admiration when he fell into one of those moods in which he found himself thinking aloud—thinking as Han Yu thought, with extraordinary violence for one so young. Hsiao Chu-chang constituted himself Mao's bodyguard, servant, nurse, and confidant. They swore an oath of brotherhood. For the next ten years they were rarely separated.

Hsiao Chu-chang was the son of a rich farmer in Hsiang-hsiang. Thin-boned, elegant, with a high forehead and unusually expressive hands, he looked as though he had stepped out of *The Dream of the Red Chamber*. He was a natural aristocrat, gentle where Mao was impetuous, subtle where Mao was ingenuous. He was older than his age, while Mao gave the impression of being either very much younger or ancient with the wisdom of aged peasants. Mao called him Hsiao San (Hsiao the third), because he was the youngest of three brothers. Years later, when Hsiao Chu-chang went to live in Russia, he received still another name, Emi Siao, and under this name achieved some fame as a translator of Chinese poetry into Russian. He learned French, Spanish, and German, and it was from him that Mao derived most of his knowledge of Europe.

It was the time when the monarchy was gradually crumbling. In 1908 it seemed that the Reform party, proscribed ten years before, was about to assume control of the government. The Empress Dowager was dying. Inevitably, the young Emperor Kuang Hsu would come to the throne and summon K'ang Yu-wei to his side. Immediately the famous edicts which were issued at a mounting pace in 1898 would be reissued, and once more China would be able to hold up her head.

Hsiao San and Mao debated the future. They were both Reformists; and they began to look forward to a time when China would become a constitutional monarchy: there would be peace and plenty for all, and there would be no need for them to disturb themselves over politics, for both would become teachers and writers. Then they learned that the young Emperor had died on the same day as, or the day before, the Empress Dowager and that the two-year-old Emperor Hsuan T'ung had come to the throne. Power was being wielded by a regent as reactionary as the Empress Dowager.

About this time there occurred an incident which later became famous. Hsiao had found a book relating the lives of great generals and rulers in foreign countries. It was called *Great Heroes of the World*. Translated from an American original, it described the lives of Peter the Great, Wellington, Washington, Lincoln, Rousseau, Montesquieu, Catherine the Great, Gladstone, and Napoleon. Not all the articles came from the American book: the article on Montesquieu, for example, had been inserted because Liang Ch'i-ch'ao the disciple of K'ang Yu-wei, had made great capital of *De l'Esprit des Lois*, until the youth of China had come to regard Montesquieu as perhaps the fountainhead of all Western knowledge. In this book it was not Montesquieu but Washington who fired Mao's imagination. Given *Great Heroes* one evening, he returned it the next morning. He had read it all. "We need great people like these," he commented. "We ought to study them and find out how we can make China rich and strong, and so avoid becoming like Annam, Korea, and India.* You know the old proverb, 'If the cart in front turns over, let the cart behind take warning.' China is very weak; she will grow strong, rich, and independent only after many years; but the important thing is that we must learn these things. And it is not impossible. After six years of hard fighting, Washington defeated the British and began to build up America."

There was nothing in the least astonishing in this incident: similar discussions were taking place all over China. What was astonishing was the peculiar expression on Mao's face when he returned the book. "It was all very strange," Hsiao San told me when I met him in Kalgan. "I can remember exactly how he looked, and I can remember his tone as he said, 'We need great people like these.' I had the feeling that he had made his decision. Many years later I read Turgenev's *Fathers and Sons*, and instantly I recognized the authoritative Mao I had known in my youth. He breathed authority, never more than at that moment, and yet he looked just like all the other students, and he differed from them in being a little more handsome than most, and because he had a quick, loping stride, and always carried a load

---

* These were the countries which the Hunanese viceroy, Chang Chih-tung, in his book *Five Objects of Knowledge*, described as "warnings."

of books under his arm. He was Bazarov, dedicated to scholarship —particulary history—and the peasants."

Though Hsiao San knew Mao better than most people, there were defenses he never penetrated. He says he never came to understand Mao intimately: there were secret springs never disclosed. Mao could read twice or three times as fast as any other man. In libraries he surrounded himself with a wall of books. No one Hsiao San had ever known hungered for such a vast quantity of knowledge on so many different levels. Mao was the first to enter the library and the last to leave. Though he was the most brilliant scholar at the school, he discounted scholarship, saying that it was perfectly easy to read but that something more was necessary—an understanding of the laws of civilization. It was a chance phrase from a famous essay by Liang Ch'i-ch'ao. So Mao talked continually about social rights and social duties, from the point of view of one who sees hope of peaceful change.

To understand Mao Tse-tung, it is necessary to understand the social theories advanced in China at the beginning of the century, the peculiar atmosphere of the times. His Marxism was a later accretion; in the most impressionable years of all he was influenced by the Taipings and by the Chinese revolutionary movements of the past, about which he was extraordinarily well-informed. He was fundamentally under the influence of K'ang Yu-wei and Liang Ch'i-ch'ao. He was passionately delighted with the Reform party. All that was modern and advanced was represented by these two fingers, one the theoretician, the other the popularizer. Both, in a sense, were nineteenth-century mechanists. They drew their inspiration from Darwin and Spencer, and from an obscure book called *Principles of Western Civilisation*, by the Englishman Benjamin Kidd. It was one of the books translated by Yen Fu, and according to Liang Ch'i-ch'ao it was destined "to influence all the races of the world, to be a great light to the future."

The book, now forgotten, possessed an incalculable influence, for it sought to answer the precise questions which disturbed the Chinese. The evidence of Western civilization they knew; the

principles by which Western civilization arose and commanded
its own strange progress were unknown. For the reformers, Kidd
was the answer to all their problems, for he traced all the forms
of society through their stages of evolution, and he did all this
more solemnly and at the same time more simply than Herbert
Spencer would ever have dared to do. This minor sociologist was
readable, and Liang Ch'i-ch'ao found him more stimulating than
Marx, and more entrancing than Huxley. "Kidd stands out above
all the others," he wrote, "and takes a step forward." He continued:

> Kidd maintains that man is like the other animals: without strug-
> gle there can be no progress. Whether is be a struggle between
> individual and individual or race and race, the outcome is that
> the unfit is defeated and perishes while the superior who is the
> equal to the situation flourishes. This is an unchanging law, and
> in this movement of evolution *there must be the sacrifice of the*
> *individual for society, of the present for the future. Therefore the*
> *man who grasps at his own immediate profit entirely misunder-*
> *stands the theory of evolution. He is indeed a criminal to the*
> *evolutionist. . . . He is not a help but an injury to the cause of*
> *man's survival.**

Marx, too, had been impressed with Spencer's development
of the theory of evolution, and it had confirmed his authoritarian
temper. So it was in China. The elements which really went to
make the principles of the West—the desire for height, the delight
in liberty, the far-ranging exaltations of the mind, and the belief
in youth—were omitted in the dry-as-dust theories of the Victorian
sociologists, who saw their categories and advanced their philosophies in terms of a sterile theory of evolution, in which evolution
itself, rather than man, acquired prime importance. Kidd did
hardly more than popularize Herbert Spencer, but he left upon
the awakening minds of the young Chinese indelible traces.

At this time Mao was reading the *Hsin Min Chung Pao*
(*The New Peoples' Journal*) once edited by the Reformers in

---

* The italics are in the original. I owe this quotation to Professor E. R.
Hughes's exceedingly significant book, *The Invasion of China by the Western
World* (New York, 1938), p. 211.

exile in Yokohama, now clandestinely printed in China. It was heady wine, full of Liang Ch'i-ch'ao's theories, his urgent demands that the "new people" take their future in their own hands. K'ang Yu-wei had believed that the great dream of *Ta Tung* could not come about until the surrender of nationality to the greater sovereignty of a world state. Liang Ch'i-ch'ao began to see increasing benefits in nationalism. Was it not their sense of overriding nationalism which had brought England, the United States, Germany, and France into their positions of power? He upheld the virile spirit of nationalism and the domination of other races, and showed that China would perish unless she set out to affirm her own nationalism over her neighbors.

The importance of the *Hsin Min Chung Pao* lay less in the particular philosophy it inherited from the English evolutionists than its insistence on the "new people," the new dedicated students who would change China from top to bottom. Hu Shih in his autobiography has explained the changing atmosphere. First, in the 1850's, the idea of *hsi hsueh*, "Western learning," had been prominent. This was followed by a period in which particular prominence was laid on *pien hua*, "reform," and this in turn was followed by a period in which the students spoke increasingly about *hsin hsueh*, the "new learning," which demonstrated the synthesis between East and West. Finally there was the period of *hsin min*, the "new people." To be new, to be modern, to be completely informed about the nature of social change, and to create an entirely new people—this was the prospect which faced the young Chinese students in the first decade of the century.

There was, however, nothing essentially revolutionary in this attitude. It, too, had origins in the ancient classics; the opening sentence of the first great classic taught to schoolboys introduced the phrase "making a new people," and Confucius himself in the *Great Learning* had pointed approvingly at the famous bathtub on which was written the words: "Everything must be made anew." Newness, and a new people, and a vast new horizon, and the whole archaic past thrown overboard—with such thoughts the students faced the future, building a theoretical world possessing greater validity than the world of the Empress Dowager which they saw around them. So Liang Ch'i-ch'ao wrote passionately, and often inaccurately, about Rousseau, Hobbes, Bentham, Spinoza, and Montesquieu, and he saw the new China emerging as a constitutional monarchy with an independent judiciary and a government responsible to the national assembly, and the laws modeled on the laws of England. Indeed England provided the model, and he particularly approved of habeas corpus; he wanted gradual change on the English pattern, and wrote that "revolution always retards the progress of a nation." In his admiration of England, however, he was almost alone; and something in the temper of the time demanded more violent solutions. The tragedy of the Chinese civil wars can be foreseen in those passionate pages in which Liang Ch'i-ch'ao, though demanding moderation, suggested solutions which could only come about by violence.

This is, of course, a digression; but it is necessary to understand the temper of Mao's mind as it was formed by the intellectual atmosphere at the beginning of the century. His mind was formed during the years 1906–1909, the years during which Liang Ch'i-ch'ao's reformist *Hsin Min Chung Pao* fought a continual running battle with another clandestine journal, called the *Min Pao*, edited by Wang Ching-wei and Hu Han-min, both of whom Mao came to know intimately later. Mao's intellectual roots are to be found in the mechanistic philosophy of the nineteenth century, and it is from Spencer, rather than from Marx, that he derived the belief that the individual must be sacrificed to the state. His beginnings lie with English sociology and the English conception of constitutional reform. He had nothing but contempt for the revolutionaries. Surely the monarchy would last forever! It was only much later that he rejoiced in the thought of revolution. Meanwhile, it was perhaps inevitable that the great debate should grow more heated as the issues of reform and revolution—precisely the same issues were debated in China at the time of the civil war—were discussed in the pages of the two journals. It is one of the more subtle ironies of history that Mao began by sympathizing with the Reformers, but by the time he came to know the revolutionaries well he was already planning a far more rigorous revolution than they had ever contemplated.

The portrait that emerges is clear: a tousle-haired boy steeped in the classics and the historical novels of ancient China, uncommonly studious, passionately fond of wandering over the low hills of Hunan, perpetually wondering why it was that in all the histories and all the novels there was no account of the peasants. It came to him, as he wandered from village to village during the holidays, that the peasants were the forgotten heroes, possessing an immemorial wisdom. They were kinder than the people who lived in towns, more resourceful, and they possessed an abundant culture of their own. More particularly, they possessed the quality of "energy" which Mao was beginning to demand of everything he respected. "Everything had to be 'energetical,'" Hsiao San remembered. "It was no good unless it displayed the qualities of energy: he tested everything by what he called his 'secret formula.'" And where was the source of energy? Clearly, it was the sun. So Mao developed a theory of nudism: one could suck up the energy of the sun by walking about naked or nearly naked. The two friends wandered over the hills, wearing blue drawers, barefoot, till they were both tanned by the sun; and when the peasants laughed at them, Mao said: "The sun is the source of health. Isn't it the sun which makes the rice grow? Then why wear too many clothes?" They learned that they were in danger of arrest, for the Manchu police frowned on the two nearly naked students who walked in the sun. They believed that a new and dangerous cult might emerge.

"I think it was at that time that Mao set his face away from the townspeople," Hsiao San said. "He approved of the peasants; he approved of no one else. What he particularly approved of in the peasants was their courtesy and their loyalty to one another. He said that the townspeople were not really loyal to one another; and they were not courteous by nature, they simply followed accepted customs. In a sense he was split between his admiration for scholarship and scholars, and his admiration for the peasants. He thought he would be a teacher, and he would spend his time teaching peasants."

Meanwhile the wanderings over the hills continued during

the holidays. Both Hsiao San and Mao came to know the reaches
of the Hsiang River. They walked to Changsha, thirty miles
away; they walked to Liuyang and Lilin in the south. There was
hardly a village in the five counties of Changsha, Hsiang T'an,
Hsianghsian, Lilin, and Hung Shan which they did not know
well. It was in these five counties that Mao was later to launch
his own insurrections. But in those days the thought of insurrection was far from his mind, and though he studied the conditions
in the villages carefully, he was more interested in theories of
government, in history, in the pure physical pleasure of wandering among the Hunanese hills. Above all, he was enjoying his
freedom for the first time, no longer at the beck and call of his
father. He said: "It was good training. I lived very simply, with
almost no money, but it was an amazing period of discovery." He
was beginning to think ahead. Together with Hsiao San, he
decided to enter the junior college in Changsha.

Early in the spring of 1911, Mao and Hsiao San were accepted as pupils, but they had hardly settled down when there
occurred the fourth Kuomintang uprising under the command
of Hwang Hsing. On April 27, between half-past-four and six
o'clock, Hwang Hsing led 130 of his followers against the Canton
yamen. These followers included the flower of the Kuomintang.
For the first time they were provided with adequate funds and
ammunition, and they were given nine supporting columns,
numbering altogether about eight hundred trained revolutionary
troops, with orders to concentrate on the outlying fortifications.
They did their work well, but they failed to reach the interior of
the yamen at the time when Hwang Hsing had entered it, and
the fierce little group of guerrillas supporting Hwang Hsing was
cut down. Forty-three revolutionaries were killed in battle, and
twenty-seven were captured and executed. The "seventy-two mar-
tyrs of the Yellow Flower Mound" became famous all over China.
"They have failed, but they will strike terror in the hearts of
our enemies," pronounced Sun Yat-sen.

In Changsha it was believed that the next uprising would
occur in the Hunanese capital. It was the year of decision, and
like everyone else Mao spent the summer in mingled exaspera-

tion and expectation, for the final revolution which would throw
the Manchus from their thrones could not be longer delayed.

In the excitement of the time, Mao began to write political
articles. They were not printed, so he posted them up on the wall,
signing them with a pseudonym. He also took part in "queue-
chopping expeditions" and claimed that he had ten queues to
his credit. He was still feeling his way. If he was now against
the Manchus, he had not yet declared his allegiance to the
Kuomintang.

In October, when the revolution broke out at Wuhan, he
was still at college, still undetermined about the future, and still
at the mercy of the minute changes in the political atmosphere
of the time. "I was a pure weathercock. I knew nothing. I simply
followed the trend," he said of this period later. It was probably
impossible to do otherwise.

The revolution broke out as the result of the accidental explosion of some gunpowder belonging to the secret Kuomintang
organizations, the casks being hidden in the Russian concession
at Hankow. From this moment onward there was to be a strange
contact with the Russians throughout the whole of the Kuomintang revolution.

Meanwhile, accident followed accident. Li Yuan-hung, the
future leader of the revolutionary army, was a liberal officer who
had sworn to defend the Manchu Empire. He had no desire to
lead the uprising. On the night when the gunpowder exploded,
he was found hiding under his bed, with only his boots visible.
Asked to sign a document calling upon the whole country to
rise against the Manchus, he explained nervously that he had
no authority to sign such a document. Hwang Hsing was away.
There was no one to command the revolutionary forces. The
times were desperate. The revolutionaries, instead of shooting the
officer for disloyalty to the revolution, threatened to shoot themselves in his bedroom if he refused. He finally agreed to sign the
document only because he was afraid that the blood of the revolutionaries who shot themselves would spoil his favorite carpet.

In this atmosphere, caught up in a wayward revolutionary
tide, hardly knowing what was at stake, trusting that the Reform

party would take over power, with K'ang Yu-wei as prime minister
and Sun Yat-sen perhaps as president, Mao decided to join the
revolutionary army at Hankow. The times were too quick for
him. Changsha itself declared its independence before the end
of the year; a student army was formed; everyone was talking
about marching on Peking and dethroning the Emperor, for the
Regent did not immediately resign his functions. In the hothouse
atmosphere of Hunan nothing went according to schedule. Not
all the army sided with the revolutionaries. There were conflicts
within the province, and armies were marching and counter-
marching up and down the Hsiang River. Mao joined the regular
army, in the hope that it would be sent immediately against
Peking, but by the end of the year agreement between Sun Yat-
sen and Yuan Shih-kai, the warlord who had assumed power
after the collapse of the Manchus, was in sight. Thirsting for a
military career, and with a desire for glory, Mao found himself a
common soldier in Changsha on garrison duty. He was paid
seven dollars a month, and his chief occupation was to be the
servant of the younger officers.

During the revolution, Mao showed no signs of military brilliance. He detested the violence of the soldiers among themselves,
the perpetual threats of execution for the slightest misdemeanor,
and he suspected that the revolution had failed in its main purpose. Yuan Shih-kai had assumed the role of Napoleon, turning
the current of revolution back again toward autocracy; and with
Sun Yat-sen's inexplicable surrender to Yuan Shi-kai, Mao found
himself for the first time leading a completely aimless existence
in Changsha. By the summer of 1912 he had left the Army and
he was living in poverty in a lodging-house.

In the lives of men who later become revolutionaries there
very often appear periods of intolerable poverty and indecision.
Uprooted, without money, suddenly confronted with harsh necessity, they withdraw into themselves while at the same time, in
order to live at all, they take on the most menial occupations.
Hitler painted his postcards and became a paper-hanger; Chiang
Kai-shek became a bartender and Lenin a proofreader.

Mao read the advertisements desperately. He was receiving

no funds from home, because his father disapproved of his becoming a soldier, and he was living on money borrowed from his friends. The first advertisement he read concerned a new soap factory. Another concerned a police school. A third concerned a commercial school. He toyed with them all. There were advantages in soap-making. Had not Liang Ch'i-ch'ao thundered in one of his editorials that the one thing China needed to learn from the West was the importance of cleanliness and sanitation? The police school pleased him, for he had been in some kind of trouble with the military police in the army. The school of commerce was a last resort: it would please his father, but he knew he had no aptitude for trade. He answered the advertisements, paid registration fees, interviewed the principals and was interviewed by them, and sooner or later he knew he would be compelled to choose between them. He had no desire to choose. He knew now what he wanted to be: the eternal student, the man who goes to college and never leaves, delaying his graduation from year to year, accepting some small position in the college—a junior librarian or a bursar's assistant—happy in his reading, and in the absence of responsibilities. He entered the Teachers' Training College at Changsha with Hsiao San, and there he stayed for nearly six years.

In those early days following the revolution, the teachers' training colleges were at the mercy of conflicting schedules and conflicting aims. An entirely new system of education, with its emphasis on Western science, had been ordered by the government. But there were few teachers trained in science, and the old "eight-legged essays"—those ancient classical essays devised to torture candidates in the imperial examinations—were still being written. All education was in the melting pot. Subjects taught one year were mysteriously removed from the curriculum the next, and incompetent professors were numerous. It was possible to become a professor of English while knowing only a smattering of English; there were professors of science who maintained their position only by reading a few pages of the textbook ahead of the students.

Mao had thought of acquiring huge areas of knowledge of

Western science and philosophy: the teaching was so inept that he revolted. He had studied ancient Chinese philosophy and history, and learned to write passable classical essays at the middle school in Hsianghsiang. These same studies were continued at the Teachers' Training College. Here, too, he met Professor Yang Chen-ch'i, who was the first to give him the kind of encouragement he needed, praising his essays, putting them in a prominent place on the notice board, and urging the other students to "follow the example of Mao Tse-tung, who writes elegantly and honestly."

Professor Yang Chen-ch'i was a short man with a small, narrow face and a dome-shaped forehead, exquisite gestures, and a delusive quietness. More than any other teacher Mao had seen, he represented the moral strength of the classical past. He developed a deep affection for Mao, lent him books, spoke about England—which he had visited, though without much profit and with something of a Chinese scholar's disdain—and he habitually gave 100 points to Mao's essays, though always warning Mao of his facility. Mao in turn never failed to show him profound respect.

It was during this time that Mao for the first time came face to face with socialism. As Hsiao San related it, he came quite accidentally upon a book written by Chiang Kan-fu, which gave an inaccurate account of the development of socialism in England and on the Continent:

> "If you read the book now, you would think it was ridiculous, it was so muddle-headed; but it contained some good quotations and mentioned the names of Owen and Marx. It was the first time Mao had ever heard of socialism, and he was wildly excited. All his sympathies, all his scholarship, all his memories of life on the farm and in the army seemed to lead to one conclusion: he would become a Socialist. He looked around, and saw no Socialist party in China, and thought the time had come to bring one into existence, with himself perhaps as the founder. Later he read three books: the *Communist Manifesto*, Kautsky's *The Class War*, and a history of socialism by someone whose name I've forgotten. He was completely thunderstruck by these books.

Hsiao San's memories of Mao are confirmed by his elder brother, who prefers to be known as Siao Yu. In his charming

autobiographical fragment *Mao Tse-tung and I Were Beggars* he
describes a journey he made with Mao across Hunan in the summer of 1917. They deliberately set out without money, and the
difficulties started almost from the moment they left Changsha,
for they had no money to pay for the ferry across the Hsiang
River. They bluffed their way across, and continued to bluff their
way through the entire journey. They spent a miserable night on a
sandbank reciting Chinese poems to one another, discussed their
ambitions—even then, according to Siao Yu, Mao liked to compare himself with the Emperor Liu Pang who overwhelmed the
Ch'in dynasty and brought the great Han dynasty into existence
—and heard their fortunes from the lips of a pretty young poetess
at an inn on the Yuankiang road. Mao's fortune was ominous. He
was told that he would become a prime minister or a great bandit
chief who would kill thousands of people without turning a hair.
If he survived to the age of fifty-five, he would inherit immense
good fortune. He would have at least six wives, and would be restless throughout his life. Mao seems to have been completely un-
moved by these revelations.

According to Siao Yu, Mao was an erratic student who occasionally wrote brilliant essays in a clumsy calligraphy. "He received
no marks at all for English, only five out of a hundred for arith-
metic, and in drawing the only thing he managed was a circle."
Happily, essay-writing was considered the most important of all
accomplishments, and Mao therefore had the reputation of being
a good student. Mao also had a minor reputation as a poet. He
was an excellent public speaker, and possessed a curious hypnotic
power over his audience.

Here is Siao Yu's portrait of the tall, clumsy, ill-dressed Mao
Tse-tung as he appeared in the Normal School in Changsha one
day in 1912:

> Mao was not unusual in appearance, as some people have main-
> tained, with his hair growing low on his forehead, like the devils
> pictured by old-time artists, nor did he have any especially strik-
> ing features. In fact I have never observed anything unusual in his
> physical appearance. To me he always seemed quite an ordinary,
> normal-looking person. His face was rather large, but his eyes were

neither large nor penetrating, nor had they the sly, cunning look
sometimes attributed to them. His nose was flattish and of a
typical Chinese shape. His ears were well-proportioned; his
mouth, quite small; his teeth very white and even. These good
white teeth helped to make his smile quite charming, so that no
one would imagine that he was not genuinely sincere. He walked
rather slowly, with his legs somewhat separated, in a way that
reminded me of a duck waddling. His movements in sitting or
standing were very slow. Also he spoke slowly and he was by no
means a gifted speaker.*

Though Siao Yu contradicts this last statement on a later
page, the portrait rings true. They were evidently close friends,
and when they parted nine years later over the question of Communism, they still held one another in high regard.

By the time World War I had come, Mao was a convinced if
erratic socialist. He no longer took his lessons at the college seriously. Except for a few professors whose courses he attended, he
was spending most of his time studying newspapers or buried
among the books of the public library, which had been founded
by Hsiung Hsi-ling. The library was excellently equipped, and its
discovery marked one of Mao's happiest days. He immersed himself in it, sometimes spending ten hours at his desk without moving, going without food, continually taking notes; and a prodigious
memory allowed him to regard the day as time spent in absorbing
knowledge which could then be conveniently reinterpreted at
night. Hsiao San says that he did not merely turn his attention to
what he read, but seemed to turn his whole body to the work in
hand, and he would come out of the library with a high fever, his
eyes like black smudges on the pale face, and immediately launch
into an excited description of the things he had read. In the
libraries, too, he was able to read the newspapers from all parts
of China, and it was at this time that he developed almost a
mania for reading newspapers, checking the accounts of events
as they were reported in different cities. Sun Yat-sen, though
powerless, was beginning to come into prominence in 1915, for

* Siao Yu, Mao Tse-Tung and I were Beggars (Syracuse University Press,
1959), p. 31.

Yuan Shih-kai was at last overreaching himself, and under Tsai Ao in Yunnan a formidable army was being raised against the dictator. Mao had paid little attention to the evolution of the Kuomintang. He reread, or read for the first time, old copies of the *Min Pao*, which had ceased publication in 1909, and made a careful comparison between the strategy of the Reformers and the strategy of the Kuomintang. The Reformers were regarded as far superior to the Kuomintang, which had failed in its evolutionary attempts because it was lacking in any carefully thought-out plans, though it was observed that Liang Ch'i-ch'ao invented a new kind of state every spring, only to demolish it by the autumn; the winters were spent in preparing the foundations for the new, imaginary state to be constructed the following year. Mao admired them, if only for their inventiveness, and when he came to found his first political society, it was a society of students gathered together to study the works of the Reformers and bearing the name long associated with the Reform party. The society, called the *Hsin Min Hsüeh Hui* ("New People's Study Organization") was subversive only in the limited sense that it disapproved of Yuan Shih-kai's dictatorship. It was, as Mao came to admit rather ruefully later, considerably less subversive than many of the radical societies then coming to birth in the large cities.

Siao Yu claims that he was the co-founder of the organization and wrote the original rules one night in the spring of 1914. The rules consisted of seven simple clauses, and the charter members consisted of eleven students from the Normal School. Siao Yu was the first secretary, and therefore empowered to receive the small membership allowed to attend. The organization eventually assumed sharp political overtones, but in its beginnings it seems to have been largely a cultural society attended by dedicated young students. A surprisingly large number of them later became Communist party officials, and were executed by the Kuomintang.

With the death of Yuan Shih-kai in 1916, the civil wars, which were to plague China for thirty-five years, began in earnest. Mao was not particularly interested in them. He was antimilitarist as a result of his own brief experience in the army, and he realized that the Chinese wars were being fought according to obsolete patterns. He read avidly everything he could lay his hands on concerning the world war. He gave elementary lectures on strategy. He had been particularly delighted with Galliéni's effort to prevent Von Kluck's encirclement of Paris in September 1914 by commandeering all the taxicabs, and he followed Hindenburg's campaigns in Russia with interest; the memory of Hindenburg's use of massive driving wedges in the battle of the Masurian Lakes, leading to the destruction of a quarter of a million Russians, delighted him and was to remain with him. These two events were the only European examples he remembered when he later came to write *Strategic Problems of China's Revolutionary Wars*.

Mao was now the leader of a progressive movement in Hunan which made no claim to being revolutionary. Surrounded by a crowd of earnest young men, which included Hsiao San and a youth called Lo Man, who was to become a high official in the Chinese Communist party, Mao was beginning to put his mind to the practical affairs of organization. The *Hsin Min Hsüeh Hui* was not a political association; it was simply a society of young students earnestly debating the problems of the day and contemptuous of officialdom. They regarded themselves as the "new people," exchanged newspapers, thought of and discarded ideas of revolutionary action, gave lectures, and enjoyed debate. Mao dominated the small group, which never amounted to more than a hundred. He was slowly testing himself, discovering the sources of his power and enjoying the role of chairman; he was older than most of the other members and considerably more widely read.

But if his age gave him authority, it was also a sign of his inability to find himself: he was developing slowly. Handsome, brilliant, restless, and always poor, with a genius for discovering intelligence among young Hunanese students, already the pedagogue saturated with knowledge on a diversity of subjects, he might have become in time one of those erratic, charming, and aimless teachers who are occasionally to be found in Chinese colleges—men with exceptionally fine minds who write one or two short books during their lifetime and have no influence outside a small circle. "At that time," said Hsiao San, "there were two things he might have become, or rather three. He could become

an editor or a teacher, or a combination of both, or he could become a great general. I was firmly convinced that he would make
a good general because he talked so brilliantly about war. Also,
he had already fought a campaign. This happened quite early
during our life at the college. It often happens that soldiers will
receive orders to take over colleges for barracks. Our own college
received an ultimatum. Mao immediately sprang to its defense.
He took charge as though he had received the sanction of the
Ministry of War. He drilled the students and professors. His
orders, even to the senior professor, were instantly obeyed. He sent
out students to buy arms and medical supplies. We kept the
soldiers out and Mao remarked: 'This is the first time I have taken
military command.' He seemed to know it wouldn't be the last."

In the summer of 1918 Mao graduated and shortly before the
graduation his mother died, so breaking the last tie which bound
him to Shao Shan. For a long while he had been on bad terms
with his father. Peking beckoned. China had declared war
against Germany and Austria in August 1917. Shortly afterward,
Lloyd George, surveying the loss of manpower on the western
front, requested the Chinese government to send laborers to
France, and now at last from Tientsin, Shanghai, and Hong Kong
flotillas of laborers were being sent, though Sun Yat-sen thundered
against the agreement, saying that imperialism had claimed these
men and imperialism would ruin them. Some young Hunanese
laborers had decided to make the journey. The *Hsin Min Hsüeh
Hui*, which had once followed the Reform party, had flirted with
Sun Yat-sen, and was coming gradually to accept the ideas of some
intellectual leaders in Peking, helped to finance their journey to
the coast, and then turned its attention to its own lack of knowledge of Europe. Should not these young students also make the
pilgrimage?

In 1915 Dr. Ts'ai Yuan-p'ei had formed a society with the
strange name of the Diligence-Labor-Simplicity-Educational-So-
ciety to encourage students to obtain their higher education in
France while performing manual labor. Inquiries were made. Costs
were carefully worked out. By borrowing, and by selling some of
their possessions, about ten students, including Mao and Hsiao

San, set out for Peking with the intention of making their way
to France. Among the travelers was one of Mao's teachers, Hsu
Teh-li, who was the exact opposite of Yang Chen-ch'i. This old
scholar, born in 1876, who never wore an overcoat and who pro-
pounded theories of vegetarianism and had a fondness for swimming in rivers, delighted Mao, who later appointed him director
of education at Yenan. He was always laughing, and the journey
to the north was made to the accompaniment of his almost super-
human talent for finding amusement in everything.

Mao was appointed commander-in-chief of the expedition,
though he had no desire to go abroad and was content to supervise the operation, delighting in the complexities of travel and
happy to leave Hunan and see the world outside for the first time
in his life. He had everything to gain. The life in the provincial
capital was like life in provinces everywhere: the glory had departed. For a brief moment the white flag with the character for
Han* written on it in blood-red letters had flown over Changsha
as a sign of its conquest by the revolutionaries; then the flag had
been hauled down, to be replaced by the five-stripe flag, each stripe
representing one of the five races inhabiting China: Chinese,
Manchu, Mongol, Mohammedan, and Tibetan, and then for a
brief while Yuan Shih-kai had resurrected the flag showing the
imperial dragon. There were to be other flags later; in less than
ten years there was to appear in Hankow a red flag with a small
hammer and sickle in a blue center. All this lay in the future. As
they tramped around the Tung Ting Lake and took ship down
the Yangtse, none of these students could have dreamed what lay
before them.

* Han was the name of an ancient warlike dynasty. The Kuomintang revolutionaries seriously modeled themselves on its leaders.

THE NEW YOUTH

IN THE SUMMER of 1918 Peking was passing through a period of desultory peace. Ruled by warlords who formed uneasy combinations of power, the city slumbered through the last months of World War I, a rich city, and now richer than it had ever been, for silver was not yet devalued currency and the Maria Theresa dollar was worth more than one and a half American dollars. The casual observer saw prosperity everywhere, and even when Sun Yat-sen thundered from the small government chamber in Canton against the *tuchuns* of the north, hardly a ripple was perceptible in the dusty streets of Peking. Far away, on the other side of the continent, the Russian revolution was stirring up a convulsive war against the remnants of czarism; huge armies were wandering across Siberia; Lenin was proclaiming the dissolution of the state; but in Peking the state remained, represented by the strange feudal monsters, resplendent in their gaudy uniforms modeled on those worn by obscure princelings of Germany. Meanwhile, from Peking there was being organized the immense army of Chinese coolies who were to be sent, usually too late, to dig

53

trenches on the western front. No one was ever to know exactly
how many coolies were shipped to Europe: the figures ran from
100,000 to 200,000. Unknown to the *tuchuns*, the mass export of
coolies from Tientsin, Shanghai, and Canton was to seal the
fate of the Chinese empire.

In later years Mao was to say that he came to Peking in order
to organize the Hunanese students who were planning to go to
France on the "work and learn" scheme invented by the French
to bolster their dwindling manpower. There were other reasons.
He had long desired to study at Peking University. He had made
sporadic attempts to learn French and English, and at one time,
according to Hsiao San, he had contemplated writing a study of
the French and American revolutions. But there were no good
foreign-language teachers in Hunan except for the missionaries, and
he had long ago set his face against missionaries of any kind. He
was perfectly prepared to spend his days reading quietly in the
great Peking libraries. He would learn languages. He would travel,
like Yang Chen-ch'i, abroad. In the end he would take some minor
position in the government. He still regarded himself as the dedicated student, a young Bazarov perfectly content to occupy a small
place in the provincial history of Hunan. He helped to organize
the Hunanese students, saw that they went through a short training period at Chung-Fa, the Chinese-French university, and then
saw them off on the boat at Tientsin. By the time they sailed,
the world was was already coming to an inevitable conclusion.

Autumn came early in 1918. With almost no money left and
most of his friends on their way to Europe, Mao found himself
alone in Peking without a job and with a desperate desire to bury
himself in libraries through the long winter ahead. He was twenty-
five, of an age when most men have already settled upon their
profession or occupation; and he was farther away than ever from
having made up his mind about what he wanted to accomplish.

In all this Mao was not alone. Peking was filled with uprooted
intellectuals who flocked to the capital, stayed there for a few
years, and then retired, defeated, to their ancestral villages. The
imperial examinations open to poor students from all over the
empire had come to an end, though for a brief period they had

been revived by Yuan Shih-kai. Peking University was still the intellectual center of China, and it was at this university that Mao had wanted to study, for here at least he could have the illusion for a few years that he was not uprooted, that he belonged to the classical tradition of the Chinese scholar. Someone reminded him that Yang Chen-ch'i was then lecturing at the college on Chinese philosophy. Mao went to him, explained his situation, and was immediately whisked off to meet Li Ta-chao, then the librarian and later to become the real founder of the Chinese Communist party.

Mao received a minor position in the library. It was his duty to fetch the newspapers requested by the students, place them on the tables, and then collect them and return them to the files. In the whole university it was hardly possible to conceive of a more menial position: he was a little above the coolies and the sweepers, but he received the same salary as the coolies, and the students poring over the newspapers treated him as though he possessed only a mechanical existence. The great professors came, demanded their newspapers, and went away; and if Mao so much as paused to ask them a question, he was treated with the indifference with which scholars at the time treated the poor. Years later, when he came to discuss the relationship between scholarship and the people, Mao openly confessed that he came to detest these high-handed professors who spoke to him, when they spoke to him at all, with such evident contempt. "I know then," he said, "that there was something wrong. For hundreds of years the scholars had moved away from the people, and I began to dream of a time when the scholars would teach the coolies, for surely the coolies deserve teaching as much as the rest."

The story of Mao's first few months in the library is one of baffled retreat before the conventions of Chinese scholarship. He saw little of Yang Chen-ch'i, not daring to show himself in his worn black gown. Rebuffed after a serious effort to engage the young radical Fu Ssu-nien in conversation—the young radical was later to become a pontifical reactionary president of the university in its exile in Kunming—he kept very much to himself, nervous and ill at ease in the huge capital, where nearly everyone

disappears into a quiet anonymity, and where it is possible to die
without anyone paying the slightest attention. He found a translation of one of Bakunin's pamphlets, and announced to his rare
friends that he was an anarchist. There were similarities between
Bakunin's anarchism and traditional Taoism. He began to think
that the only solution for China's problems was a complete decentralization of government, and that the government itself must
be violently overthrown, forgetting that decentralization would
only make China still more powerless to resist the demands of
Japan and the Western powers. He corresponded with other
anarchists. He even thought for a while of founding an anarchist
society. Anarchism was in the air, and in Hunan especially there
were small anarchist groups among the industrial workers. But as
winter came on, the rage for an anarchist China gave way to
simpler pleasures. He saw more and more of Yang Chen-ch'i, and
he began to forget the loneliness and misery of his life in the
contemplation of Peking in a calm, snow-bound winter.

In his youth, Mao had walked barefoot and bare-chested
across the desolate fields of Hunan, where there are few trees and
almost no palaces. Here there were more trees and palaces than
he could even count, all of them shining in the frosty sunlight.
Most of the Forbidden City was now thrown open to the public.
He could wander at leisure over marble bridges and painted colon-
nades; around the North Lake stood the sloping yellow roofs of
the palaces emerging among the bare branches of the willows,
and he could pace the borders of the lake, where all the lotuses
were frozen, remembering that only a few years previously it
would have been a capital offense to enter these immense parks
reserved for the emperor's family and attendants. In summer
Peking is hidden in a green carpet of trees; in winter the city
shines clear, but the trees themselves form a kind of silvery frame
for the magnificence of blood-red walls and gleaming yellow roofs.
Mao was perfectly aware of the imperial magnificence, and he
took careful inventory of the trees. Nearly twenty years later the
memory was still vivid. "I saw the white plum-blossom flower
while the ice still held over the North Lake. I saw the willows
over the lake with the ice crystals hanging from them and remem-

The farm at Shao Shan,
where Mao Tse-tung was
born.

LEFT TO RIGHT: *Mao Tse-tung, his father, an uncle, and his younger brother Mao Tse-hung.*

Mao Tse-tung while librarian at Peking University, 1919.

The young revolutionary, about 1924.

BELOW: *Mao Tse-tung's first wife, Yang K'ai-hui.*

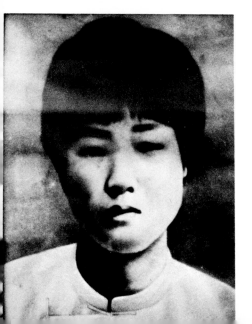

LEFT: *Mao Tse-tung and Chu Teh in Yenan, 1937.*

BELOW: *Mao Tse-tung delivering a speech, 1936.*

The valley of Yenan

Chou En-lai, Mao Tse-tung, and
Chu Teh on the airfield at Yenan,
1945.

General Marshall and Mao
Tse-tung, Yenan, 1946.

*Chiang Ching and Mao
Tse-tung, Yenan, 1945.*

Chu Teh
General Nieh Yung-chen

P'eng Te-huai
General Lin Piao

General Chen Yi
General Yeh Chien-ying

Chou En-lai
General Lin Po-cheng

Mao Tse-tung with bodyguards, during flight from Yenan, 1948.

Mao Tse-tung in triumph in Peking, October 1949.

bered the description of the scene by the T'ang poet Ts'en Ts'an, who wrote about Pei Hai's winter-jeweled trees, looking like 'ten thousand peach trees blossoming.' "* It was characteristic of Mao that he should have chosen to remember the most vigorous and pellucid of the T'ang poets; and in fact his own poetry borrows as deeply from Ts'en Ts'an as his prose borrows from Han Yu.

Though he was living in great poverty, this winter was probably the happiest in Mao's life. He fell in love with Yang K'ai-hui, the daughter of his professor of philosophy; he rode over the western hills on pony-back; he attended lectures at the university and immersed himself in poetry. More important, he found himself turning away from anarchism to socialism, and he discovered that the indifference with which he was treated in the library had been due partly to his own nervousness. He made friends and found himself caught up in all the social and literary movements which centered around the university. Hu Shih had returned the previous year from America with a bold program for substituting *pei hua*, the language of the common people, for the traditional literary language of the classics. Ts'ai Yuan-p'ei, the "great innovator," had become president and chancellor of the university and was dedicating himself to renewing the springs of Chinese youth.

More influential than any of these was the dean of the faculty of Chinese letters, Ch'en Tu-hsiu, who had been editing the magazine *New Youth* (*Hsin Ch'ing Nien*) ever since the famous day in September 1915 when the students of Peking were suddenly made aware from his first editorial that a new, iconoclastic force had arisen, urging them all to sweep away the corrupt Confucian past. "The task of the new generation," he proclaimed, "is to fight Confucianism to the death, all the old traditions of virtue and ritual, all the old philosophies and all the old political subtleties: and the old learning must go altogether. We must break down ancient prejudices and build a new society based on democracy and science."

It was heady wine, but though the students of Peking hung on his words and repeated them endlessly, Mao was not wholly impressed. He was making his way slowly. There were other reviews

* Edgar Snow, *Red Star over China* (New York, 1938), p. 151.

besides *New Youth.* In the four years between 1917 and 1921,
nearly four hundred student reviews appeared in China, most of
them short-lived, many of them containing the character for
"new" in the title. There were reviews called *New Woman, New
Light, New World,* and even *New Air.* Mao read them avidly in
the library, delighted that he no longer had to starve himself in
order to buy magazines, surrendering to the intellectual ferment
of the time, but wary of making decisions.

He met Ch'en Tu-hsiu briefly. At their first meeting neither
seems to have made any impact on the other. Intellectually, Mao
was more impressed with some of the young students in the classes
he attended, men like Cheng Kung-po and Chang Kuo-t'ao, both
of whom were to hold high office—the first as puppet prime minister under the Japanese, until his execution by Chiang Kai-shek
in the summer of 1946, and the second as Mao's own superior
within the Communist party, until his desertion to the Kuomintang. Nearly all his friends of this period came to violent deaths.
Intellectual violence was in the air. At this time were sown the
seeds of the conflicts that came later.

Though Mao failed to come under the direct influence of
Ch'en Tu-hsiu at their first meeting, he could not escape the per-
vading influence of the professor who almost singlehandedly had
changed the intellectual atmosphere of his time. Not until Wen
Yi-tuo subtly exercised an intellectual mastery over the exiled universities of China during World War II did any professor exert
so vast an influence on young Chinese students. Short and wiry,
with a fine forehead and very large, questioning eyes, nearly always
wearing a simple black scholar's gown, with an eye for women and
a fine taste in food, Ch'en Tu-hsiu at the age of forty could
already be counted as among the first four who were influencing
the course of China, ranking with Sun Yat-sen, Liang Ch'i-ch'ao,
and K'ang Yu-wei, and in opposition to all of them. His influence
was prodigious. It seeped down among the poverty-stricken coolies,
if for no other reason than that the students themselves often became coolies. He had the habit of writing in short epigrammatic
phrases. "The universal laws of science must take the place of the
Chinese heaven," he wrote, and with this single phrase he swept

Buddhism, Confucianism, and Taoism, which all concerned themselves in different ways with the interpretation of heaven (tien), into limbo. He approved and rejoiced in the Russian revolution, insisting that the Chinese should find comfort in a revolution directed not only against the Czar but against monarchism and imperialism; and at the same time he wrote superbly on the character of Jesus, insisting on the heroism of the Crucifixion, and he gave his blessing to the missionaries, who had, whatever their faults, brought Western culture to China. He flirted with Comte's positivism, and he was the first to comment intelligently on Marxism, devoting a whole issue of the review to a series of interpretations of Marxist philosophy. He was also in a very real sense a historical figure, for New Youth had come into being not long after Yuan Shih-kai had accepted the infamous Twenty-One Demands imposed upon China by Japan, and his review represented the only effective response to Japanese hostility.

Of all those Chinese who influenced Mao, Ch'en Tu-hsiu's influence was the greatest. Though the brief meeting in the winter of 1918 counted for little, there were to be endless meetings later. Ch'en Tu-hsiu not only influenced Mao's mind, but he influenced his style; and even the famous phrase "New Democracy" derives directly from Ch'en Tu-hsiu. Whole phrases, first written by this dean of the department of Chinese letters, are echoed and sometimes copied verbatim by Mao in the books he wrote years later in Yenan. It was a style which mingled exhortation with a vast hope, a concise, brutal, and entirely new style, deliberately denuded of the graces which previously informed Chinese apologetics. No one before had addressed the Chinese students in this way:

> What I want to say, and to say with tears, is that I hope those of you who are young will be self-conscious and that you will struggle. By self-consciousness I mean that you are to be conscious of the power and responsibility of your youth, and that you are to respect it. Why do I think you should struggle? Because it is necessary for you to use all the intelligence you have to get rid of those who are decaying, who have lost their youth. Regard them as enemies and beasts: do not be influenced by them, do not associate with them.

O young men of China! Will you be able to understand
me? Five out of every ten whom I see are young in age, but old
in spirit; nine out of every ten are young in health, but they are
also old in spirit. When this happens to a body, the body is
dying. When it happens to a society, the society is perishing.
Such a sickness cannot be cured by sighing; it can only be cured
by those who are young, and in addition to being young are
courageous. We must have youth if we are to survive, we must
have youth if we are to get rid of corruption. Here lies the only
hope for our society.*

To those who were brought up on classical Chinese, the
new trumpet notes, deriving from Ch'en Tu-hsiu's reading of
Nietzsche, were demonstrable evidence that China had come to
the turning of the ways. Famous old scholars approached Ts'ai
Yuan-p'ei and begged that Ch'en Tu-hsiu be removed from his
post. Ts'ai Yuan-p'ei refused. He could hardly do anything else,
for Ch'en Tu-hsiu was an excellent administrator, a scholar in his
own right—he published voluminous surveys of T'ang dynasty
poetry—and he had also taken part in the revolution of 1911. In
himself he represented the new youthful China, and at the same
time he was a bridge between the past and the future, for his ancestral roots lay deep in the mandarinate, and for centuries his
family had been powerful in Anhwei. He had one further advantage: he had traveled in France and Japan and knew the languages of both perfectly. Finally, he was well liked by his students
and the faculty.

The Peking over which Ch'en Tu-hsiu ruled with invisible
power resembled Moscow or St. Petersburg in the 1870's. There
were the same dedicated youths living in poverty and desperately
attempting to work out solutions for the crisis in which China
found herself. But while the young nihilists and anarchists of the
seventies envisaged a single enemy solidly entrenched on the
throne, the students saw countless *tuchuns* parading over China
and maintaining a precarious balance of power. The task seemed
almost hopeless. Before a new social state could come into being,

* Tsi C. Wang, The Youth Movement in China (New York, 1927), p. 98.

they would have to be removed one by one; and every time a
tuchun was removed, another might take his place.

For Mao the long winter in Peking was also a period of withdrawal. He took almost no part in political activity. He learned
some French and some English, courted Yang K'ai-hui—whom he
married a year later in Shanghai—visited all the imperial monu-
ments, walked around the walls of Peking, and attended to his
duties in the library. And since the library was open from seven
o'clock in the morning to nine o'clock at night, he had little
leisure. He saved no money. He wore a threadbare gown and allowed his hair to grow long. He had very bright eyes, and was
almost excruciatingly thin. Before the winter was over, he had
absorbed almost all that he wanted of Peking, and when another
detachment of students bound for France left for Shanghai, he
accompanied them as far as Tientsin, and there, finding himself
penniless, he stayed for a few days until a chance encounter with a
friend allowed him to borrow some money to continue the journey
to Shanghai.

As usual, he made most of the journey on foot. Wandering
was by now in his blood, and he was determined to wander over
all the historic places, walk around all the historic walls, and make
his way down all the historic roads. Yen Huei, one of the favorite
disciples of Confucius—the only one for whom Confucius
mourned—had lived, according to tradition, in a village along the
Huai River. Mao visited the place as an act of homage. He held
Yen Huei in great honor. It was not only that Yen Huei was
the most humble and the most devoted of the disciples, but he
was also the one who had received more traditional respect than
any of the others. Of him it was said that he was able to preserve
an attitude of "perfect virtue" for three months, while others were
unable to attain that level for more than a month or a few days.
Some particular virtue lived in him, and since nearly a half of
the Confucian Analects is concerned precisely with the problem of
"perfect virtue" and the characteristics of the sage, which were
never defined, except obliquely, Yen Huei has become a symbol of
all that Confucian tradition meant by the superior person.

In all this Mao was perfectly at home. Like Bazarov, he

had long ago decided to become a superior person, and the visit
to Yen Huei's birthplace was more than an act of desultory
homage.

Mao's wanderings led him to the tomb of Confucius at
Chufu, and from there he went on to ascend the T'ai Shan, the
Great Eastern Mountain, the highest in all China and the most
sacred—a strange enough journey for one who confessed to being
an anarchist, vowed to combat Confucianism. In fact, he had
never wholly departed from Confucianism, and a hard Confucian
core remained, to torment his enemies, who were neither so
learned as he nor so conscious of the role to be played by the
superior person. There had been a famous sacrifice at the tomb of
Confucius by Liu Pang, the first emperor of the Han dynasty.
Liu Pang rose from obscurity to the conquest of an empire, raising
the standard of revolt when he was still a shepherd, and creating
his capital in Sian, a few miles south of Yenan. Mao was saturated
in history and followed in nearly all their details the famous travels
of the historian Ssu-ma Ch'ien in this territory—as though he were
attempting to see through the historian's eyes the past grandeur
and the present decadence of the empire. When he climbed the
T'ai Shan, he must have been perfectly aware that the Han emperors had performed their sacrifices there and that it was on the
topmost summit that they had received the secret utterances of
Heaven as they waved their jade batons.

It is impossible, of course, to see too much in this journey.
Mao was marking time. He had not yet decided upon a course of
action. He was escaping from his librarian's job in Peking. He had
neither duties nor responsibilities. It is at such times that ultimate
decisions are made: at such moments of weariness and wandering
the mind plunges forward and scoops out its own pathways. Later,
he was to destroy Confucianism root and branch; it is inconceivable that he would have been able to destroy it without having
submitted to its power, without, in fact, being a Confucian himself.

Meanwhile he was the wandering scholar, continually on the
move, hardly to be distinguished from the hundreds of other
wandering scholars who were conscious of the power to be de-

rived from attending upon the holy shrines. Mao went everywhere. He walked in the dead of winter on the ice in the Gulf of Pei Hai, he visited the tomb of Mencius, and he continued to walk around the walls of historic cities, as though he was already possessed with the desire of conquering them: in ancient China the ceremonial march around the walls by the conquering general was a mark of his triumph. Finally, still nearly penniless, he returned to Changsha, but not before he had spent a week wandering around the Tung Ting lakes. He was fit and well. He had even managed to borrow a little money in Shanghai. He knew more than he had ever known before about the world outside Hunan, and he was prepared to "exert himself to the utmost" on whatever political issues confronted him, for at some time during his wanderings he had determined to enter politics, and if possible overthrow the men in power.

In Hunan, the times were ripe for change. While Mao was away in the north, an expedition was sent against the Hunanese, then in one of their customary rebellions, by Tuan Chih-jui, the prime minister. The generals in command of the expedition were Wu P'ei-fu and Chang Ching-yao. Wu P'ei-fu was a Buddhist, a scholar, and a poet, possessing many of the graces usually absent among Chinese warlords. Chang Ching-yao was the pure type of the corrupt tuchun. When Chang Ching-yao was appointed governor of Hunan, and Wu P'ei-fu was relegated to the subordinate position of vice-inspector of the military forces in Chihli, Shangtung, and Honan, all Hunan was in ferment. Wu P'ei-fu had recently written a bitter epigram describing his rival as "one whose fatty remains will serve to fertilize only a few yards of Chinese soil."

Mao, who had become editor of the Hsiang River Monthly Review, threw himself into the conflict, organized a student strike, and prepared to use the forces of Hsin Min Hsüeh Hui, which had continued in his absence, to attempt to overthrow not only Chang Ching-yao but all the military governors who followed; and under the banner of the League to Renovate Hunan he proposed some kind of wide-scale antimilitarist revolt. Ch'en Tu-hsiu had proposed such leagues in the past. Mao thought the time had

come to put the revolt into operation, for it was clear that the
Kuomintang revolution of 1911 had abundantly failed. He sent
himself on a mission to Ch'en Tu-hsiu, received the professor's
benediction, and returned with the necessary blueprints of revolt.
Ch'en Tu-hsiu had insisted upon some dramatic action, though he
never made clear what kind was appropriate to the occasion.

Events were moving fast. Mao was continually on the move.
Previously he had attended an antimilitarist conference, organized
by students, in Peking in January 1919. This followed a mass meeting held during the previous November in the National Central
Park, attended by nearly all the students of Peking University. At
the second meeting it was agreed that "if the world refuses to
give up militarism, China should lead the way," and with this
avowal of nonviolent resistance Mao was perfectly in agreement.
The problem of the *tuchuns*, however, remained.

There were, of course, innumerable other problems. There
was the deep restlessness of the student body, now replenished by
many students returning from abroad; there was growing industrial
unrest, a growing feeling of insecurity. China felt herself defenseless in a world at arms. Then, in the spring, came the explosion.

On May 4, 1919, there occurred one of those rare critical
events which completely alter the course of history. Revolutionary
action had been employed by peasants and by guerrillas; it was
now to be employed by students, and out of the student revolution, which canalized all the intellectual and moral frustrations
of generations of Chinese, there was to emerge the pattern of a
new, revolutionary China. With this movement, according to
Mao, the Chinese Communist party had its beginnings.

Outwardly, it did not give the impression of being a Communist revolt. What had happened had little enough to do with
social change. May 4, 1919, was the fourth anniversary of the
presentation of the Twenty-One Demands on China by Japan, a
day of national mourning. It happened that on this day there came
news that the peacemakers at Versailles had granted the former
German concessions at Shantung to Japan. It was an affront to
Chinese dignity. It was also an indication of Japan's further de-
signs. Immediately a violent excitement swept over Peking. There

was a sense of furious protest and at the same time a sense of relief. The time for direct action had come. What kind of direct action? Against whom? With what weapons? Ch'en Tu-hsiu had for some time been awaiting an explosion of this kind. His plans were prepared, and he carried them out with a masterly sense of order. He addressed the five thousand students of Peking University, told them to elect committees to tour the neighboring colleges, and urged them to elect by ballot a supreme committee to be devoted to direct action. There was to be a student cabinet and a council of wardens to carry out the decisions of the supreme committee. There was to be nothing casual: everything must be done quietly and systematically. The purpose of the new political movement was to overthrow the government, which contained the three cabinet members who had signed and accepted the Twenty-One Demands.

At ten o'clock in the morning of May 4, the students assembled in the Law School of Peking University. In the afternoon they held a mass meeting outside the Tien An Men, the "Gate of Heavenly Peace," at the entrance of the Forbidden City. They were more than ten thousand strong and they were armed with wooden clubs, iron bars, and cans of gasoline removed from the laboratories. Afterward they marched to the Legation Quarter to ask the Allied ministers to help in securing justice for China. The American Minister, the first to be approached, refused to see them, though four students were allowed inside the legation compound. It was a Sunday, and the Minister was perhaps perfectly reasonable when he declared afterward that important business should not be contracted on Sunday. The students, however, were angry. They had hoped to receive at least some sympathetic advice, perhaps even their recommendations might be transmitted to the Allied governments. Furious at what they considered the treachery of the Allies, they then marched to the house of Ts'ao Ju-lin, the minister of communications. The house was guarded by soldiers and policemen. They threw small paper flags over the high walls. Their intelligence system was excellent. They learned that all three of the hated pro-Japanese ministers were in the house. Thereupon they forced their way in, found the ministers

in consultation with some Japanese officials, and would have attacked them if the police had not suddenly fired over their heads.
The house caught on fire, whether from a police bullet or from
a match laid by a student, no one knows, and eventually the
students were thrown out. They marched back to the university.

Except for the incident in the house, the procession had
been orderly. So it was to remain. Every move which followed
was calculated and deliberate; it was as though the students were
working coldly and scientifically against the government. They
called the role and discovered that thirty-two students were miss-
ing. They then called upon the chancellor, Ts'ai Yuan-p'ei, for
advice. They wanted to march in procession to the police station,
but Ts'ai Yuan-p'ei dissuaded them. He went alone. He was told
that the students had been arrested for disturbing the peace.

The students now possessed a weapon with which they could
cajole the government. On the next day they called another mass
meeting and decided upon a provisional strike. Two days later
the thirty-two students were freed, but arrests continued, and on
May 14, while the strike was spreading to Shanghai and Nanking,
the government issued two special rescripts which exasperated
the students still further. The government ordered that the
student activities should be suppressed by military force, and
they announced that the decisions of the students would have no
effect on a responsible government. The students then employed
their strongest weapon: they declared a general strike. They had
absolutely no warrant for the declaration, and were not empowered to make the declaration; but for a long time there had
been an absence of any leadership, and the declaration was
obeyed. The shops closed in Peking. The railwaymen on the
Peking-Tientsin railway refused to allow trains to pass. Shortly
afterward the industrial and craft workers in Peking went on
strike, to be followed by those of Tientsin, Shanghai, Nanking,
and Hankow. The government gave way. The "three national
traitors" escaped to Japan without even the formality of resigning
from the cabinet.

The success of the student movement surprised the students.
For the first time they became aware of their power. The move-

ment did not end with the defeat of the three ministers. The supreme committee of the Chinese students ordered an embargo on Japanese goods and throughout the rest of the year there were continual clashes between students and Japanese. Not only Japan was blamed. Bitterness was deep: it was especially deep against America because the Chinese felt that the Americans possessed a privileged position at Versailles and were ultimately responsible for the offer to Japan.

America's inexplicable disinterest in China's recovery was commented upon at length in the magazines and broadsides which began to be issued in increasing numbers with the words, "Remember May 4th," on their covers. The movement had arisen entirely from within the intelligentsia, who had never until this moment known that they could have such a prodigious influence over the shopkeepers and the workers. The peasants were unaffected; it was a purely urban movement, and it marked the beginning of student influence in politics.

Mao must have known from his talks with Li Ta-chao that something of this kind was in the air. Insofar as the movement could be planned, it was planned by Ch'en Tu-hsiu with the assistance of Li Ta-chao, both of whom regarded themselves by this time as at least under the influence of Marxism. It was no accident that in the same month New Youth issued a special edition consecrated to a lengthy study of Marxism by Li Ta-chao. The impact of Marxism and Leninism was now being felt on an increasing scale, and clandestine printing presses began to produce more and more translations of the writings of Marx and the speeches of Lenin. Among these speeches the most important was one delivered by Lenin early in 1918 calling upon the whole of the Orient to rise against the imperialists.

Actually, it was not a speech but a manifesto; yet it was couched in the phrases employed by oriental monarchs, with a strange mingling of revolutionary fervor and monarchical trumpeting. The more famous Manifesto to the Orient, issued two weeks after the Bolshevik revolution, had set the keynote. In it, together with a proclamation renouncing all czarist possessions in the Far East and pledging support in the struggle for emancipation, there were apocalyptic references to "the empires of the unrighteous that are breaking down" and "the earth that is trembling under their feet." These references, which show signs of having been written by Bukharin, showed the temper of the times, the belief that the fire of revolution was about to sweep the whole world. Years later, with something of the same fervor, and at a comparable stage in the progress of a revolution, Mao Tse-tung, in the great palace at Peking, was to remember some of these phrases when, having declared the beginning of the dictatorship, he thundered: "Let the world tremble!"

With a more skillful administration, Li Ta-chao and Ch'en Tu-hsiu might have brought about a revolution in 1919. The students, the shopkeepers, the merchants, and the workers were on their side. Japan had been singled out as the main enemy, but all imperalists were included in a general denunciation. Inevitably, mistakes were made. It was one thing to accuse the foreigners of all the evils in China; it was altogether another thing to discover that many of the evils were the result of ancient Chinese traditions and a corrupt social system; and by directing the revolt outward, the leaders of what came to be known as the "May Fourth Movement" failed in their main purpose. Feudalism and the rule of the *tuchuns* remained unaffected, political cliques and warlords retained their power, and nothing was done to heal the breach between the Kuomintang in the south and the warlords in the north. Even more important was the fact that the soldiers and the peasants took no part in the movement.

Mao was swept up in the movement, and some of his original excitement appears in his account of it in *New Democracy*. He saw it as "a Communist revolt without Communists," and with some exaggeration acclaimed it as "the greatest and most thorough cultural revolution in Chinese history." He wrote:

> The May Fourth Movement was an anti-imperialist as well as an antifeudal movement. The outstanding historical significance of the May Fourth Movement lies in the fact that it possessed a feature not present in the 1911 revolution—it opposed imperialism and feudalism in the most thorough and uncompromising way. The reason the May Fourth Movement possessed this char-

acteristic is that the capitalist economy of China had made a
new step in its development at that time. At the same time the
revolutionary intelligentsia was witnessing the disintegration of
the three great imperialist countries, Russia, Germany, and Austria, the weakening of Great Britain and France, and the construction of a socialist state by the Russian proletariat. Also,
Germany, Austro-Hungary, and Italy were in the grip of proletarian revolutions. All these things gave new hope for the liberation of the Chinese nation.

It must be understood that the May Fourth Movement
broke out at the call of the world revolution, of the Russian
revolution led by Lenin, and formed a part of the world proletarian revolution of the time. Although we did not have a Chinese
Communist party during the May Fourth Movement, many
intellectuals did accept the primary Communist ideas, and they
approved of the Russian revolution. In its beginnings the May
Fourth Movement was a united-front revolutionary movement
absorbing the energies of three kinds of people: the Communist-
inclined intelligentsia, the revolutionary petit-bourgeois intelligentsia, and the bourgeois intelligentsia, who formed the right
wing. The cultural revolution of the May Fourth Movement
opposed feudal culture in a thoroughgoing way, and there was
never such a great and thorough cultural revolution in the history
of China. It achieved success in two ways: it opposed the old
morality and promoted the new morality, and it opposed the old
literature and promoted the new literature.

When Mao speaks of the "outstanding historical significance"
of the movement, he is not essentially exaggerating. Professor
John Dewey, then in Peking, visited the university at a time when
it had been transformed into a vast student prison surrounded
with the tents of soldiers, and wrote: "To say that life in China is
exciting is to put it mildly. We are witnessing the birth of a nation, and birth always comes hard." When the thirty-two arrested
students were released and marched down the streets of Peking
to the sound of brass bands, while flowers rained on them, he
wrote that "it was a victory for public opinion, and all set going
by these little schoolboys and girls." They were not for the
most part schoolboys and girls, but the implications were clear.

Ts'ai Yuan-p'ei, resigning shortly after the incident because he feared assassination by the police, described it more accurately. He said simply: "It is war between the deluge and the wild beast." But the wild beasts were to remain, and the flood was not to roll over China for many years.

Mao's insistence on the importance of the victory should not surprise us. It was a small war in which no one was killed. The casualties amounted to a solitary student who committed suicide. A foreign minister was thrashed, and a young lecturer cut off the tip of one finger in order to write on the palace walls in his own blood, without using a pen, "Tsingtao must be given back to us." Except for the abrupt flight of three ministers, almost nothing was gained. Yet in another sense everything was gained. Never before had the political power of the students shown itself so successfully. Nor was Mao exaggerating when he wrote that "the May Fourth Movement broke out at the call of the world revolution," for Ch'en Tu-hsiu and Li Ta-chao both regarded themselves as Communists.

During all this time Mao was in Hunan, armed with his blueprint from Ch'en Tu-hsiu and attempting to formulate a policy of revolt, obsessed with the idea that the policy must be "correct" and must be calculated to follow the complex laws of revolution he had learned from his study of Marxism; for after the May Fourth Movement he had come to regard himself, too, as essentially a Marxist. But the situation in Hunan demanded characteristically non-Marxist solutions. The *Hsiang River Monthly Review* was suppressed by Chang Ching-yao, but the May Fourth Movement was already in full stride, and the *tuchun* was confronted with interminable waves of protest coming from the students. He threatened to close the colleges; the students went on strike, following the pattern already carefully worked out in Peking; and all the time the *Hsin Min Hsüeh Hui*, which was coming to assume something of the character of a revolutionary secret society, grew increasingly powerful. Eventually, Chang Ching-yao was overthrown by Tan Yen-k'ai, who had held power in the early days of the 1911 revolution. There was no peace. A new army under Chao Heng-ti launched an attack on the new governor. It was as though Hunan was dedicated to perpetual unrest.

Mao was now finding himself. During one of these wars he led an antimilitarist attack on the provincial parliament. There were scuffles. Blood flowed. But no one was seriously hurt, and the attack altered nothing whatsoever. In the winter some anarchists working in a cotton mill at Changsha came out on a strike. The success of the strike suggested to Mao that antimilitarism and demands for a democratic government led nowhere, and confirmed him in his belief in Marxism, so much so that on the anniversary of the Russian revolution he organized a parade through the streets of Changsha. This, too, was foiled by the police. Thereafter, he saw no hope except in mass action and the formation of a Communist party.

The First Congress of the Communist Party of China was held in Shanghai sometime toward the end of June or the beginning of July 1921. No one now remembers the exact date, but Mao Tse-tung has selected the date June 30, rather arbitrarily, so that the founding of the party can be celebrated annually. This was not the first attempt to inaugurate the party, for in the Petrograd edition of *Pravda* for July 30, 1920, there appears a short paragraph saying that an organization of the Chinese Communist party then existed in Shanghai, but giving no further details. Pavel Miff, a delegate of the Far Eastern Bureau of the Comintern, who was on the scene shortly afterward, made inquiries and says that about thirteen delegates were present at the original conference, but they included "anarchists, biblical socialists, legal Marxists and camp followers," and that the anarchists broke away and the conference ended in a fiasco. The meeting which followed a year later was carefully arranged by Ch'en Tu-hsiu and Li Ta-chao, both of whom had by now resigned their posts at Peking University. They established themselves in Shanghai and began sending out invitations to the conference in May. Among the first arrivals was Mao Tse-tung, who helped to arrange the conference and whose friendship with the two leaders gave him a predominant position.

A complete list of the members of the original congress is

difficult to put together. Mao says there were twelve members, while others have spoken of seven, eleven, and fifteen. Among them certainly were the following twelve:

Ch'en Tu-hsiu, who was deposed from the Chinese Communist party in August 1927, and died in 1942.

Li Ta-chao, who was executed by Chang Tso-lin in 1927.

Chang Kuo-tao, expelled from the Chinese Communist party in April 1938.

Chou Fu-hai, who later became the secretary of Chiang Kai-shek and still later went over to the Japanese.

Ch'en Kung-po, who was executed by Chiang Kai-shek in 1946.

Shih Tseng-tung, who went over to the Kuomintang.

Pao Hui-sheng, who also went over to the Kuomintang.

Tai Chi-tao, who obtained high position under the Kuomintang.

Li Han-chün, who was executed in Wuhan in 1927.

Li Ta, who became a professor of social sciences at Peking University and appeared to drop out of politics.

Shao Li-tzu, who became Kuomintang ambassador to the Soviet Union and was governor of Shensi during the time of the Sian incident.

Mao Tse-tung.

Of the original members only three survived to become members of the Presidium which assumed the governing powers of China in September 1949. Three were executed, six went over to the Kuomintang, and two were expelled from the party. The survivors were Li Ta,* who continued his work as a professor of social sciences in the Kuomintang areas under another name while remaining in close touch with the Communists, Shao Li-tzu, whose extraordinary career embraced many of the highest offices of the Kuomintang, and who came to Peking to discuss surrender terms on a mission from Chiang Kai-shek, and Mao Tse-tung himself. Except for the two founders, all of them were young men under thirty, and the greater number of them were students from Peking University.

* In Red Star over China, Edgar Snow says that he was told by Mao that Li Ta had been executed. It is probable that Mao simply did not know what had happened to him, and execution was the probable fate of all those who had disappeared from the scene.

Mao seems to have been conscious from the beginning that the party as it was constituted was unwieldly. Because they were mostly students from upper-class families, with no roots among the people, they were far from being the revolutionary material which, according to Mao, the times demanded. Their speeches were elegant, but determination was lacking. They were in contact with Maring (Hendricus Sneevliet), who had been dispatched by Lenin to confer with Wu P'ei-fu and Sun Yat-sen, but Maring had only suggested that they establish study groups, though he also made promises of support. Maring, who had been Lenin's secretary, was himself confused by the extremely complex situation. A far more capable Comintern emissary was Grigori Voitinsky, who had reached China the previous year. Older than Maring, with a talent for seeing political shapes in broad outlines, he was the first to suggest that the final power would reside neither with Sun Yat-sen in the south nor with the warlords in the north, and he violently disagreed with Maring's contention that the Communists should work through Sun Yat-sen's Kuomintang party based in Canton. There were to be innumerable consequences of Voitinsky's disagreement. For years the official Communist thesis remained: Work within the Kuomintang, assume power through the Kuomintang, make the Kuomintang the servant of the Communists. Of all the Communists who worked on the problem, Voitinsky seems to have been the only one in 1921 who foresaw the future.

The work of the First Congress consisted in passing resolutions, forming various secretariats, and devising a blueprint for political action. It was decided to create a secretariat in charge of labor, but no one suggested a secretariat to deal with the problems of the peasantry. Resolutions were passed condemning anarchism, which had now extended over Hunan and Szechuan as a result of the strikes in the cotton mills. An even more significant resolution was passed: the Chinese Communist party rejected affiliation with the Comintern, apparently on the advice of Maring, who saw the danger of adding fuel to the "anti-foreign feeling" always present in China.

The Congress was held in a girls' school in the French Con-

cession. Students and teachers were away for the summer holidays
with only a cook and a guard on duty. The cook prepared meals
for the revolutionaries, and the guard saw to it that no unwanted
visitors appeared. Originally the Congress was scheduled to last for
seven days, but on the evening of the fourth day a stranger
described as "a man in a long cloak" blundered into the house,
asked questions about a certain Mr. Wang, the chairman of the
Association of Social Organizations, and then vanished. The building owned by the Association of Social Organizations was a few
doors away, but the chairman's name was not Wang. The revolutionaries decided that the visitor was a police spy, and most of
them hurriedly decamped, taking their documents with them. Ten
minutes later ten policemen arrived and made a search of the
building. They found some Marxist literature, but since it was
perfectly legal to possess such books and pamphlets in the French
Concession, no arrests were made.

The work of the Congress was still unfinished; no formal
resolutions had been passed; and it was decided to move to the
Western Lake at Hangchow, until someone remembered that in
summer the Western Lake was full of holiday-makers and the
chances of detection would be all the greater. Finally, it was decided to move Chiahsing, a watering place halfway between
Shanghai and Hangchow which would be less crowded. Here they
hired a boat, bought food and wine, and spent the whole day on
the lake debating their problems while pretending to be holiday-
makers. A light rain fell, and this helped them to avoid detection.
A good part of the day was spent in debating the relations between the Communists and the Kuomintang, and it was generally
agreed to support the Kuomintang while keeping a watching
brief for a more drastic program. No minutes of the Congress
were kept, or perhaps they were lost. Some of the more important
delegates were absent from the meeting on the lake, but Mao was
present. Surprisingly, he had invited his friend Siao Yu to ac-
company him, and though Siao Yu as an unregenerate Taoist
refused to have anything to do with the Communists, foreseeing
the appalling consequences to China if they obtained power, they
remained friends, and after the conference on the lake they spent

the night in the same bed hotly debating the issues. Then they returned to Shanghai.

While the First Congress of the Chinese Communist Party was in session, other Chinese Communists, unknown to them, were meeting thousands of miles away. In Paris, Berlin, Tokyo, and Moscow, Chinese gathered, deliberated, passed resolutions, and quietly determined that China would become a Communist state. Chu Teh, studying philosophy at Marburg in a desperate attempt to understand the motivations of the West, turned toward communism with a passionate singlemindedness, seeing it as the last recourse of the underprivileged; the simplicities of communism delighted his fundamentally complex mind. So with Chou En-lai, Lo Man, and Li Li-san, who founded a Chinese Communist party in France. Even in America there were small Chinese Communist parties. Hardly any of these parties knew of the existence of the others. It was dangerous to admit to an interest in communism, still more dangerous to say that one was a Communist, for postal censorship existed throughout all that part of China controlled by the warlords. Chu Teh, for example, wandered aimlessly over half of China before he journeyed to Germany, hoping to discover Communists, but finding none.

In this haphazard way, slowly and secretly, continually making mistakes, a handful of people were hoping to make China understand that communism supplied the answer to all political problems; very few of them knew what communism was, or what its Chinese equivalent would be. They spoke in terms of the dictatorship of the proletariat, which is inconceivable in China. They translated Marxist and Hegelian terms into characters which had little enough meaning in Chinese. But gradually the trap was being sprung.

THE YEARS OF WARNING

CHINA DURING the first half of the 1920's was divided into six large areas, each controlled by a warlord. The survivors of the warlords who inherited Yuan Shih-kai's empire were in the north, but most of the provinces were ruled by independent satraps. The country seemed, indeed, about to split into its provincial elements, and an observer might be excused if he thought, as Lord Henry Beresford thought at the end of the nineteenth century, that the only remaining question was: Which of the foreign powers will pick up the pieces? Yet, though a fatal instability seemed to be increasingly accepted as a permanent condition, there were nevertheless forces at work tending to weld the pieces more tightly together.

What were these forces? First, there was the remarkable growth in national consciousness, arising as a result of the May Fourth Movement among the students. Then, like water perpetually falling on rock, there were the actions of the Kuomintang in Kwangtung—a small party, with little financial power, dependent upon the whims of merchants whose profits derived from Hong Kong, but devoted to the task of breaking the power of the northern warlords.

Mao was now working on one of the few tasks which showed promise of affecting the political structure of the country, and which lay outside the orbit of the political parties. He delegated himself to Hunan, where he organized trade unions among the miners and the railway workers. He also organized trade unions among the printers and the workers in the government mint, as though deliberately attempting to influence people who would be most useful to the Communist party, if it ever emerged and acquired power. The Marxist theory demanded that the "vanguard of the revolution" should consist of the "awakened proletariat"; and now for the first time he came to know the small factory towns of Hunan. The peasants were temporarily abandoned, not because he no longer had any interest in them—he still spent a considerable part of his time at Shao Shan—but because they had no place in Marxist theory.

1922 was a year of Kuomintang failure. When in the early summer Sun Yat-sen gave orders for the punitive expedition to the north, his armies failed even to reach the borders of Hunan. There were uprisings in the rear of his army. Yet the center of Chinese revolutionary activity was now Canton rather than Shanghai. Here, in May, was held the First All-China Labor Congress and the First Congress of China Socialist Youth League, both Communist-inspired organizations. But Mao attended neither of these meetings. On May Day a general strike was called in Hunan, and he was too busy attempting to organize it to leave for Canton. The Second Congress of the Chinese Communist Party was held in Hangchow in July, and this, too, Mao failed to attend, though he made a journey to Shanghai—someone having misinformed him about where the Congress was being held.

Mao was still feeling his way. Separation from Ch'en Tu-hsiu, the decision to remain in Hunan, the extraordinary success of the general strike on May Day—all these things tended to make him a purely provincial leader. During the following year, too, except for a brief visit to Shanghai, he remained in Hunan; and the Third Congress of the Chinese Communist Party, held at Canton

in June, was held without him, though some of the preliminary
work for it was done by him in Shanghai, where he worked with
the Central Committee of the party. He was already one of the
members of the Central Committee, with the title of "delegate
representing Hunan," but his influence was still peripheral. The
third Congress was one of the most important of all, for here it
was resolved to allow the Communists to co-operate with the
Kuomintang, a decision brought about by the arrival of Borodin
and the gradual Russian orientation of the Kuomintang itself.
During the same summer Sun Yat-sen sent Chiang Kai-shek on a
mission to Moscow, with a letter of introduction to Lenin. By
November the Kuomintang party itself was being reorganized,
with Borodin's assistance, on the model of the Communist party
in the Soviet Union. The Chinese Communist party, therefore,
had reason to believe that it would inevitably be able to influence
the Kuomintang, and during November and December the gates
of the Kuomintang were thrown wide open to Communist members.

This time Mao did not fail to seize the opportunity. He
attended the First National Congress of the Kuomintang Party
in Canton, which was held during the last ten days of January,
as a member of the Kuomintang. At the same time he was a
member of the Central Committee of the Communist party. There
was nothing particularly reprehensible in being a member of both
parties. Borodin had become Sun Yat-sen's conscience, and this
heavy man with the drooping mustache and the puffed cheeks
dictated the policies of the Kuomintang just as he dictated the
policies of the Communists. It was an enviable position. He
knew no Chinese and had made only a cursory study of Chinese
history; but he had the sense to make a profound study of the
Taiping Rebellion, and with this to guide him he attempted to
work out a policy acceptable to both wings of the combined
Kuomintang-Communist party. But from the first it was the
Communists who were most suspicious of him.

The orientation toward Russia had been gathering momentum ever since Sun Yat-sen signed the famous agreement with

Adolf Yoffe in January 1923. The agreement encouraged Sun Yat-sen to believe that Soviet communism was preparing to make no claims on the Chinese revolutionary movement. By the end of the year, with Borodin in command, the Comintern was already in the position where it could dictate Kuomintang policy. Canton began to be filled with those strange international adventurers who, knowing little of China, and with no loyalty to the Chinese, argued among themselves, passed resolutions, and considered themselves authorities on "the broad currents of Chinese history" in the name of international communism. There is no evidence to suggest that they ever served the cause of the Chinese revolution, and Mao, who knew no foreign language well and possessed a considerable contempt for foreigners in general, mentions them rarely, and then with scorn.

Now for the first time he was arriving at the stage where he could influence policy. He met Chiang Kai-shek, who had returned from Russia with glowing accounts of Russian industrialization. He was introduced to Sun Yat-sen and the other leaders of the Kuomintang party. When the Communists insisted that their own members be included within the Central Committee of the Kuomintang, Mao's name was put forward. He was not a good speaker, but he was an excellent manager of debates: he would corner speakers and urge them to discuss certain topics and give them a desired "slant." He was beginning to be a power behind the scenes.

It was during this period that Mao became the secretary of one of the most powerful people thrown up by the 1911 revolution. Hu Han-min is hardly known outside China, yet he played a dominant role in the early days of the Kuomintang revolution. Complex, sometimes mischievous, a reactionary by instinct and a revolutionary by choice, he was second only to Sun Yat-sen at the time Mao became his secretary. Because being secretary to a minister often involves assuming many of his tasks, Mao possessed at this time quite extraordinary powers. He was taken into Hu Han-min's confidence, and the documents that the aging minister was expected to see and approve were chosen by the

secretary who four years before had been wandering in rags over
the province of Shantung. For the first time Mao was presented
with the opportunities of power.

Hu Han-min professed a deep interest in communism. He,
too, had been born a peasant—he was one more of those peasants
who were born in obscure villages near Canton and who came
to high positions. He had passed the imperial examination and
received the title of chu jen, been a schoolteacher, studied in
Japan, and taken part in the abortive risings led by Sun Yat-sen
in 1910. Immediately after the revolution of 1911 he had become
governor of Kwangtung, and afterward, during Sun Yat-sen's brief
presidency, he was appointed secretary to the president. He was
one of the editors of the Min Pao, and all of Sun Yat-sen's
writings had passed through his hands, to be edited by him.
Sun Yat-sen did not entirely trust him. Nepotism, a tone of
casualness in his voice, the suspicion that he desired power over
all things—all these reflected on the character of the dark-skinned
man whose large, heavy head and cruel mouth and intelligent
eyes gave him the appearance of the pure revolutionary.

Mao was his secretary for about three months. He seems to
have gained considerable power over the Minister, who increasingly came to favor the Soviet Union—in the following year he
made a pilgrimage to Moscow, where he was greeted as the
"hope of the Chinese revolution" and addressed continually as
Generalissimo. Mao possessed a real admiration for him, if only
because he had edited the Min Pao at a peculiarly receptive
period of his own adolescence. Hu Han-min had supported the
Russian orientation in a number of speeches at the First National Congress of the Kuomintang, and like Mao he had risen
from poverty. It was Hu Han-min who appointed Mao a delegate
of Hunan to the Central Committee of the Kuomintang.

The Manifesto of the First National Congress of the Kuomintang—the most important of the documents to be issued
during the historic meeting—was written not by Sun Yat-sen but
by the strange, mercurial, and faintly sinister Wang Ching-wei.
He, too, supported the Russian orientation. He had a simple,
handsome face, which rarely revealed what was going on in his

mind, and he looked twenty years younger than he was. Bland, polished, a delightful host, he regarded himself as the historian of the movement. He wrote nearly all the Kuomintang manifestoes, rewrote sections of the *Three Principles of the People*, and rewrote, emended, or entirely revised, where he did not entirely invent, the last speeches and testaments of Sun Yat-sen made on his deathbed. He modeled himself on Julius Caesar, whose *Commentaries* he admired; and though incapable of generalship, he thirsted to be generalissimo. He was a senior member of the Kuomintang Executive Committee, and when the Whampoa Military Academy for the training of officers to lead a punitive expedition to the north was opened, he appointed himself "chief professor of the history of the Kuomintang party." Hu Han-min introduced Wang Ching-wei to Mao, who for a short period fell under his spell. Wang Ching-wei had taken part in the movement to send young Chinese students to France, and for Mao this was also a recommendation. But it was from Hu Han-min that Mao derived the close knowledge of the workings of the Kuomintang, and from him too that he came to understand the ineradicable weaknesses of the party. In later years Mao suggested that the Kuomintang destroyed itself through pride. In Hu Han-min the flame of pride burned very brightly indeed, so brightly that he was hardly able to see the party without seeing himself as its most glorious defender and most potent organizer.

There follows in the life of Mao a period of extraordinary tightrope-walking. A member of both the Communist party and the Kuomintang, devoted to the conspiratorial overthrow of one to the benefit of the other, working in close touch with the leaders of both, curiously anonymous and detached, appearing rarely in public, he was beginning to exert a subtle, invisible influence. He was constantly traveling between Shanghai and Canton. He inspired trust, and the most important missions were given to him, but his whole existence was lived on the borderline of history, and his name appears in none of the registers of membership of the Kuomintang party.

In the winter of 1924, the affairs of the Kuomintang were

moving toward a crisis. Sun Yat-sen launched another unsuccessful
punitive expedition to the north, and once more he was compelled to withdraw because of treachery in his own ranks. When
the "Christian General," Feng Yu-hsiang, invited Sun Yat-sen to
Peking to discuss a situation which was getting out of hand,
Sun Yat-sen believed the heaven-sent opportunity had at last
arrived: with the help of Feng Yu-hsiang he would call for a
National Assembly, and all China's problems would immediately
be solved. For a few months an astonishing hopefulness reigned
in China, and Wang Ching-wei became dithyrambic in his utterances, pronouncing a blessed state of harmony as the inevitable
result of Sun Yat-sen's journey to the north. There was to be no
harmony. Sun Yat-sen fell ill on the journey, to die of cancer in
the spring. That winter, working at the headquarters of the Communist bureau in Shanghai, Mao had become ill from overwork,
and as a hopeless state of chaos began to descend upon China, he
removed himself from the scene, retiring to Shao Shan, leaving
his brother to represent him in Shanghai.

This retirement was to have prodigious consequences. The
Chinese Communist party under Ch'en Tu-hsiu was dedicated
to the overthrow of the existing government by the methods
Lenin had introduced: the proletariat, as the advance guard of
the revolution, would take over the functions of the government
through its elected representatives. It was the classical thesis clas-
sically understood. Now for the first time, as he lay in bed in
his small village, Mao began to question the validity of the Communist thesis. Accustomed to compromise through his work in
merging the Communist and Kuomintang parties, he began to
see that the evolution of Chinese communism could come only
through a period of compromise. The theory of proletarian
uprisings was dubious; the force of China lay in the peasantry.
Not in Canton or Shanghai, but in the millions of small villages
like Shao Shan, lay the seeds of the revolution.

When spring came, Mao was out in the fields, organizing the
peasants. Previously he had attempted to organize miners, railway
workers, even the small tradespeople. Now he abandoned them
completely. Traveling mostly at night, hiding in the villages by

day, talking to the farmers who remembered him from the days when he walked barefoot over the Hunanese hills, he formed in the spring of 1925 the nucleus of the peasant armies he was to unleash in the spring of 1927. The adventure lasted three months. There was a price on his head, for his activities were becoming known to the landlords and the militarists who ruled over Hunan. He became a legend, for legends grow rapidly in the countryside, only to die in the towns. A tall, thin, sunburned man in a sun helmet, traveling under many names, looking like a land agent, he was beginning to set the spark to the peasant kindling.

The mission he had given himself—he was alone throughout this period—was dangerous. The price on his head increased, and from various directions small groups of soldiers were sent out after him, questioning the villagers and demanding knowledge of his movements. Mao could trust the smaller peasants; the middle peasants, he knew, could be bribed; and his horror and fear of them dates from this time. By the late summer he was fleeing for his life over the Hunan border and making his way to Canton, where his activities in Hunan were unknown, or only guessed at.

In Canton the whole political atmosphere had changed. The battle of the satraps, following the death of Sun Yat-sen, ended with the victory of Wang Ching-wei, who now exerted the real political power. Hu Han-min was sent to Moscow, the possesser of wide ambassadorial powers, an aging man who babbled polite irrelevancies to Stalin, promised the unyielding support of the Kuomintang to the Comintern, and drank more vodka than was good for him. But though the real political power lay in Wang Ching-wei's hands, another power was slowly emerging in the shape of a handsome young Chekiangese officer, who wore gold earrings and held himself with the stiffness of a Prussian parade-ground sergeant. His name, in the Cantonese dialect, which he never learned to speak, was Chiang Kai-shek.

Wang Ching-wei had not forgotten Mao. In Canton and Shanghai the young, resourceful Hunanese had admirably performed the duty of forging co-operation between the Communists and Kuomintang. Now, as the plans for a final punitive expedition against the north took shape, this co-operation became all the more necessary; and Mao's genius for tightrope-walking was given full play. A host of duties were given to him. He became editor of the *Political Daily*, the informative secret newspaper placed before all the highest government officials every day; he lectured or supervised lectures at Whampoa Academy; he continued to supervise the co-operation of the two parties in Canton, assuming the position of chief spokesman for Communist affairs, since the greater number of the Communist leaders remained in the comparative safety of Shanghai. Ch'en Tu-hsiu was still the Communist power in the country, but he was almost permanently resident in the French quarter of Shanghai. It was the year that Ch'en was elected a delegate of the Chinese Communists to the Third International, and in the same year he was also elected a member of the Central Executive Committee of the Kuomintang. Never had the two parties collaborated so closely; nor were they ever to collaborate very closely again.

Mao had become the symbol of the collaboration. Given his talents, it was an ironical situation. Though, outwardly, he performed his Kuomintang functions well, he was essentially a Communist by the conviction, now completely formed in him, that the peasants could lead the revolt. The Kuomintang at this time was prepared to recognize the privileged position of the peasantry. Laws were passed concerning land tenure, and the expropriation of the large landlords was debated at length in the Kuomintang headquarters. It was recognized that the northward march would be completely impossible without the aid of the peasants. Mao could, and did, exert pressure in favor of the peasants. He organized a seminar where men were trained in the organization of peasant movements; and here, for the first time, safeguarded by the whole Kuomintang apparatus, he worked out methods of arming the peasants and made blueprints for peasant revolts, revolts which would break out during the northern punitive expedition. Wang Ching-wei was credited with the belief that an inevitable revolutionary era would be ushered in by this northern march. Borodin approved of it. Hu Han-min had given it his blessing shortly before leaving for Russia. It was assumed that

Chiang Kai-shek, the commander of the First Army, would obey the government which had assumed the mantle of Sun Yat-sen. No assumption could have been more incorrect. Chiang Kai-shek had many virtues, including a belief in his own star, but he resolutely opposed revolutionary uprisings among the peasants. "The task of the peasant," he wrote, "is to provide us with information concerning the enemy, food and comforts in our encampments, and soldiers for our armies." He said nothing about the duties of the army toward the peasants.

By the end of the year, Mao was assuming even wider functions. He became a candidate for membership in the Central Executive Committee, he broadened out the whole scheme of seminars for training peasant leaders, and he became head of the Propaganda Bureau of the Kuomintang. Communists were now taking increasingly high positions within the Kuomintang. Tang Ping-shan was head of the Peasant Bureau, and other Communists were to be found in the Bureau of Finance, the Bureau of Supplies, and the Bureau of Foreign Affairs. They were prominent at the Whampoa Academy and, because they were a cohesive group, they exerted an influence out of all proportion to their numbers. Whatever else happened, they were determined that the success of the northern march would be followed by a greater Communist influence within the Kuomintang; and since they, and particularly Mao, were in charge of bringing the peasants on the side of the punitive expedition against the warlords, the chances of success increased.

Mao wrote some articles on the peasant situation in relation to the forthcoming expedition; and though Ch'en Tu-hsiu opposed the more radical policies advocated by Mao, he could do nothing to prevent him from exerting his radical influence. When, on July 9, 1926, the northern expedition set out, its success in occupying Hunan, Hupeh, Kiangsi, Anhwei, and Kiangsu within the space of three months could be set down to the co-operation of the peasants, and the Communists could claim with some justice that they had prepared the ground.

Whenever events of dramatic importance occurred, Mao usually found himself in Hunan. It was almost as though he was deliberately placing himself as far away from the scene of major operations as possible. During the May Fourth Movement he was in Hunan; he was again in Hunan during the May Thirtieth Movement of 1925, when a vast anti-British campaign was launched after the shooting of some demonstrators in Shanghai's Nanking Road by Sikhs under British command; and he was in Hunan at the time of Sun Yat-sen's death. When the northern expedition marched out of Kwangtung, he was once more in Hunan, this time as an inspector of peasant unions, preparing the collaboration of the peasants with the revolutionary army which came marching up from the south.

The period 1925–1927 has come to be called the Great Revolution. It is difficult to understand why. Chiang Kai-shek's army reached the Yangtse, and then turned east. By the following spring his Cantonese soldiers were outside the walls of Shanghai. The government, meanwhile, remained in Wuhan. It was a government predominantly under the control of left-wing members of the Kuomintang. Chiang Kai-shek had treated it with contempt throughout. There had been quarrels on the march, strange silences, curious pauses while the armies reformed.

Suddenly, on April 12, 1927, Chiang Kai-shek gave the orders for the occupation of Shanghai and, at the same time, commanded the complete extermination of the Communists and Socialists in the city. This entirely unexpected development— neither the order for the occupation nor the order for the extermination of the left-wing workers had the sanction of the government in Wuhan—revealed that entirely new forces were at work. In March 1926, Chiang Kai-shek attempted a coup d'état in Canton. It failed. The Kuomintang government was re-established, and Chiang Kai-shek offered himself for punishment, only to be excused on the grounds that he was perhaps only exerting his "great zeal." He had, in fact, been testing his own powers. In Shanghai he showed proof that he was under no illusion about their extent.

The massacres of Shanghai were never to be forgotten by the Communists; and the merciless vendetta which lasted until 1950 had its origins during those days when, without warning,

Chiang Kai-shek attempted to put down once and for all any opposition that might come from the revolutionary proletariat. He excused himself by saying that information had been received that Communists in Shanghai had been ordered by Moscow to bury their arms, and would inevitably endanger his rear as he pushed toward Peking; but it was observed that he received large sums of money from foreign and Chinese merchants to finance the northern expedition, and it was reasonably surmised that one of the conditions attached to these grants was the extermination of Communist influence within the party.

On the day of the Shanghai massacre, Chiang Kai-shek inaugurated a new government at Nanking. He declared bluntly that the power had now fallen into his hands, and he would treat with Wang Ching-wei only on his own terms.

Exactly what happened in Wuhan will probably never be known. There seems to have been confusion, purposelessness, sudden decisions made at night, then long periods of waiting upon orders never made clear. Wang Ching-wei possessed a brilliant mind, but it was hardly a clear mind; he hesitated and delayed. In sympathy with the workmen massacred in Shanghai, the Communists brought about a general strike—the first general strike in China successfully accomplished by them. At night there were Red Guards patrolling the streets, but Borodin no longer gave orders, and Ch'en Tu-hsiu no longer felt any impulse to exert his authority. Three hundred thousand workers were silent, and none of them knew what to do. Meanwhile, on the highest levels, there were endless discussions, endless efforts to avoid unavoidable issues.*

---

* The incredible confusion has been described by Tsou Lu, an associate of Hu Han-min and Sun Yat-sen: "When Wang Ching-wei sent the telegram saying he would resign, I didn't take it seriously. Suddenly I heard that Wang Ching-wei had gone to Lushan in Kiangsi, and then I heard that Ch'en Kung-po had gone to Kwangtung, and then I heard that a branch Political Council was established in Wuhan, and then that Wuhan opposed the Extraordinary Commission. Then I heard that Wang Ching-wei had gone to Wuhan, explaining that there was a precedent for the Extraordinary Commission, and then I heard that Wang Ching-wei proposed the opening of the Fourth Plenary Session of the Central Executive Committee to recognize the Extraordinary Commission, and then I heard that the mass meeting

There were reasons for the strangely hesitant atmosphere in Wuhan. The left wing of the Kuomintang was without capable leadership. Left behind during the Kuomintang advance on Shanghai, shocked by the massacres of April 12 and the bombardment of Nanking by British and American warships—with thirty-five foreign warships at anchor in the Yangtse outside Hankow—they realized that the slightest decisions would have endless, unpredictable consequences. They were not alone there. The Chinese Communist Party was also in session, attended by a strange medley of Comintern advisers—Borodin, Pavel Miff, Earl Browder, Jacques Doriot, and, the most powerful of all, Manabendra Nath Roy. Most of them were incompetent, and all were useless at this turning point in Chinese history. Ch'en Tu-hsiu presided over this, the Fifth Congress of the Chinese Communist Party, but he seems to have been as baffled as the rest.

The issues were not simple. From Nanking, Chiang Kai-shek was threatening to launch a punitive expedition on Wuhan. On April 5, Ch'en Tu-hsiu and Wang Ching-wei issued a manifesto which exhorted the Communists to be faithful to the Sun-Joffe Agreements, and there seemed to be some hope among the left-wing Kuomintang that a common program, including wide-scale land reform, could be put into operation. Moreover, there were three armies, under Cheng Ch'en, Tang Sheng-shih, and Tan Yen-k'ai, ready to support the Wuhan government, but only on conditions presented by their commanders. These conditions included the immediate cancellation of all the plans for agrarian reform, for the army officers were themselves proprietors. Any attempt at agrarian reform would be crushed by the army; any attempt to use the army against Chiang Kai-shek would probably

---

to support the Extraordinary Commission in Canton had been postponed, and then I heard voices in Canton proclaiming against the Extraordinary Commission, and then I heard that Wang Ching-wei had gone from Wuhan to Shanghai, and then I heard he had gone to Canton from Shanghai and proposed to convene the Fourth Plenary Session and dissolve the Extraordinary Commission, and then I heard that he had returned to Shanghai, and then I heard that Canton had been occupied by the Communists, and then I heard that Canton was recaptured. It was like a movie film." Tsou Lu, *Reminiscences* (Chungking, 1943).

lead to defeat, for Chiang Kai-shek possessed a navy, overwhelming manpower, and considerable foreign support; finally, if the three armies were not employed, they might be expected to take over Hankow and rule by military junta. All these possibilities were clearly foreseen by the government in Wuhan, and no solutions were in sight. At last, apparently through the mediation of Wang Ching-wei, Chiang Kai-shek advanced northward and abandoned his threatened attack on Wuhan. At the same time the three Wuhan armies marched against the forces of Chang Tso-lin, in the north. But the revolutionary problems remained exactly as they were before, and the most urgent of these problems concerned the peasant uprisings through Hunan and Hupeh.

Early in 1927 Mao was sent to Hunan to report on the farmers' associations. Traveling overland from Shanghai, he arrived in January. He spent only thirty-two days in the province, but during those days he laid the seeds for a revolution which affected the whole development of the Kuomintang and Chinese Communist parties. In the previous year, as secretary of the Kuomintang Peasant Committee, he had gathered considerable material concerning landownership in China. The figures showed that poor peasants, numbering perhaps 65 per cent of the population, owned only 10 to 15 per cent of the cultivable land; another 15 per cent was owned by the "middle peasantry"; the remaining 70 per cent was owned by the absentee landlords, rich peasants, and money-lenders. On the basis of these figures Mao concluded that the peasants were ripe for rebellion. Returning in 1927 to the counties in Hunan he knew best, he was determined to bring the rebellion about. He inspected the counties of Changsha, Lilin, Hsiang T'an, Hung Shan, and Hsianghsiang, where he had wandered in his early youth, and secretly brought about a revolt, explaining what he was doing in a short report addressed to the Interprovincial Peasant Union.

This report should be studied at some length. Much that came later is explained by it, and the first stage of the revolution as Mao saw and guided it bears a close relationship to the violent strategy evolved during the month-long walking tour in central Hunan. In the history of revolution, this report is probably as important as the theses written by Lenin during the October revolution.

The armies of the northern expedition preached revolution but hardly practiced it, with the result that the peasants came increasingly to take power in their own hands. By October 1926, the peasant associations were in control of large areas of central Hunan. They were a force to be reckoned with. Mao estimated that during the period from July to September 1926, their total membership did not exceed 300,000 or 400,000, but after October their numbers rose sharply to 2,000,000, and half of the entire peasantry was organized under the control of the peasant associations. These were the associations which Mao himself had brought into being. He had also largely directed the propaganda campaign preceding the northern expedition, and his responsibility for the peasant uprisings was therefore twofold: he had helped to form the associations, and he had fed them with a continuous stream of propaganda from Canton. The effect was astonishing, and out of all proportion to the means employed; and the violent "revolution within a revolution," the peasants taking over power while the Kuomintang armies marched north, could only be explained by the long-pent-up despair of the poor peasants in Hunan.

The flame, lit in Canton, traveled across Hunan. No landowner's life was safe. The richer ones fled to the safety of Shanghai; those who were less rich fled to Hankow; others escaped to Changsha. Those who remained, or were caught by the peasants, were compelled to renounce their riches. Those who wore long gowns or owned more than fifty mou of land were fined, required to make contributions to the peasant association, and had their sedan chairs smashed before their eyes. The final affront consisted in taking their opium pipes away from them, and then the pipes were broken. With some relish, Mao noted that "the ivory beds of the daughters of the landlords were stepped upon by the dirty feet of the peasants." Revenge was in the air. Tragic excesses were sometimes committed. Landlords who had committed grievous crimes according to the peasants were killed; others were compelled to march down the streets wearing tall paper hats with their sins written on them. Mansions on large estates were burned to the ground. "There was a huge storm, and only those who bent to the storm could survive."

In his report on the revolutionary outbreak, Mao was wholly on the side of the peasants. He went to some length to defend the peasant terror. "Revolution," he wrote, "is not a dinner party, nor a literary composition, nor a painting, nor a piece of pretty embroidery; it cannot be carried out 'softly, gradually, carefully, considerately, respectfully, politely, plainly, and modestly.' " With this eightfold declaration against revolutionary gentleness—the last five terms are borrowed from the Confucian *Analects*—he launched into a studied defense of the uprisings. Even their excesses, he said, were necessary and possessed revolutionary significance. He defended the peasant leaders against the charge that they were rabble who "go about in worn-out shoes, carry broken umbrellas, wear green gowns, and gamble." No, they were reasonable men, behaving in a reasonable and revolutionary way. They fought, they organized, and they performed all the complex tasks of the revolution. The report is almost a hymn to the peasantry, "who placed their muscular, sunburned hands on the heads of the gentry." The reign of the *t'u-hao*, which literally means "local ruffians" but came to mean the "local gentry," was at an end, and it was the poor peasants who were most responsible for their defeat. "To reject the poor peasants," wrote Mao, "is to reject the revolution." Sun Yat-sen had devoted forty years of his life to bringing about the revolution which the peasants had accomplished in a few months. The real heart of the revolution was here, and—with a characteristic use of mathematical symbols—Mao came to the conclusion that if the whole revolution was represented by the figure 10, then its success in the cities might be accounted as 3, and among the peasants as 7. He therefore demanded urgent action by the Wuhan government: their mistakes must be immediately corrected. Why? Because in a short time hundreds of millions of peasants would arise in China with the fury of a hurricane, and there was no power on earth able to restrain them. "All the imperialists, all the warlords, corrupt officials, and t'u-hao will meet their doom at the hands of the peasants. Are we to lead them or criticize them behind their backs or fight them from the enemy camp? Among these three alternatives every Chinese can choose freely."

For the first time Mao was now demanding direct action by the peasants, without the formalities of discussion with the Kuomintang, and without the agreement of the Central Committee of the Chinese Communist party. The report was tabled before the Central Committee in Wuhan. Ch'en Tu-hsiu immediately ordered Mao out of Hunan and refused to allow the report to be discussed within the party. The damage, however, had been done. The peasant rising, as Mao had expected, produced panic in Wuhan. And still the Wuhan government vacillated, wondering what the consequences would be if they, who were supposed to represent the left wing of a revolutionary party, threw their military force against the peasants, who were demanding no more than Sun Yat-sen's "equalization of land."

The Communists at Wuhan were equally unsure of themselves. In one of those strange directives which Stalin occasionally issued from the Kremlin to the Far Eastern bureau of the Comintern, then sitting at Wuhan, he had explained in the previous year that full-scale agrarian reforms were impermissible at this stage, because immediate difficulties would arise from within the revolutionary army. Mao was presumably aware of the directive; and on his own initiative he acted entirely against it. By the time Mao left Hunan the revolutionary flame was lit, and there was no way, except by military invasion, to put the flames out. The Wuhan government could deliberate to its heart's content, Chiang Kai-shek could decide to attack Wuhan, or he could march north: for Mao none of these possibilities had any importance whatsoever, for he saw clearly, as Borodin had failed to see, that there could be no real revolution until the absentee landlords were dispossessed and the peasants brought into the current of the revolutionary wave. The concessions of the Wuhan government consisted largely in a general surrender of the peasants to the cause of Chiang Kai-shek's betrayal. By forcing the hand of the Wuhan government, Mao hoped to change the whole course of the revolution.

He did not succeed. He may have guessed that the peasant rebellion would be put down with ruthless efficiency, but for four months the peasants in the five counties resisted. In the areas controlled by them the peasant associations possessed the sole power, and the privileges of the landlords were taken from them. The landlords fought back. Apparently writing early in March, Mao said:

The Hunan peasants at the present time cannot be said to have overthrown the landlords. We can only say that they are now rebelling against them. Those who do not know the real conditions say that in Hunan the conditions are terrible, that too many landlords and their hirelings have been killed. But the facts are otherwise. . . . The landlords killed numbered only tens, but the number of peasants killed by them is astounding. . . . Many people know that the peasants are conducting a revolution in Hunan, but few know the cunning and cruelty of the landlords. . . . It has been very common in all countries for the *min tuan* [landlords' militia] to lynch peasants. Torture was freely used. After being arrested, peasants would either be killed outright or mutilated: muscles of the feet extracted, genitals cut away, etc. . . . The *min tuan* in Tsalien burned alive in kerosene a student who had come to the district to work in the peasant movement. . . .

After being driven from the villages by the peasants, the landlords and the dregs of the *min tuan* often sought alliances with bandits to fight the peasant associations. Nine reports out of ten coming from the provincial peasant association tell about the gathering of the *t'u-hao* with the bandits to drink wine and cock's blood for the overthrow of the peasant associations, for the extermination of the party commissioner. . . .

They also formed reactionary organizations. In Hsiang-hsiang they called it the Association for the Maintenance of Town and Village. In Henyang it was the White Party. In Lilin and Liuyang, the San-Ai Party. In Lilin, there was also the Association for Beating Dogs, the dogs meaning the peasants. In many parts of Hunan, there was the Party for the Preservation of Property. These organizations planned and carried out the massacres of peasants and raids on peasant associations. Sometimes these plots were uncovered by the peasants, but the organizations were never dissolved.*

The desire for land by the landless peasantry could not be resisted indefinitely. In October 1926, the Kuomintang itself had recognized that something would have to be done. Then for the first time the peasants and workers had been given the right to form unions. Land rents were reduced to 25 per cent of the annual income from the land. A surprisingly moderate reform program had been passed without any serious dissensions. The peasants were allowed to form volunteer self-preservation corps. Now, when they applied to Wuhan for arms with which to defend themselves, they were turned back empty-handed, to struggle on with meat hooks, flails, scythes, spears, and bamboos.

Only one of the members of the Comintern present, Sydor Stoler, a Russian, seems to have approved of Mao's action, saying that failure to help the peasants was a "fatal error." But he was fresh on the scene, and it was supposed that he understood very little about the problems of the peasantry.

The Wuhan government was in a quandary, and Wang Ching-wei carefully arranged that the Ministers of Agriculture and Labor within the Wuhan government should both be Communists. If they failed to settle the disturbance, they would be discredited.

On May 20, T'an P'ing-shan, who had been a student at Peking University and possessed more experience of labor problems than of problems concerning the peasantry, was formally installed as minister of agriculture, a position specially created for him by Wang Ching-wei. Wang Ching-wei's duplicity—he was

* Harold Isaacs, *The Tragedy of the Chinese Revolution* (London, 1938), p. 266, where the passage is quoted from the "Report of the Delegate of the Hunan Provincial Peasant Association," *Min Kuo Jih Pao*, Wuhan, June 12, 1927. The anonymous delegate was Mao Tse-tung. The text given in Mao's *Selected Works* is a revised version of the original.

playing everyone against everyone else—became only too evident when, the next day, the military forces in Hunan for the first time attacked the peasants.*

Previously, the landlords, the gentry, and their armed defense corps had had to deal with the peasant situation alone, unaided by the three armies under the control of the Wuhan government. Now in Changsha, General Hsü K'o-hsiang, the garrison commander, ordered a general massacre of the revolutionary peasants and workers, throwing around the city a cordon of Yunnanese soldiers with white armbands. These armbands, usually provided with a single character written in red ink, were to distinguish his own men from any others who might disguise themselves in uniform. The Hunan Provincial General Labor Union, unmolested previously because of its close connection with the Wuhan government, was attacked in the early morning, and all the pickets and delegates found sleeping there were taken outside, propped against the wall, and shot. All the other organizations connected with peasants or workers were similarly raided. The west gate of Changsha, facing the river, was selected as the place where the executions would have maximum effect.

An incredible wave of terror and torture now swept over the Hunanese capital, to be remembered long afterward as one of the most terrifying of a long series of massacres. It was to avenge this particular terror that the Chinese Communists kept turning their minds to the capture of Changsha in the months that followed.

In all the five counties which Mao had visited, the garrisons received orders to strike terror among the peasants. The peasants of Liuyang fled for safety to Changsha, only to be mown down by Hsü K'o-hsiang's machine guns. A hundred and thirty men and women were killed outside the city gate. The peasants outnum-

---

* Wang Ching-wei's responsibility for the massacres has been disputed, but the clue is to be found in a book written by his secretary. "On May 21, 1927, riots had broken out among the Wuhan forces at Changsha, the capital of Hunan, as a result of the unauthorized policy of land seizure of the Communists, working through the Provincial Kuomintang and the Provincial Government. The insurrection of military forces, which Wang had foreseen, had occurred." Tang Leang-li, *Inner History of the Chinese Revolution* (London, 1930), p. 273.

bered the local garrison and decided upon a counterattack, taking cover in the low hills to the east of Changsha and at the same time urgently inviting the assistance of Wuhan. On May 27, the All-China Trade Union Federation and the All-China Peasant Association sent a telegram from Wuhan to the provincial unions in Hsiang T'an and Hsianghsiang:

> The Central Government has appointed a Committee of Five which left here this morning for the settlement of the Changsha incident. Please notify all peasant and labor comrades to be patient and to wait for the government officials in order to avoid further friction.*

These orders were not received by the two detachments from Liuyang, which marched up to the walls of Changsha, and were mown down. T'an P'ing-shan headed the delegation from Wuhan, but never arrived in Changsha. Another general, Ho Chien, was sent by Chiang Kai-shek to support Hsü K'o-hsiang, with orders to put down the peasant uprisings mercilessly. Chiang Kai-shek was preparing his advance on the northern warlords, and he was determined that his rear be protected from the uprisings of dissident peasants. The fate of the rebellion, sparked by Mao in January and February, was sealed during the last days of May.

At the beginning of June there occurred an incident which has never been fully explained. Roy, the chief delegate of the Comintern, received a telegram from Stalin addressed to Borodin and himself. According to Roy's account of what happened—an account corroborated by Wang Ching-wei's secretary—he immediately called upon Wang Ching-wei. "I thought," Roy said, "that at this juncture a final effort must be made to regain the confidence of Wang Ching-wei. I communicated to him the message from Moscow. Though not addressed to him, it was obviously meant for him, because it was a repetition of a promise made to him personally in Moscow."† The telegram urged that land seizures take place, except in the areas owned by officers, and that

---

* Harold Isaacs, The Tragedy of the Chinese Revolution (London, 1938), p. 283, who gives the only complete account available in English of the Hsü K'o-hsiang massacre.
† M. N. Roy, My Experience in China (Calcutta, 1945), p. 51.

the Communist party immediately raise an army twenty thousand strong consisting only of Communists, together with battalions of armed peasants numbering fifty thousand. It was furthermore ordered that pressure be put on the Kuomintang to organize revolutionary courts to try anti-Communist officers. Showing Wang Ching-wei the strange telegram, Roy said, "Borodin does not like to show you this telegram, but I, on the other hand, think it is most advisable that you should know what it is about, as I am quite sure you would approve of it."*

The consequences of the telegram were entirely unlike those which Stalin contemplated. Wang Ching-wei immediately informed Chiang Kai-shek, whose suspicions were confirmed. Roy had acted with calm deliberation. There is no reason to believe that he did not know what he was doing. He regarded Mao as a completely unstable element, saying that he was "one of those who persistently and deliberately sabotaged all plans of revolutionary action in 1926–27." According to Roy, Mao was an opportunist who even then was planning to set up "romantic soviet republics in the mountainous wilderness" instead of organizing proletarian mass movements.

When Eugene Chen, the Wuhan government's foreign minister, saw the telegram, he turned pale and said, "You understand, this means war between the Kuomintang and the Communist party."† It was a war precipitated by Mao Tse-tung. From that moment there was never again to be any real understanding between the Chinese Communists and the Kuomintang. In this war, fought bitterly and without quarter, the genuinely subversive or revolutionary forces in China went underground, to emerge as small scattered groups of armed peasants, destined finally to grow and to conquer the whole of China.

In Hankow the confusion only increased during the long, hot summer. Steam rose from the flooded yellow Yangtse, the warships of the foreign powers still trained their guns on the shore, and the left wing of the Kuomintang government fought a losing battle for power, until it submitted completely to Chiang

* Tang Leang-li, *Inner History*, p. 280.
† *Ibid.*, p. 281.

Kai-shek's government in Nanking. The official power of the Chinese Communists was broken.

For a brief while Ch'en Tu-hsiu attempted to hold the party together. He ordered Mao Tse-tung to report on the situation in Szechuan, where Mao could do least harm. Instead, Mao slipped into Hunan, only to be recalled immediately as soon as his destination became known, with orders to remain in Wuhan and to take no part in the organization of peasant uprisings.

On June 30, T'an P'ing-shan, who had at last been able to make a cursory examination of the situation in Changsha, resigned office on the grounds that he had failed to direct the peasant movement. Two weeks later the Communist party was officially proscribed by the Kuomintang, Ch'en Tu-hsiu resigned from the chairmanship of the Central Committee, and, on July 27, Borodin and the remaining foreign Communists prepared to leave the country which they had never understood. Borodin was a large, quiet man, rarely given to showing emotion, but at the railway station it was observed that he shivered and wept unrestrainedly.

For Mao the departure of the Comintern representatives was a blessing in disguise. Ch'en Tu-hsiu had stopped the Hunan uprising on the advice of Borodin, who had completely failed to understand the slogan, "The land to the tillers." Without foreign advisers the Chinese Communists were left to their own resources. There were no Borodins or Roys in attendance on the secret meeting of the Central Committee of the Chinese Communist Party held on August 7.

The meeting was attended by Mao Tse-tung, Chang Kuo-t'ao, Li Li-san, Chou En-lai, Chiu Chiu-pei, Chang Tai-lei, Tsai Ho-sheng,* Peng Kung-ta, and Liu Wei-han, who was also known as Lo Man. At this meeting, Ch'en Tu-hsiu was drummed out of the party, although he had already resigned, and his letter explaining the defeat as due to the fact that "the revolutionary mood of

* Chang Tai-lei became head of the Revolutionary Committee during the Canton Commune and was killed in battle on December 12, 1927. Chiu Chiu-pei was captured and executed in Fukien during the retreat from Changchow, in 1934. Tsai Ho-sheng was executed in 1931.

the masses was not then at a high point, the Kuomintang could not be quickly overthrown, and untimely risings only weakened the power of the party" was regarded as sufficient proof of his own incapacity. A lengthy letter detailing his "errors" was sent to the remaining members of the party, and a new program, authorizing the confiscation of the property of the large landowners, but protecting the small landowners, who were merely ordered to reduce their rents, was issued by the committee, which scattered shortly afterward.

Like a moth eager for the burning, Mao immediately set out in disguise for Changsha, presumably believing that it was the last place anyone expected him to go, and there he could hide most successfully.

The white terror of the Kuomintang was now being launched all over the Yangtse Valley, and in all the provinces of the south. The unaccountable failure of nerve in Wuhan led to the disappearance or execution of at least 10 per cent of the members of the Chinese Communist party. In Shanghai alone four hundred were executed, and among them were some of the highest members of the party. Others, like Chou En-lai, escaped only by ruse. Inevitably, the effect of the white terror was to harden the Communists' resolve to fight back. Only those who have known a Chinese terror know how it makes men determined upon revenge. The Communists had nothing to lose.

Proscribed, humiliated, the party dissolved by government order, their communications made increasingly difficult, the Communists had no weapons. For the most part the army remained loyal to Chiang Kai-shek. Only one section, the Twentieth Army, under Ho Lung and Yeh Ting, declared its independence at Nanchang on August 1. Nearly the whole garrison in the capital city of Kiangsi immediately drove against Swatow, hoping to establish a soviet on the coast. They were beaten back. They then turned into eastern Kwangtung and invaded the Hailofeng area, famous because it was inhabited largely by women who remained on the Chinese mainland while their husbands went abroad to seek the family fortunes. They were a hard and handsome people, and they had already devised a kind of rule by village council which approximated a soviet. The survivors of the battle of Swatow were welcomed, and the Communists might have thought they now possessed a base in Kwangtung from which they too might begin a new march to the north. They were mistaken. By the end of October the Hailofeng area was surrounded by Kuomintang troops, and there was only a handful of Communists left at the end of the battle. To the women who had welcomed the column under General Chu Teh, no mercy was shown. Whole villages were put to the flames, most of the women were raped, and nearly all of them received bayonet wounds.

The failure of the Hailofeng occupation was complete. Leading a small column of three or four hundred men and women, including some railway and porcelain workers from Nanchang, Chu Teh spent the winter beating off Kuomintang attacks.

Mao's fortunes were hardly better. He is heard of for a moment in Changsha itself, a ghostly figure attempting to bring together the scattered remnants of the *Hsin Min Hsüeh Hui,* only to discover that they were too frightened by the terror to go with him. He went south, to Liuyang and Lilin, his customary stamping-ground, determined once again to bring about peasant uprisings. There was every reason to believe that if he continued long enough, he would succeed in overthrowing the Kuomintang. Had not Sun Yat-sen led thirteen separate uprisings before accomplishing the revolution of 1911? Now he paid particular attention to the Henyang miners, men who seemed to belong to a race apart. Pock-marked, fearless, revolutionaries by instinct, nearly all of them deaf because underground explosions of dynamite had shattered their eardrums, they presented only one problem: it was necessary to hold them on a leash, for they thirsted for war against the Kuomintang, or against any authority whatsoever. They had been anarchists; Mao was determined to make them Communists; and he succeeded in making them the spearhead of the First Peasants' and Workers' Army.

For some time Mao had been working in the dark. Borodin's last words had been, "The revolution must now go underground." The Comintern, after a succession of hopelessly mistaken interpretations of the Chinese revolution, had come out on July 13 with a simple thesis: "The revolutionary role of the government in Hankow is finished. It is now counter-revolutionary and must be thwarted. Therefore, Communists must spread an agrarian revolution and arm the workers and peasants." How this could be done was not explained. Nor was it explained why the Comintern had ordered the workers in Shanghai to bury their weapons, thus leaving them defenseless against Chiang Kai-shek's Cantonese troops. And finally, no one had explained why the logic of revolutions demanded that the Hankow revolutionaries be put down by a counter-revolutionary force. The Comintern, previously possessed of an extraordinary influence in China, now surrendered its influence and left the Communists to their own resources; and to men of Mao's stamp it was almost unnecessary to repeat that "the Communists must spread an agrarian revolution and arm the workers and peasants."

Not all Communists, however, agreed with him. These small detachments of armed peasants, located chiefly in Pingkiang and Liuyang, with a seasoning of miners and some troops from Wuhan who had marched south after the dissolution of the Wuhan government, were derisively called "rifle brigades."

By September 12, Mao was ready. He had worked with astonishing rapidity. He planned to attack Changsha but the revolt, which came to be known as the Autumn Harvest Uprising, failed. The peasants were cut down and surrounded, and once near Liuyang Mao was arrested, but succeeded in slipping away from his guards and hiding a whole day in a reed-grown pond. A month later he was marching south at the head of three regiments. He had a thousand men and less than two hundred rifles.

Some memory of the mountain near Shao Shan, where a member of the *Ko Lao Hui* had taken refuge when Mao was a child, or one of the stories in *All Men Are Brothers*, led him to believe that the small Red Army could make a fortress out of a mountain; and he chose the mountain called Chingkanshan on the Hunan-Kiangsi border. Chingkanshan was more than a mountain: it was a whole range of mountains some 150 miles in circuit, wildly romantic with its great forests of pine and spruce and bamboo, with flowering creepers and desolate little pathways leading into the heart of the mountain fastness. It possessed one advantage overriding all others—for the greater part of the year the whole area was hidden in fog and mists. Also, it lay close to the borders of three provinces. Attacked by an army belonging to one province, he had only to retreat over the provincial border. There were only five passes leading to the mountain, and these could be defended. There were other advantages. All over the mountain there were Buddhist temples which could be used as hospitals, offices, and dormitories. The monks were ordered to leave; and in the temples, the Red Army soldiers used as clothes racks the gods who were falling to pieces and who stood in rows in the dark-painted halls. A printing press was brought from Liuyang. Within a week of establishing themselves on the mountain, the first number of the newspaper appeared, printed on the backs of Buddhist scrolls.

The interlude of Chingkanshan was heavy with future consequences. From this moment until October 1934, the Red Army was to find itself among high mountains. Other Communist armies were being formed. Ho Lung had ridden alone to Hupeh, and there he was to found a soviet over which he ruled with uncommon gentleness and understanding of peasant problems. Hsu Hsiang-ch'ien, a former teacher, and Chang Kuo-t'ao, a former student of Peking University, were already forming soviets in northern Szechuan. But it was the army of rather less than a thousand men living in Buddhist temples above the volcanic cliffs of Chingkanshan which formed the nucleus of the main fighting strength of the Chinese Communists.

Their lives on the mountain were not without incident. Two local bandits, Wang Tso and Yuan Wen-tsai, had long ruled over the mountain with six hundred armed peasants to defend them. They threatened to attack. They had more rifles than the Communists. By diplomacy Mao succeeded in winning them over, though for about a month they kept demanding that the Red Army be placed under their command or be annihilated. In the end, by appointing Wang Tso a regimental commander and

Yuan Wen-tsai a battalion commander, and by allowing them extraofficial powers in dealing with the peasants, the six hundred bandits were incorporated into the Red Army. Mao allowed them to deal directly with the peasants only on condition that they willingly assented to undergoing political training. When they agreed, their power was curbed, for they were immediately trained to obey the army commander—Mao himself.

On Chingkanshan in the winter of 1927 it was deathly cold. There was no store of food, and there were no sources of military supplies. Mao's own fortunes were at their lowest ebb, for since the Autumn Harvest Uprising had not been sanctioned by the Central Committee he could expect no help from them, and might indeed find himself summarily court-martialed by the party. Communication with the other soviet areas was slow and undependable. Mao sent his brother Tse-t'an in search of the remnants of the Hailofeng soviet. He did not return for two months. They had no radios. They were constantly being attacked by small local forces, and they seemed to be completely isolated on the obscure mountain on the border.

Living high up in a cliff monastery, surrounded by hostile armies in command of all the roads, Mao was compelled to revise all his thinking on revolutionary tactics and strategy. Previously he had commanded small guerrilla battles where his own troops possessed swift mobility. He had suffered dreadful losses. He could no longer afford to lose soldiers. The first step was to acquire the good will of the villagers in the plains, the second was to employ them as his intelligence staff, and the third was to invite the provincial armies to attack, so that he could replenish his diminishing supply of ammunition. He said later that there was not a single machine gun among his troops at the beginning of their stay on Chingkanshan. He ordered concealed entrenchments to be dug on the mountain, chiefly to keep the soldiers occupied, and sent couriers to link up with the other scattered Communist armies. Rice was planted in the mountains. Three crops a year could be grown there, and they hoped to hold out if necessary with their own food. Meanwhile, in the plains, Mao assembled the villagers and encouraged them to redistribute the land.

The prospect remained bleak. The winter was strangely variable, one bitterly cold day being followed by several unexpectedly warm ones. There were mutterings in the army, which was gradually increasing in size. A mutiny was suppressed with terrible forcefulness. It was a time that tried men's souls. Speaking of this period, Mao said afterward that he kept remembering Wu Sung, the bandit in *All Men Are Brothers*, who found himself confronted with a tiger on the Chingyang mountains. "The tiger," he said, "would eat people whether it was provoked or not, and you had to choose between killing the tiger and being eaten by it." Wu Sung killed the tiger with his own hands.

During this time Mao introduced a famous series of guerrilla slogans. With slight changes, these slogans were recited by Red Army soldiers during all the years of the struggle to power. Originally they consisted of three rules and six injunctions:

1. Obey orders at all times.
2. Do not take even a needle or a piece of thread from the people.
3. Turn in all confiscated property to headquarters.

1. Engage in propaganda wherever we go—spread the revolutionary policy far and wide.
2. Respect and protect public property—do not waste the wealth of the revolution.
3. Adopt a courteous attitude when talking with anybody—we should never lose our temper or quarrel with anyone.
4. Pay a reasonable price for everything bought—never lower than the market price.
5. Return furniture borrowed from the people once it is finished with —do not let it be lost, but let the borrower return it in person.
6. If a piece of furniture is damaged in use, the owners should be paid compensation.

In time it was discovered that the six original injunctions were too long and too repetitive, and they were given a pithier, more coherent form. In the process the number of injunctions was increased to eight:

1. Replace all doors when you leave a house, and return the straw matting.*
2. Be courteous to the people, and help them when you can.
3. Return all borrowed articles and replace all damaged goods.
4. Be honest in all transactions with the peasants.
5. Be sanitary—dig latrines at a safe distance from homes and fill them up with earth before leaving.
6. Don't damage crops.
7. Don't molest women.
8. Never ill-treat prisoners-of-war.†

Together with these slogans went a short rhymed verse intended to convey the basic military tactics of the revolutionaries:

When the enemy advances, we retreat.
When he escapes, we harass.
When he retreats, we pursue.
When he is tired, we attack.‡

Nothing could be simpler; but these verses, which were sometimes to lose some of their effect by becoming incantations, had deep roots in ancient Chinese history. They were not original, though the form was original, and all of them can be found in the remarkable military writings of Sun Wu, the military technician who lived at some time during the period known as the "Spring and Autumn dynasties," between 722 and 481 B.C.

---

* Wooden doors of Chinese peasant huts are supported on iron pins. They can easily be detached and in summer are often used as beds.
† There are minor variations to the list of eight injunctions. The list, as it is printed here, is based on the official version published in 1947.
‡ Extraordinary importance was attached to slogans by the Chinese Communists from the beginning. The original four military slogans were adapted and subtly altered to suit changing circumstances, usually after long debates. They were more than slogans in the Western sense: they enshrined principles, and sometimes they were extremely dangerous, for the words seemed to develop an existence of their own, and after the Fifth Annihilation Campaign, Mao bitterly attacked the twenty slogans employed at the time. When the Japanese introduced the scorched-earth policy under the slogan, "Kill all, burn all, loot all," the Chinese Communists countered with a further development of Mao's slogan:
When he retreats, we return.
When he burns, we put out the fire.
When he loots, we attack.
When he pursues, we hide.

Mao's debt to Sun Wu cannot be overestimated. In his military lectures he constantly quotes him, particularly emphasizing such doctrines as: "Know yourself and know your opponents, and in a hundred battles there will be a hundred victories," or "Use the resources of the occupied country, and take your supplies from the enemy." He did not always obey Sun Wu. "If you have ten times as many troops as your opponent, surround him; if five times, attack him; if you are equal in numbers and superior in fighting power, engage him; otherwise avoid the conflict." Here Mao violently disagreed, though he insisted that at the point of contact even guerrilla forces must outnumber the enemy. He was most completely obedient to Sun Wu in his conception of espionage. There were five kinds of spies, and all, according to the ancient military philosopher, should be used simultaneously. The first group consisted of "native spies," men who knew the terrain well; then there were "inside spies," who knew the highest secrets of the enemy; then there were "spies in reverse," who were in fact fighting for you, but were employed unknowingly by the enemy; then there were "dumb spies," poor creatures who were fed with knowledge which they unconsciously gave to the enemy; finally there were "daring spies," men who went over to the enemy lines and discovered military secrets at great risk to themselves. To survive, Mao had to use all five kinds of spies.

Sun Wu's ideas on war are exceedingly adaptable. In its present form the book is divided into thirteen arbitrary sections. There is very little attempt toward outlining a complete summary of the art of war. There is no argument, no progression. The author simply offers a series of disconnected apothegms, nearly all of them demonstrating how the commander of a small force can overcome a powerful enemy, given suitable conditions of his own making. These apothegms have a peculiarly Chinese flavor, hardheaded, deeply philosophical, often showing a disturbing knowledge of the human soul under stress. Here are a few of Sun Wu's apothegms:

> If you plan the movement of your troops well, they will do what you did not even plan.

War is nothing but lies.

Be as swift as the wind, as secret as the forest, as consuming as fire, as silent as the mountains, as impenetrable as darkness, as sudden as thunderbolts.

In throwing in troops, drop them like a millstone on an egg, the solid on the void.

Very obscure and without form, very mysterious and without voice is this, but it is the arbiter of the enemy's destiny. We advance, and he cannot resist: for we strike where there is only emptiness. We retire and he cannot pursue, for we are too quick for him to reach us. When we wish to fight, though the enemy be ensconced behind high walls and deep moats, he will have to give battle because we attack a place that he must assist. So we locate him, but he does not locate us, and we keep together while the enemy is defenseless. We are one united body, while the enemy is divided into ten parts, so that with our ten parts we attack his one. Since we are many and the enemy few, and many can easily attack few, our victory will be easy: for the place where we give battle will be unknown, and being unknown, the enemy will have to prepare in many places. So it is that victory is a thing we make ourselves.

When discipline exists, disorder may be simulated; when there is courage, timidity may be simulated; when there is strength, weakness may be simulated.

The best plan is to strike at his war plan, the next is to strike at his communications, the next is to strike at his armies, and the worst of all is to strike at his strongholds.

Nothing is to be gained by numbers.

Mao's understanding of these apothegms derived from continual study, and he was able to adapt them to all existing circumstances. He was also able to adapt them in the merciless in-fighting which occurred within the Communist party itself.

That winter there occurred the Commune in Canton, in which Yeh Ting played a major part. For three days the Communists held the city, only to be overthrown by Kuomintang forces; and though some escaped to Hailofeng, and others survived to join forces with Mao on Chingkanshan, the destruction of Communist power in Canton was complete. The time had not come for the capture of cities, and though, as his forces increased, there

were continual demands for one more attack on Changsha with
Chingkanshan as a base, Mao refused to allow the Red Army to
be used for a purpose which could only end in disaster.

During the whole of the year 1928 Mao remained on Chingkanshan. In May, Chu Teh arrived at the head of his ragged
column. They had not met before, but they took each other's
measure during a night and a day when they talked to one
another without ceasing, and thereupon they decided to join
forces. They provided an extraordinarily brilliant combination.
Chu Teh had fought in rebellions against Yuan Shih-kai, and he
had been among the first Chinese Communists in Germany. He
spoke German well, and had a wider knowledge than Mao of the
history of military strategy. More than Mao, he resembled a
hardbitten, humorous peasant, with a broad mouth and small eyes
and a habit of grinning pleasantly at the foibles of mankind,
though he could, and did, look ferocious, with the terrible ferocity
of the Chinese war god, when occasion demanded. Agnes Smedley
has recounted how his face turned a sickening deep green when
he walked over a battlefield where his own men lay dying. Like
Mao he had no instinct for adventure: he was cautious, and his
boldness derived from an exemplary understanding of the enemy's
powers. Yet they were antithetical. Mao remained the scholar by
habit, and Chu Teh, though a scholar in his own right, desired
action and thirsted for glory, though he would sometimes mock
his own ambitions—as when, years later, possessing the title of
commander in chief of all the Red armies, he designed for himself a purple cloak, like the one worn by the Generalissimo, and
around the collar scatterings of frayed rabbit fur. Mao was aloof,
conscious of his general superiority. Chu Teh genuinely liked
men, shared their simple pleasures, joked with them incessantly,
and his jokes came with the freshness of someone who understood
their casual secrets. From the moment of their meeting they
were almost inseparable; and together they dominated Chingkanshan, where previously Mao had dominated alone. Both had
experienced the same failures, both had attempted uprisings in
southern Hunan: on his journey to Chingkanshan, Chu Teh had
made one last effort to lead the peasants of Hunan against the

Kuomintang. Now, having failed completely, they shared the same hopes.

In the comparative security of the mountain stronghold, they waited upon events. Their first hope was to carve out of the border villages a soviet consisting of six counties linked together. Failing this, there were possibilities of withdrawal into the uplands of Kiangsi. Most of the younger officers desired quicker profits. They would go north to Changsha or south to Canton, for these were rich cities, and once established in them, the Communists could hope to provide themselves with armaments and armies. What was the use of living like bandits? Mao shook his head. He realized that the quickest advance might be the slowest. He counseled caution. They were fighting small battles all the time. They had insufficient resources for attacking the Kuomintang. Sooner or later they would have to meet the full brunt of the Kuomintang campaigns. They counted fifty-seven minor engagements, and thirteen battles during the year they spent on Chingkanshan; and though they destroyed the opposing armies, they were perfectly conscious that an almost inexhaustible manpower would in time enable Chiang Kai-shek to annihilate them.

The Sixth Congress of the Chinese Communist party was held that summer during July and August, in a suburb of Moscow. It was attended by the leading Communists who had escaped the White Terror during the previous year, and who had been ordered by the Central Committee to take refuge in the Soviet capital. The report of its resolutions did not arrive in Chingkanshan until the late autumn. The resolutions were curiously ironical, for though Mao agreed with them in principle, it was clear that they were formed by men who had no knowledge of the situation of the Communists in China. The resolution stated:

At the present time the party must everywhere propagate among the masses the idea of soviets, the idea of the democratic dictatorship of the proletariat and peasantry, and the inevitability of the coming revolutionary mass uprising. It must emphasize in its agitation the necessity for overthrowing the ruling bloc, and the mobilization of the masses for revolutionary demonstrations. . . .

It must consistently and undeviatingly follow the line of the seizure of state power, organization of soviets as organs of insurrection, expropriation of the landlords and big property owners, and the expulsion of the foreign imperialists. . . . The future growth of the revolution will place before the party as an immediate practical task the preparation for, and the carrying through of, armed insurrection as the sole path for the completion of the bourgeois democratic revolution and the overthrow of the power of the Koumintang.

The dull, repetitive document could be read to mean anything anyone desired. It came, however, with more authority than the decisions of the Central Executive Committee, which still existed in the isolation of Shanghai; and the Central Executive Committee, disposed to believe that Changsha and Canton were the supreme objectives of the Communist campaign, had to bow before the resolutions made in Moscow, which offered only a few vaguely worded suggestions about how these industrial towns could be captured for the revolution. The major importance was still given to the industrial proletariat:

The chief tasks of guerrilla warfare are: first, the immediate realization of the slogans of the agrarian struggle (such as the confiscation of land of the landlords for distribution among the peasants, killing of oppressive gentry and landlords, setting up of peasant delegates, committees, and village soviets, etc.) in order to mobilize more peasant masses to join the fighting front of the revolutionary struggle; second, the setting up of the Red Army. The brave young fighters, particularly those of proletarian and semi-proletarian backgrounds, should be gradually absorbed, during the course of guerrilla fighting, into the guerrilla units in order to expand them gradually into a worker-peasant revolutionary Red Army.

Very little of the authoritative hopes and despairs included in the report of the Sixth Congress had any meaning for Mao and Chu Teh, who were doggedly concerned with the realities of the situation. They needed an assured base, and without it they were lost. When they heard in the spring of 1928 that there had been uprisings in Tungku and Hsingkuo, they began to believe that the secure base might be somewhere near these two large towns, deep in the Kiangsi hills.

Meanwhile Chingkanshan was becoming untenable. It was not only that larger and larger armies were being sent against Mao's army, but they had been unable to provide enough food for all the new volunteers who flocked to the mountain. There were now about eleven thousand men, comprising Mao's original thousand, two thousand more who had followed Chu Teh, and about eight thousand armed peasants from southern Hunan.* The mountain was overcrowded. Most of the military supplies they had captured were lost; they had been unable to grow much food; and they were dependent upon the peasants, who were themselves still afraid of the power of Wang Tso and Yuan Wen-tsai. The Communists were faced with a desperate situation. There were already defections to the Kuomintang. At dawn on January 4, 1929, Mao and Chu Teh led their small forces down the mountain, leaving P'eng Teh-huai, a Kuomintang officer who had mutinied while in Ho Chien's army, in command of the mountain.

Chu Teh has described the miserable beginning of the march which was eventually to lead to the conquest of China:

> At dawn the column of gaunt and ragged men and women began creeping single file along the jagged crest of this mountain spur that connected Chingkanshan with the mountain range that runs southward along the Kiangsi-Hunan border. The stones and peaks were worn to slippery smoothness by no one knows how many eons of fierce winds, rains, and snow. Snow lay in pockets and an icy wind lashed the bodies of the column that inched forward, crawling over huge boulders and hanging on to one another to avoid slipping into the black chasms below.
>
> By nightfall they reached a small, sloping ridge of solid volcanic rock where they ate half of the cold cooked rice which each had brought along. Huddling together and linking arms they sat down on the slope and spent the night, shivering and coughing. At daybreak they were again creeping southward, and by late afternoon reached an overgrown trail that led down a

* *Räte China—Dokumente der Chinesischen Revolution* (Moscow, 1934), p. 253.

wooded mountain slope toward the village of Tafen, where a battalion of enemy troops was stationed. Here they halted to eat the last half of their cold rice. When darkness fell they began moving stealthily down the trail, under strict orders not to make a sound, forbidden even to cough.

Reaching the foot of the trail, they surrounded Tafen village while the squads with ammunition moved in and overpowered the enemy garrison.*

Such was the small beginning: there was very little improvement as the months passed. Exactly a year later the *Military Bulletin* of the Central Committee of the Chinese Communist Party published an interim account of the small column which left Chingkanshan for Kiangsi. It read very simply:

The masses completely failed to understand what the Red Army was. In many places the army was even attacked, like a bandit gang. The army had no support from the masses There were great difficulties in finding encampments, carrying on military operations, and securing information. We marched across snow-covered and icy mountains, closely pursued by the enemy. We sometimes covered thirty miles in a single day. Our sufferings increased.

* Agnes Smedley, *The Great Road: The Life and Times of Chu Teh* (New York: Monthly Review Press, 1956), p. 236.

FIVE BATTLES

THE FANTASTICALLY small Red Army, wandering into the hills of Kiangsi, had not the least resemblance to a real fighting force. As they came down from Chingkanshan, they still wore their cotton uniforms, they were covered with lice, their hair fell down to their shoulders, and many of them walked barefoot. Mao was desperately thin with the strain of commanding the mountain outpost. Less than half the soldiers on the march had rifles: it was assumed that the small column would be able to recoup its armaments from the enemy.

The mountains were deep in snow, very beautiful with their tall pines and small secluded villages among the ravines. Though the villagers supplied them, there was rarely enough food to go around, and quite often they lived on roots, and many died of exposure at night, dying silently. They were four thousand when they left the mountain, but a month later there were four or five hundred more peasant boys from the villages. They marched up mountain trails, camped on the mountaintops, and sometimes lost themselves. Of all the places they had been to in China, this was the hardest, the most legendary, and the most ripe for rebellion.

Kiangsi at this time was full of underground movements of protest against the Kuomintang. A succession of corrupt governors had left the province poverty-stricken. The landlords built large stockaded fortresses and kept their own private militia; they had power of life and death over the villagers, who were treated like serfs. Indeed, there had hardly been a time when the Kiangsi peasants were not ripe for rebellion. One of the most famous of their rebellions had been quashed at the end of the T'ang dynasty by one of the ancestors of Sun Yat-sen, who received a dukedom and a large gift of cash in reward. Here, too, among the desolate, sharp-cragged mountains, lay the heart of the Taoist religion. The Taoist temples were the richest in all China. And from one of these mountains, called the Dragon Tiger Mountain, the most famous of the Taoist popes, Chang Tao-ling, had ascended to heaven. The name of the mountain was not a misnomer: even to this day, in those hills where the bedraggled Communist armies wandered, tigers are to be found.

There were continual skirmishes, but in the first month there were no severe losses. Nananfu was occupied, and so was Namyung, but gradually it was being impressed upon them that two large towns in the heart of Kiangsi, both high up in the mountains and almost inaccessible, would provide the best base. These towns were Tungku and Hsingkuo. The latter in particular was formidably defended by high mountains, for it lay in a circle of mountains whose crests were invisible in winter. All over the mountains lay the scattered Taoist temples. To get to these towns it was necessary to pass through Tapoteh. They deliberated. It was known that Tapoteh was well defended, but they needed ammunition and decided to attack, though some of them had only sticks, stones, branches, and rifle stocks to fight with. It was a merciless battle, fought in late February, while the snow was still on the ground. It lasted from three o'clock in the afternoon to noon of the next day. At the end of the battle there were two thousand dead Communists. Half the army had been wiped out.

There had been bad defeats before, but this was the worst, and the most unnecessary. "It was more like a mutual blood-letting," said Chu Teh afterward, "than a battle. It was indescribably horrible." When evening came down on the second day, Mao, who had directed the operations with Chu Teh, and who sent himself on missions to the front lines, walked over the battlefield, seeing the small clumps of dead soldiers on the icy ground, and the women coming from the villages with pots of tea and small bowls of rice for the soldiers who remained alive. There he and Chu Teh swore to avenge the defeat. By the end of February the Red Army had reached Tungku and Hsingkuo, which were to become famous bases during the "annihilation campaigns." On Chingkanshan the Red Army had flown a red banner with a five-pointed white star crossed with a black hammer and sickle. Now, as though the starkness of their purpose demanded something simpler, they flew only a red flag with a black hammer and sickle in the center.

There followed a year and a half of strange and sometimes purposeless wandering. It was almost as though the Red Army was driven by internal forces to be perpetually on the march, in order to show itself, in order to attract an increasing number of volunteers. There were forces which held them to the remote villages of Kiangsi; other forces, following the demands of Li Li-san, proclaimed that they should launch attacks on cities. Between these two poles they oscillated.

P'eng Teh-huai had been forced to leave Chingkanshan in April, four months after Mao had left the mountain. By July of the next year he thought he had strength enough—he had ten thousand men armed with bayonets, mattocks, and a few rifles— to attack Changsha, which was held by Ho Chien with thirty thousand men. The city favors the defenders, but the resolution of the peasant guerrillas led to its capture. For ten days they held it, retiring only because vastly larger forces than Ho Chien's original thirty thousand were being brought up against them, and because foreign warships were already bombarding the city. Thereafter, P'eng Teh-huai moved south, to join forces with Chu Teh and Mao. There were long sweeping operations along the Fukien border; preparations were made for an attack on Nanchang; and once more there arose the promise of a victory at Changsha.

At Kutien, in December, Mao had warned against the Li Li-san line at a military conference. He was overruled by his field commanders, who saw no future in the aimless wandering over high mountain passes in winter: better to settle in an industrial city in the heart of China and from there spread out over the whole nation. What was the use of the small abandoned villages in Kiangsi? Would they support an army? By June 1930, preparations for the second onslaught against Changsha were made, and though the Red Army reached the walls of the city, they made no dent in the city's defenses.

Just as Changsha, to the Communists, had become the symbol of a necessary victory, and the beginning of a great campaign which would embrace the whole of China, so the same city was regarded by Chiang Kai-shek as his most important defense line; and the huge armies which wheeled into Hunan in September were designed to stamp out the small forces of the Reds forever.

They did not quite succeed. The Red Army withdrew to the pine-clad hills of Kiangsi, to face another winter; and they half guessed that at the height of the winter the Kuomintang troops would be launched against them. This was, in fact, what happened. Then, in the course of three years, while the Reds retained their bases of Tungku and Hsingkuo, five "annihilation campaigns" were thrown against them.

The First Annihilation Campaign

Four of the five annihilation campaigns which occurred in Kiangsi—all of them in roughly the same region—have been commented on at length by the Chinese Communists, by the Kuomintang, and by foreigners who discussed the battles at Yenan with the Communist leaders years afterward. They were battles fought against almost overwhelming odds. The Red armies survived only by employing great mobility and ingenuity. And mostly, as the Kuomintang generals admitted later, the Red armies were successful because they knew their terrain better, because they were trained for guerrilla warfare, and because they observed all the classic tenets of guerrilla warfare without ever forgetting their main objective: loot, elbowroom, secure footholds.

The Red armies were ragged, underfed, without cannon or airplanes or any heavy equipment, without reserves, and with only a handful of trained officers, and in all their battles they were outnumbered ten to one. Yet they nearly always succeeded in inflicting heavy defeats on the enemy, and it was by an exhaustive study of these battles that the Red armies were able to defeat the Kuomintang in 1949. From 1934 onward the study of these campaigns became obligatory in the Red Army. In the first four annihilation campaigns the Red Army in Kiangsi was directed by Chu Teh and Mao. Surprisingly often, Mao's contribution to the strategical operations can be detected. Mao is the surgeon, exploring the wound, insisting above everything else on the delicate probing, the discovery of the enemy's weakened nerve, the dangerous point where weakness is balanced by strength: at this point he will order the attack. There follows a cunning interweaving among the enemy columns—as Mao describes his tactics, they have something of the inevitability of a dance—and finally there is the withdrawal to the chosen terminus, which may be within the enemy lines or deep in enemy territory or safely within the territory the Reds have circumscribed for themselves. The theory, as he relates the battles, seems to be pure Mao; the practice, the knowledge of the possible, the way in which forces can be grouped together for maximum effectiveness, seems to come from Chu Teh. Yet they learned from each other, and it is hardly possible to say where one begins and the other ends. When they came to the borders of Kiangsi and Fukien, Mao was almost entirely inexperienced in warfare. There had been the Autumn Harvest Uprising, followed by the minor guerrilla battles at Chingkanshan. None of these was of any great importance. But in Kiangsi, Mao demonstrated that he was a military genius of the first magnitude.

At the beginning there was almost nothing to show for it. There was the famous four-line slogan invented at Chingkanshan, and there was the knowledge that among the hills of southern

Kiangsi the enemy might be lured beyond the reach of its supply columns—the slogan "lure enemy deep penetration" was invented by him during this time. He had not yet begun to think out all the consequences of a strategy of "luring." He was still, as he admitted later, contaminated by Li Li-san's theory of "proletarian uprisings in the large urban districts," but it was impossible to correlate this theory with the small vagrant army, consisting mostly of peasants with a sprinkling of Henyang miners, wandering in the winter hills. His mind fought for certainties, and by the use which he made later of his conceptions of the "first engagement" and the "terminus of withdrawal" it is clear that he found his certainties in these two things.

But where should the first engagement take place? Clearly, the guerrilla troops can choose their own terrain. The Red Army was concentrated along the road from Yungfeng to Hsingkuo, with its main concentrations near Kian, a large and prosperous town, the economic capital of Kiangsi province. Should the guerrillas occupy the towns? There were heated arguments, for Li Li-san had insisted on the primary importance of the towns, but Mao and Chu Teh were already planning a withdrawal into the hills between Kian and Kwangchang; and though the debates were endless, and Mao commented ruefully that the decision to leave the towns had to be fought tooth and nail, the slogan "lure enemy deep penetration" prevailed.

By the end of December 1930, at least seven Kuomintang columns were driving down from the north under the command of Lu Ti-p'ing, who was governor of the province and commander in chief of the whole expedition. He had not been idle. Even during the brief Red occupation of Kian, he had organized what came to be known as A-B (anti-Bolshevik) groups in the towns east of Kian, and in the Red Army itself there were these dissident elements: men who joined the army during the hurried reorganization at Kian, and who were determined to make havoc. Futien and Tungku were particularly dangerous to the Reds. But now, skirting Futien, they marched out of Kian and took Tungku in a short battle. Then they waited. The Kuomintang columns came down the Yungfeng-Kian road, and were elated to find the city

abandoned. Leaving Lo Ling's division to guard Kian, the rest
took to the mountains and began to pursue the Reds. It was a
particularly cold winter, with mists hanging over the mountains.
Some Kuomintang columns lost their way, and there was sporadic
fighting in the hills. Reports came to the 18th Division under
Chang Hui-chang that Tungku had been abandoned, as Kian
had been abandoned before it. On December 31st, the 18th
Division entered Tungku. The trap was sprung. The Red Army
made a forced march and arrived under cover of darkness outside
the walls of Tungku, capturing the town by surprise and taking
nine thousand prisoners. The Kuomintang general was captured
and put under arrest. He was a big, burly man, very sure of himself, and he seemed to be under the illusion that he had been
captured by bandits and would soon be released against a ransom
to be paid by the Kuomintang government. To the surprise of
Mao and Chu Teh he had no interest in his own army, and gave
information about Kuomintang troops which later proved to be
entirely accurate. He seemed to be perfectly prepared to act the
traitor, and even offered to teach military science to his captors.

"In our opinion," Mao wrote later, "a battle is of little significance when there are no spoils of war, or when the spoils do
not exceed our losses." The spoils were beyond all their expecta-
tions, including eight thousand rifles, machine guns, trench mortars, field telephones, medical supplies, provisions for many
months of active campaigning, and the entire payroll for three
enemy divisions. The most valuable acquisitions were two radio
transmitters, together with the staff to run them.

Among the spoils Mao was inclined to include the enemy
general, for his capture proved to be a considerable propaganda
advantage. Some weeks later he was put on trial before three
thousand of his own troops and the civilian population of Tungku.
He was condemned to death, together with his entire staff. Villagers whose villages he had destroyed were permitted to execute
them. All of them were beheaded. Ironically, within a few days
of their execution Mao received a message from Chiang Kai-shek
offering a ransom of $200,000 for the lives of the general and his
staff and the promise to release a large number of Communist

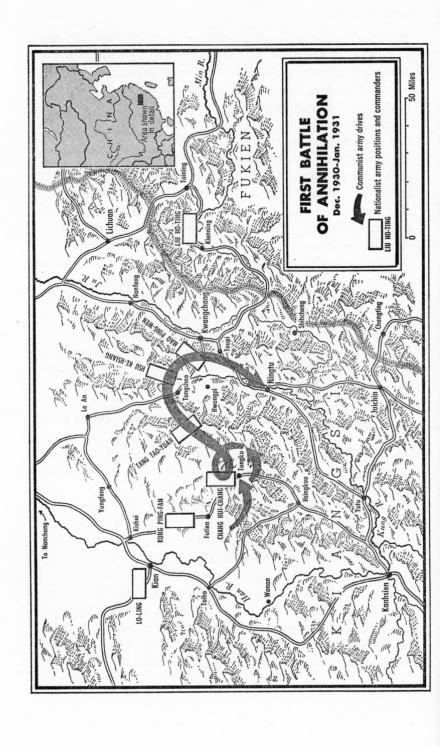

FIRST BATTLE
OF ANNIHILATION
Dec. 1930-Jan. 1931

Communist army drives

Nationalist army positions and commanders

LIU HO-TING

0   50 Miles

CHINA

Area shown
in detail

Min R.

Taining

LIU HO-TING

Kienning

FUKIEN

Nanfeng

Kwangchang

Shihcheng

Changting

HSU KE-HSIANG

MAO PING-WEN

Toupi

Ningtu

KIANGSI

Juichin

Tungshao

Hwangpi

TANG TAO-YUAN

Tungku

Hsingkuo

Yutu

Kung

Lo An

Lichuan

R.

Kishui

KUNG PING-FAN

Fufien

CHANG HUI-CHANG

Yungfeng

To Nanchang

Kian

LO-LING

Taiho

Tan R.

Woman

Kanhsien

prisoners. Learning later that the Communist prisoners had been executed in jail, Mao bitterly regretted that he had permitted the trial to take place.

In fighting against Chang Hui-chang the Red Army was leading from strength. It was not in fact a very notable victory, for the Communists had thrown forty thousand men into the combat and heavily outnumbered the enemy. "On a front of vital importance," Mao noted, "it is always necessary to have an absolutely superior force."

After the defeat of Chang Hui-chang, the full weight of the Red Army was hurled against the Fiftieth Division under Tan Tao-yuan, which was wandering in the mountains east of Tungku. This time they employed a trick which came straight out of *All Men Are Brothers*. They wore Kuomintang uniforms and carried Kuomintang banners. Tan Tao-yuan had no radio contact with Chang Hui-chang's division, and he was overjoyed when he saw the Eighteenth arriving. His enjoyment was short-lived: half his division was virtually annihilated before he realized what was happening.

The enemy originally possessed one hundred thousand troops; sixteen thousand were now accounted for, comprising nine thousand who had entered Tungku, about three thousand caught in the hills and villages, where there were the same tactics of withdrawal and speedy return, and four thousand in the mass slaughter of half of Tan Tao-yuan's forces at Tungshao. Mao had hoped that the complete division might be destroyed, and later he complained bitterly against the lack of concentration of the Reds at this point—it was a lesson he took to heart. Kung Ping-fan's division pulled out under the threat of a small independent division of Reds at Hsingkuo, which moved up and appeared to be about to encircle the Kuomintang rear. The army under Hsu Ko-chang and Mao Pin-wen reached Toupi, and then drove north along the road to Yungfeng, only too glad to avoid the Red Army. The first annihilation campaign was over.

For the first time the Kuomintang realized that the normal processes of war were no longer applicable. The "luring" operation had been wonderfully successful. Two divisions had been trapped, one in a town and another in high mountains, where its rear had been cut off. The Reds had employed a vast knowledge of the mountain paths. The Kuomintang troops lacked this knowledge, and they were deliberately misled by the hostile villagers; also, many of the village people slipped out of their villages and took to the hills, sniping at them, or leading them to small concentrations of Red troops, who mowed them down from their higher positions. The Kuomintang troops had no training in mountain warfare, did not know the strength of the Reds or realize the desperate poverty of the villagers and all its consequences, and did not co-operate with one another, each divisional commander hoping to avoid the responsibility of a direct engagement with the Reds. The most prominent commander, Chang Hui-chang, made the basic error of leading his troops too close to the main concentration area of the Red Army. Finally, three divisions at Kian, Futien, and Kienning, made no effort to support the Eighteenth Division, probably because they had no idea what had happened to it. The Kuomintang generals had hoped to annihilate the Red Army between the Kan and Ju rivers, but they were themselves annihilated. There were skirmishes until the end of February, and at least one major engagement was fought near Ningtu, the original "terminus of withdrawal" selected by the Reds. There, once again, Mao complained of the Communists' occasional inability to concentrate all their forces at the psychological moment on the enemy: too many were allowed to retreat. But the lessons had been learned, and with the destruction of the Eighteenth Division they discovered their own power for the first time. Also, they now possessed the two captured radio transmitters, which were to be of inestimable use to them in the kind of guerrilla warfare they practiced. "In this battle," said Mao, "we faced the enemy with poise and ease."

The Second Annihilation Campaign

One of the major advantages possessed by the Red Army was the completeness of its intelligence. The positions of the enemy were known, if only because the Kuomintang forces allowed their positions to be published in newspapers; the positions of the Red Army, hiding among the hills, were nearly always unknown. There were also disadvantages. The Red resources were limited. They had lost about seven thousand men in the first campaign, and they had made up their forces to the original thirty thousand, but they knew that Chiang Kai-shek was preparing to launch an even greater expedition than before. Lo Ling's division was retained to guard Kian, but from the north, east, and west seven columns were advancing on Ningtu. In the first campaign Mao fought his first battle against the strongest opposing force; in the second, he deliberately hurled himself at the weakest, avoiding the Nineteenth Route Army under Tsai Ting-kai, who was regarded as the best of the opposing generals. In the following year Tsai Ting-kai was to achieve lasting fame for his valiant resistance of the Japanese attacks in Shanghai, and for some time to come he was to remain a thorn in the flesh to the Communists.

Now that they possessed radios, diversionary movements of guerrillas—even on a large scale—became easier, and Red forces were scattered behind the enemy lines. The main forces, however, were to travel 250 miles in fourteen days, fighting four battles and capturing more than twenty thousand rifles. Nanfeng was taken, and then abandoned, and exactly as Mao had calculated they were to find a "terminus of withdrawal" inside the Fukien border, south of Kienning.

Mao's notes on the battles, compiled with the help of Chu Teh, give an illusion of ease to the whole campaign. It is almost a dance, or a game of skittles. In fact, far greater risks were taken by the Reds in this campaign than before. Absolute superiority in manpower did not exist. There were none of the advantages which come with the winter mists—the attack began in late spring—and the country was less mountainous. The enemy was learning his lesson. Ho Ying-ching, in command of the expedition, urged the commanders to move more slowly and cautiously, consolidating the territory recovered before advancing further; and already there was emerging in embryo the idea of an enclosing ring of blockhouses. Mao's deliberately dry account of the campaign is here quoted in full:

The situation was:

1. The advancing enemy forces numbered two hundred thousand with Ho Ying-ching as the commander-in-chief with headquarters at Nanchang.

2. As in the First Campaign all the troops did not belong to Chiang Kai-shek's own faction. The strongest units were the Nineteenth Route Army (in the southwest) and the armies under Sung Lien-chung and Chu Shao-liang (in the east inside the border of Kiangsi province). The rest were weaker.

3. The A-B group was purged, and the Red Army enjoyed the support of the people of the Soviet Area.

4. Wang Chin-yu's division (in the Futien area northeast of the Nineteenth Route Army position) had just arrived from north China, and was frightened. A similar situation obtained with the two columns of Wang's left wing, the divisions of Hao Meng-ling and Kuo Hua-tsung.

5. If we were to attack Futien first and then sweep to the east, we could extend the territory of the Soviets in the vicinity of Kienning, Lichuan, and Taining on the Fukien-Kiangsi border and amass provisions for smashing the coming encirclement campaign. If we strike in the western direction, then we would come up against the Kan River, leaving no space for expansion after the conclusion of the campaign. If (after the western operations) we turn back to the east again, our army would be fatigued and our time lost.

6. Though the strength of our troops was slightly reduced, to thirty thousand odd, our men had had four months for rehabilitation and training.

Basing ourselves on these considerations, we decided to engage the forces of Wang Chin-yu and those of Kung Ping-fan (on Wang's western flank), totaling eleven regiments, for the initial battle, and after defeating them, we would beat the troops of Sung Lien-chung, Chu Shao-liang and Liu Ho-ting (in the Kienning and Taining area in Fukien). For fifteen days in succession, from May 16 to May 30, 1931, our troops covered a distance of seven hundred *li*, fought five battles, and captured more than twenty thousand rifles. The encirclement was broken dramatically and punctually.

Our battle with Wang Chin-yu took place between the positions of Tsai Ting-kai's (Nineteenth Route Army) and Kuo Hua-tsung's division some ten *li* away from Kuo and forty *li* from

Tsai. We were derided for forcing ourselves into a tight position, but we succeeded in getting in. This was mainly due to the conditions of the Soviet area, plus the disunity among the enemy's units. After the defeat of Kuo's division, Hao's division fled to Yungfeng during the same night and was saved from disaster.

This is not, of course, an attempt to tell the whole story. Mao contents himself with offering the *logical* plan of a guerrilla campaign, a plan which revolves around the utmost daring and the reversal of generally accepted rules of warfare. Deliberately, the Red Army set itself the task of entering a fortified area, smashing a comparatively weak army, though strong armies were on both its flanks, and then slicing through the three remaining armies in the northeast, taking each by surprise. Elsewhere, Mao has remarked that the battles were not completely satisfactory, and dangerous risks were taken; but when he speaks of these risks, he does not mention the first onslaught against Wang Chin-yu but the fact that the Red Army, after the capture of Nanfeng, was compelled to divide its resources, and he regards it almost as an act of weakness that they did not possess absolute superiority at Kienning. Ten thousand Red Army troops were employed against the seven thousand of the Fifty-third Division. The superiority was not great enough. "Even in guerrilla war, there is complete assurance of victory only when a vastly superior force strikes at any given point: in this way, a very small army, by concentrations, can *eat* away at a vastly superior enemy."

Though Mao was aware that he had no great preponderance of forces at Kienning, he was not surprised by the outcome. The battle followed all the copybook maxims. As soon as the Red Army struck, Liu Ho-ting fled from his headquarters into Kienning, and his troops followed him. The Red Army chased him right through the town and onto the bridge over the Min River, and on the opposite bank of the river Red Army forces were already waiting for him. Then came the massacre, with the Kuomintang troops jumping into the river, where they were easily picked off by machine-gun fire. After capturing Kienning the Red Army wheeled and destroyed the remaining earthworks and

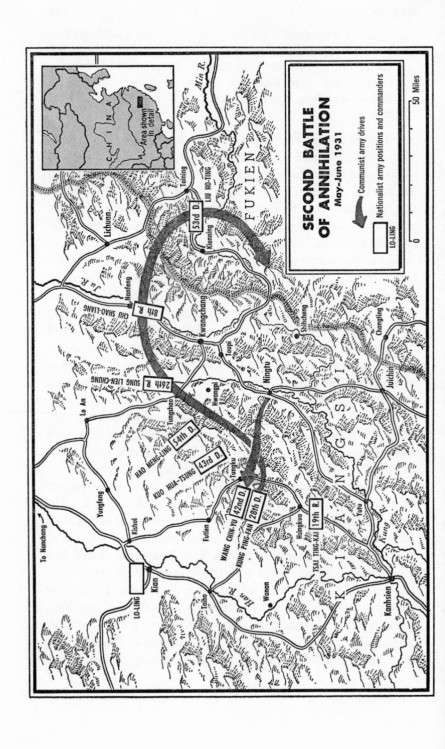

SECOND BATTLE OF ANNIHILATION
May–June 1931

→ Communist army drives

Nationalist army positions and commanders

[ ] LO-LING

0   50 Miles

fortifications of the Kuomintang, which ran for a distance of nearly two hundred miles to Kian.

Mao's campaigns suggest a brilliant daring, but their success came from caution, from a very careful evaluation of the enemy's strength, and from the patient study of the "first engagement" and the "terminus of withdrawal." Mao places an almost mystical trust in these concepts. During the second campaign, the Red Army, after a night march, actually occupied Tungku, and then, just as silently, evaporated. For twenty-five days they led a secret existence in the town, waiting for Wang Chin-yu to advance from his strong position at Futien. "During the interval of waiting we were closely quartered by the enemy," Mao relates in his book, *Strategic Problems of the Revolutionary Wars.* "Despite the danger that information about our presence might leak out, we rejected all impatient suggestions for a quick attack. At last our desire was realized."

The success of the second campaign was evidently even greater than the Communists had hoped. Near Tungku the Kuomintang Fifth Army was cut to pieces, and the equipment of two divisions captured; more equipment was captured in the three remaining battles, and once again their losses were made up by the prisoners. It looked as though the same tactics—a quick breakthrough at the weakest point followed by a quick succession of battles while they were still flushed with their first victory, and then withdrawal into the mountains—would be continually successful. But the third campaign was to last longer and was to be fought harder than any of the others. By the first week in June the second campaign was over. On July 2, Chiang Kai-shek launched the Third Annihilation Campaign, which was to last for three long months. This time there were variations of the theme of guerrilla warfare, and this time the Reds escaped encirclement largely by luck.

The Third Annihilation Campaign

The second campaign ended about June 4, 1931. The third began four weeks later with a complete abandonment of the theory of consolidation. The Kuomintang troops, now under the command of Chiang Kai-shek, who had arrived at Nanchang with a staff of German advisers on June 22, were ordered to march twenty-five miles a day through the torrid heat of a Kiangsi summer. Their tactics were carefully prepared. It was agreed that the Communists were now a more pressing menace than ever, and a final blow was necessary: a huge force of three hundred thousand men were to drive the Reds across the border into Kwangtung, where other Kuomintang armies were preparing to receive them. The Kuomintang generals calculated that high summer would have the effect of wearying the Reds, whose extraordinary mobility would perhaps be reduced; and this time the Kuomintang armies were heavily equipped, with about two hundred cannon and a hundred airplanes, and they were under some of the best commanders the Reds had ever fought against.

The map on page 129 shows a series of battles fought toward the end of the campaign. At the beginning the area between Tungku and Kwangchang was in the hands of the Reds, who were compelled to retreat within the borders of Futien. Tungku, because it had harbored the Red forces, was treated like Lidice: it was burned to the ground and all its inhabitants massacred. In the first stages of the campaign the Reds lost heavily; airplanes were able to bomb their concentrations in the forest and make careful reconnaissances. But after August 1 the tide began to ebb. Heavy rains set in, and the lines of communications of the Kuomintang armies were already too long and unwieldy. Having occupied the triangle Kian-Kwangchang-Yutu, they concentrated their forces on the right bank of the Kan River, though four divisions were left in the mountains. In an effort to cut the rear of these "lost divisions," the Reds deliberately courted danger by taking the least likely path to the north. Intending to make a wide encircling movement, they found themselves detected near Futien, two divisions rushed down to intercept them, and they were then compelled to return to a small village west of Hsingkuo. They were exhausted and bedraggled. They knew they had only a single day in which to re-form their ranks, and they had been fighting continuously for over a month. Then, by one of those

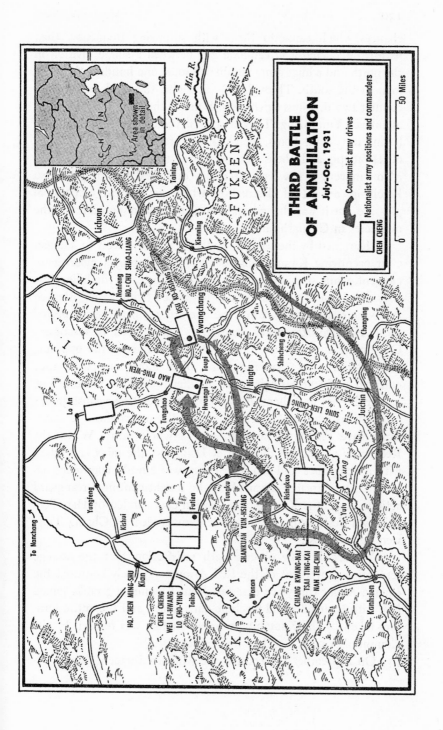

chances which came to them with surprising frequency, their patrols discovered a fifteen-mile gap between a single division in the north and a huge army numbering some one hundred thousand men in the south. Through this, at night, they fled, only to encounter two divisions driving south under the famous commander Shankuan Yun-hsiang. They destroyed these divisions in a battle lasting forty-eight hours, marched for three days in the direction of Hwangpi, and there destroyed still another division, under Mao Pin-wen. A few days later they destroyed the army of Hsu Ko-chang, an act of destruction which gave them exceptional pleasure, for it was this general who had been responsible for the massacres in Changsha in May 1927.

Heartened by these victories, the Reds drove west to Tungku after occupying Kwangchang, deliberately inviting a close encirclement, while spreading a net of partisan forces in the hills. Here they were almost trapped. As the ring closed tighter, they attacked the Nineteenth Route Army, the one army which they respected most. Finally, after heavy losses they were forced to disengage. Once more they found a providential gap between the opposing armies, and after climbing some high mountain paths they emerged again at Hsingkuo, where they were able to rest. The enemy did not find them: it was too busy operating against groups of guerrillas who kept descending from the mountains and sometimes gave the impression of being a whole army. When the Red Army was at last detected at Hsingkuo, the rains had set in with a vengeance and Ho Ying-ching was already counseling retreat. As he retreated toward Kian, he fought continual rear-guard actions. An entire Kuomintang division commanded by Han Teh-chin was destroyed, and a brigade commanded by Chiang Ting-wen was also lost.

Mao could now observe with satisfaction that the strange serpentine movement of the Red Army completely confused the enemy. About thirty-five deserters from Kuomintang ranks joined him with their rifles and machine guns intact, and the entire territory taken by the Kuomintang troops in July was retaken by the Communists by the end of September.

On September 18 occurred the Mukden Incident, which became the signal of the Japanese occupation of Manchuria. Shortly afterward the Kuomintang divisions withdrew from southern Kiangsi, leaving only some supporting troops at Kian. The Kuomintang contended that their morale had been affected by the Mukden Incident and that this was the sole cause of their withdrawal. It seems unlikely. The destruction of Tungku resulted in a widespread increase of peasant partisans. As so often before, a huge, unwieldy army had disintegrated because every divisional commander had been anxious that every other divisional commander should bear the brunt of the fighting. The Kuomintang troops were underfed because the Reds had carefully hidden all food supplies in the villages; their officers were corrupt; and both the troops and the officers terrorized the local populations. Toward the end of the battle one of the Kuomintang brigadiers was heard to say sadly, "The fat has worn thin, and the thin has been worn dead."

Of all the engagements which occurred during the third campaign, Mao was proudest of the first, the short, sharp battle near Lientang which was fought by a weary army after marching three or four hundred miles continually in the hills, after a single day's rest, and after a dangerous march between the enemy armies. It was a battle fought with the energy of despair, with tremendous speed and fury, and it could not be otherwise, for they were encircled and hopelessly outnumbered. Tactically, the decision to fight this battle went against all Mao's military beliefs except one: the belief that the first engagement determined all the rest. He was least proud of the dogged battles fought against the Nineteenth Route Army, which wasted the efforts of both armies, and ended in stalemate.

The third campaign was decisive. They had defeated, or broken, seventeen out of the enemy's thirty-three divisions, and increased their own strength. They had set up soviets throughout the south, and there were even soviets behind the enemy lines. They had made some military mistakes—Mao came to the conclusion that it was probably a mistake to have made the long march through Juichin to Hsingkuo, when it should have been possible to lure the enemy into the hills of western Fukien, for the idea of "lure enemy deep penetration" had not been utilized during this campaign; but he was dubious whether the victory would have been so complete. He noted with pleasure the remark of a Kuomintang general: "Wherever we go we are in darkness; wherever the Reds go, they are in brightness." It was a shadow game, played by one invisible enemy against another only too visible—a game played with exquisite cunning and furious violence. At its best, it was played by gradually circling around the enemy, threatening him, feeding him with suspense, and finally accomplishing his demise with a blow falling from an entirely unsuspected quarter, so that he was almost unconscious that the blow had fallen at all. Not only was Mao good at the game, but in a sense he had invented it, and no one else knew the rules.

These rules were re-examined after the conclusion of the third campaign. A completely new set of operational principles was formulated. There were developments in tactics and strategy, and the rudimentary character of the earlier principles was abandoned, though their essentials remained. In particular, Mao found no quarrel with the sixteen-word slogan he had made up at Chingkanshan. They were simple words, but they contained the answers to all the problems of encirclement. They rang like a bell, and Mao said that if you wanted to put the matter in more pompous military terms they provided "the basic directives for a countercampaign against encirclement, and the phases of both the strategic defensive and the strategic offensive, as well as those of strategic withdrawal and the strategic counteroffensive in a defensive operation." They are long words, in Chinese as in English, and Mao preferred his simple doggerel. "In a sense," he wrote, "all that came afterward was but an elaboration of those sixteen words."

For a few months the Red Army rested on its laurels. Preparations were made for holding the First All-China Congress of Soviets. The Kuomintang had reached a crisis in its activities: it had failed to prevent the Japanese occupation of Manchuria, just as it had failed to prevent the growth of the Red Army. In December 1931, at the end of one of China's most disastrous years, which had seen floods in the Yangtse Valley and the failure of crops over large areas, and the first onslaught of the Japanese as well as the third annihilation campaign, the congress was convened.

This congress is important, for here the Communists drew up their blueprints for the "democratic dictatorship of workers and peasants," and this blueprint was to remain relatively unchanged throughout the course of Communist expansion. When Mao came to power, exactly the same phrases, the same laws, and the same interpretations were used. Most of the declarations of the congress bear Mao's characteristic imprint. Nearly all of them are signed by him as president of the provisional government, though the names of the two vice-presidents, Han Ying and Chang Kuo-t'ao, are included.

In the constitution, the aims of the "democratic dictatorship" are defined. These aims include "the destruction of all feudal remnants and the destruction of the power of the warlords; the unification of China; the systematic delimitation of capitalist expansion; the development of the organization and class-consciousness of the proletariat; and the rallying of the broad masses of the village poor to our banners in order to effect the transition to the dictatorship of the proletariat." Not all of the constitution is so dry or so formidable. A special article is reserved for education—"all the peasants and toiling masses are guaranteed the right to education." Another article gives minority races equal rights and privileges. The electors are given the right to recall their deputies. Nationalization is to be on the broadest scale. The concessions are to be unconditionally returned to China. Outright confiscation of customhouses, railways, mines, and factories in foreign ownership is demanded. Asylum is offered to foreign revolutionaries. Compulsory military service occupies a special place in the constitution. Finally, "the Soviet Government in China proclaims the Soviet Union, the land of proletarian dictatorship, to be its loyal ally."

The constitution outlined a rigid program, and though it spoke of rights, it spoke more often of harsh duties and final judgments. The labor code, on the other hand, though some of its articles were clearly impracticable, did show a desire to im-

prove labor standards in a way which had never been seen in
China before. It called for a universal eight-hour day, a six-hour
day for youths between sixteen and eighteen, a four-hour day for
younger workers, and special privileges for women. No work
would be allowed on New Year's Day, the anniversary of Lenin's
death, the anniversary of the Paris Commune, the anniversary of
the inauguration of the Soviet Union, May Day, and the anni-
versaries of the Canton Uprising and the Shanghai Massacre.
Only six hours of work was permitted on days before holidays.
Wages were to be arranged by collective agreement. A list of
places where women and children were not allowed to work was
provided, including "forest work in places too high or too low."
Women were to receive the same wage rates as men. Special
machinery to prevent the exploitation of apprentices was put
into force, and labor inspectors were given complete powers over
the establishment of all new businesses. Unions were granted the
right to strike, and two per cent of all wages were to go to union
funds, and another one per cent to cultural undertakings. Social
insurance, with benefits of free medical attention, unemployment
relief, disablement and old age pensions, and special relief to
cover funerals, childbirth, and payments to the survivors after the
death of the wage earner were also introduced. The whole labor
code was to go into effect on January 1, 1932.

Admirable in many of its provisions, impracticable in others,
the new labor code was never completely put to the test. But it
did show the direction in which the new soviet state was progressing. Curiously enough, it had more to say about the conditions
of the workers than of the peasants, as though preparation was
already made for the moment when the proletariat would take
over power according to the Marxist theory. Yet the proletariat
was noticeable by its absence.

At this conference, too, Chang Kuo-t'ao prevailed upon the
Communists to accept a new interpretation of strategy. The old
and well-tried principles of guerrilla warfare and the breakthrough
during encirclement were to be abandoned, or at least partially
abandoned, in favor of the wresting from the enemy of whole
provinces. He argued that it was wrong to lure the enemy into

deep penetration, because so much Communist territory was necessarily abandoned: it would be better to defeat the enemy without abandoning any territory. Were they not two states confronting one another? The Soviets possessed huge settled areas, with regular armies, and for such armies guerrilla warfare must be accounted an anachronism. In this war of theory against practice, no final decisions were made, though the ghost of Li Li-san's ideas, which tormented them in 1927, now confronted them again at the moment of their triumph. It was a ghost which was not to be entirely laid for many years.

On this subject Mao had brooded at length with a kind of derisive horror against all those who objected to his simple and constantly repeated maxims of guerrilla war. He mocked at the strange new concepts: "absolute centralized command," "lose not an inch of land," "the division of the army into six advancing columns," "a war of blockhouses against blockhouses," and the strangest of all, which can be translated as "big-rearism." "All these theories," he wrote, "are undoubtedly erroneous. They are mechanical expressions of revolutionary hysteria and impatience. This is the theory and practice of reckless and naive elements who, when circumstances become difficult, move from sheer desperation to conservatism, and from conservatism to escapism."

In 1932 no annihilation campaigns were fought. In February the Nineteenth Route Army under Tsai Ting-kai found itself battling the Japanese at Chapei, without help from Chiang Kai-shek. The Reds were forced to withdraw to Fukien, where they set up an independent state. China was beginning to crack along the seams. The provinces of Manchuria were under Japanese control, the Japanese having employed the same tactics as the Communists: night marches, sudden surprise attacks, the wearing of enemy uniforms. Against the constant use of surprise, Chiang Kai-shek, with a faulty system of intelligence, had no weapons. Through most of the year the Red Army continued its sporadic attacks against the Kuomintang armies. On April 20, the Red Army attacked Changchow in Fukien, and held it for six weeks. There were short guerrilla attacks in the areas between the Kan and

Ju rivers. Lo An, Kienning, and Lichuan were stormed, and more deserters from the Kuomintang ranks came to join the Red Army. Even airplanes were captured, only to be burned, because at this stage there were no pilots available. Gradually the Red Army had come to possess about eighty thousand front-line troops, and perhaps fifty thousand partisan units. Yet it seemed to be losing its original vitality. Observers noted a curious sense of apathy, arising perhaps from the failure of the revolutionaries to solve the economic problems of the border regions.

In April the Communists prepared a solemn declaration, urging the Kuomintang troops to destroy the Kuomintang before launching an attack against the Japanese. Exactly the same kind of demand had been made by the Kuomintang, who urged that the Communist armies be destroyed before the Kuomintang armies were thrown against the Japanese. When winter came, and the mists closed in on Kiangsi, Mao decided that the time had come for a complete revaluation of policies, he abandoned his role as military commander and set about creating a new survey of conditions in the Soviet areas under his control. One thing was evident: the soviets in China, spread out in pockets over Hunan, Hupeh, Szechuan, Honan, Anhwei, Fukien, and Kwangtung, had completely failed to form a large central soviet. Different policies ruled in the different Soviet areas. Worse still, as Chu Teh admitted to the American writer Nym Wales, "the economic situation was not good, because we had already expropriated all the landlords and had no further sources of revenue."*

Meanwhile, the fighting went on. A fourth annihilation campaign was launched, and then a fifth. The fourth lasted from April to October 1933 and was fought out in the area between Lo An and Nanfeng, ground which the Reds knew intimately. The Kuomintang armies made the mistake of driving south in three columns. Two columns were cut to pieces, and the third was turned back. Mao described the battle briefly, and without much interest. The opening battle near Nanfeng had been a failure, and though the encirclement was broken and a battle at Hwangpi led

* Nym Wales, *Inside Red China* (New York, 1939), p. 256.

to the capture of thirteen thousand men, the tactical employment of the Red Army no longer showed its former brilliance.

The fifth campaign followed immediately on the fourth. Chiang Kai-shek had concluded a truce with the Japanese and thought his rear safeguarded. He destroyed part of the Honan-Hupeh-Anhwei Red Army, which could no longer provide diversionary assistance, prevailed upon foreign bankers for loans, and promised that within three months he would completely annihilate the Red armies. He very nearly succeeded. The first battle was inconclusive. Mao complained bitterly against the commanders who allowed the retreat. From that moment the Red armies lost their advantage.

On January 22, 1934, while the Fifth Annihilation Campaign was in full swing, Mao called the Second National Soviet Congress, at Juichin, and there, before about eight hundred delegates, he made a speech outlining the successes of the Chinese soviets. It was a curiously perturbing speech. He made great claims, and admitted mistakes. He claimed, for example, that the Chinese soviets now controlled so vast a population that numerically they were second only to the Soviet Union. He admitted that there were economic difficulties, and the system of land tenure had not yet been completely worked out. He spoke with pride of the victories of the Red Army, and anyone reading the speech today could derive the impression that the position of the Soviet armies could not be bettered and that all five annihilation campaigns had proved unsuccessful. In fact, the military position was alarming. The Red Army was being bled white. Only a few days before the speech was delivered the Kuomintang had sent a naval landing party to Fuchow, captured it from Tsai Ting-kai, and put an end to the independent Fukien government. Thus they established a Kuomintang base southeast of the Communist forces.

With the help of his military adviser, General von Falkenhausen, Chiang Kai-shek now introduced a maneuver known as the "fiery wall." Small, heavily fortified posts were carried forward into Communist positions, and all the land traveled by these posts, and all the land between them, was put to the flame. It was the scorched-earth policy. But worse than the scorched-earth policy was the growing hysteria of the peasants, who turned to the Communists in alarm, but could no longer be relied upon to fight. Hysteria led to panic, and for the first time there appeared a strange process of dissolution. It was as though, under the weight of fear, the whole Communist system was about to crack wide open. New sects appeared. Quarrels which at other times would have been settled amicably now acquired increasing acerbity. There had been, as Agnes Smedley noted, a Red Terror, but the White Terror which followed was incalculably more terrifying, for the Kuomintang soldiers no longer trusted the peasants, and because they could not trust them, over a million peasants of Kiangsi were starved to death or killed as the "fiery wall" drew closer to the Communist concentrations. Years later, Mao blamed his German adviser, Li Teh, for strategical errors at this time. The Communists should, he said, have linked up with the independent Fukien government under Tsai Ting-kai, and later they should have thrown all their available forces in the direction of Shanghai.

At the conference Mao spoke at moments as though they were faced with no pressing dangers. With memories of four successful campaigns, he conjured up a picture of vast accretions of Communist power. He stated unequivocally the party's reliance on the peasantry, and at the same time he announced that "the war is becoming more acute with every day that passes, and the time must come when the two contending parties must fight a decisive battle." "The whole world," he said in the same speech, "is passing through a transitional phase leading to a new development of war and revolution." But he did not define the new development, and indeed he did not know which direction the revolution would take. Not for a moment did he suggest that ten months later the Chinese Communists would have to break through the encirclement of Juichin and begin their long wandering march through nine provinces of China.

Yet there were occasional hints of shadows, disturbing repetitions, strange emphases. He was perfectly conscious that the revolution would assume more and more violent proportions, and with the Fifth Annihilation Campaign a critical stage had been reached, so critical indeed that he urged the formation of an army a million strong and demanded the immediate strengthening of the Central Revolutionary Military Committee.

However, there were good prospects in store. "The enemy has far more difficulties than we have," he said, "since his soldiers are continually wavering, the broad masses of the peasants hate them, the militarists themselves are disintegrating, there are continuous clashes and conflicts between the Kuomintang supporters, and they are facing economic and financial bankruptcy."

Mao's speech at the Second National Soviet Congress was the most important of the statements he had made since the famous report on the conditions of the Hunan peasantry in 1927. It is not, however, easy reading. It seems to have been composed hurriedly and under considerable strain. Three times, in slightly different terms, as if he felt it necessary to remind his listeners repeatedly of the basic problems involved, he defines the task of the revolution:

> The fundamental task of the Soviets is revolutionary war and mobilizing all mass strength to fight this war. Around the fundamental task are gathered many urgent tasks. We have to practice a broad democracy; we must suppress with absolute determination the counterrevolution within our territory; we must promote the class struggle of the workers and the agrarian revolution of the peasants; we must promote the militancy of the masses of workers and peasants under the principle that the workers shall lead the alliance of workers and peasants; we must administer correct financial and economic policies in order to guarantee the material needs of the revolutionary war; and we must wage the cultural revolution in order to arm the leaders of the masses of workers and peasants. All these are directed toward a single goal: to overthrow the imperialist rule of the Kuomintang through revolutionary war, to consolidate and develop the democratic dictatorship of the workers and peasants, and so progress toward the stage of proletarian dictatorship.

Here were the seeds of the "new democracy" he advanced six years later, and it is significant that the "new democracy" appears under the guise of a "democratic dictatorship of workers and peasants."

Though reliance on Marxist theory gives a curious air of unreality to his discussion of the stages through which the Chinese revolution must pass, the speech only rarely refers to theory. The practical benefits of Communist rule, as distinguished from "the desperate stratagems of our enemies," are related at length. In the soviets, women share equality with men; corporal punishment is abolished; real wages are raised; the period of apprenticeship has been shortened; marriages may be arranged by simple registration; private investments are permitted, for "the soviets shall not monopolize all the productive enterprises but concentrate on those beneficial to the state." Usury is prohibited. The eight-hour day is enforced. School children may spend only a small part of their day working in the fields: the rest of the time must be spent in playing and reading in school. Private merchants are to be encouraged to break the enemy blockade, and taxes are no longer to be paid when goods travel from village to village. Mao notes sadly that the blockade has affected two of the things he has always held most precious—paper and tobacco. He reveals that during the land inspection conducted in the summer of 1933, "in the central Soviet district 6,988 landlord families and 6,638 rich peasant families owning a huge excess of land were discovered and their land seized and money taken from them to the total of $606,916."

He shows the men and women of the soviets at work on the farms, with their slogan: "Liquidate all fallow land." He admits that the soviets have not progressed as far as they should have done. New tactics are necessary. "A struggle," he says, "must be waged against bureaucracy and the habit of dictation among soviet functionaries: persuasion must replace dictation in everything that concerns the masses." It is a theme he was to repeat many times later, but the very repetition of the theme suggests that bureaucracy was inefficient, and often culpable. In fact, though very remarkable changes had taken place under the Kiangsi soviet, and the best of them followed the principles of the Taiping rebels, the soviet had not yet proved itself. Sometimes the government was ignorant. An eight-hour day must be meaningless to farmers during the spring sowing. It was absurd to take children off the land when all the traditions of Kiangsi made it inevitable that children should work as soon as they could walk. As the Kuomintang armies, numbering half a million, drew nearer, the apathy of the peasant increased, and Po Ku, one of the wisest of Communist commissars, could say with some truth that "there is only the peasant: if he should lose faith with us, it is all over." It was Po Ku also who spoke openly about the "Lo Min line," saying that Lo Min, a Fukien party leader, was perfectly right to make complaints. What Lo Min had said was, "Even if our best leaders were to come, or to bring Stalin himself, or even resurrect Lenin from the tomb, and were to speak all together to the masses for three days and three nights, I do not think it would help change the mood of the people."

In spite of the defeat which came shortly afterward, Mao's speech contained too many truths to be neglected. In Nanking it was read as the testament of an expiring leadership, and Chiang Kai-shek thought hopefully of clearing all the Reds out of Kiangsi by June. "The long-drawn-out campaign is now coming to an end," he said, "and only three counties, out of more than a thousand, remain infested by the Communists. These are isolated by a ring of troops and will be cleared up soon."

This opinion was not shared by Dmitri Manuilsky, who claimed in Moscow that the Chinese Communists were on the eve of important successes and had already emerged as the second great Communist power, "in control of territories larger than France or Germany or any other imperialist country outside the United States." He praised their offensive against "English tanks and armored cars, French artillery and American airplanes," and he prophesied an immediate and final defeat of the Kuomintang armies. Both Nanking and Moscow were wrong. The war dragged on through the summer and autumn, and by the beginning of July Chiang Kai-shek was regrouping his forces for the long promised thrust at the heart of the Soviets. The end did not come until October.

Mao's speech had defended the Communist case as well

as it could be defended. Most of the time he was speaking about reconstruction, about the need for consumers' cooperatives, about the ways in which the peasants could be freed from bond slavery, about increases in real wages, facilities for education, and the improvement of land tenure. For the peasants in that hardbitten province these were matters of huge importance. Though the "fiery walls" of General von Falkenhausen burned the countryside, and whole villages and towns were depopulated, the need for a social program comparable to the one he had outlined had never been greater. The Red Army might be defeated; the message of the Communists to the Chinese peasants, in the absence of any comparable message from the Kuomintang, would remain.

The end came with surprising suddenness. Early in the campaign there had been a furious victory at Hsingkuo, a model village where "experimental sovietism" had been tried out successfully. In this battle a corps of women soldiers, fighting with spears and sabers, had distinguished itself and a whole enemy division had been defeated. But thereafter the tide turned. Repeated attacks against enemy strong points failed. The Red armies were reduced, in Mao's words, to "moving backward and forward as we sought battle between the enemy's main forces and his chain of blockhouses, so that for long periods we sank into a kind of passivity, retaining no initiative at all." The strategical directives were given by the German Communist Li Teh. They were almost fatal. The ring grew tighter. The Communist leaders seemed to be hypnotized by the huge forces arrayed against them. The cardinal mistake was the division of their forces into six columns, for it was thought hopeless to engage the enemy at any one place on the circumference: the Kuomintang was advancing from every direction. The old axiom was, "Lure the enemy into the depths of our territory, then attack with all our force at the enemy's weakest place." Unaccountably, the axiom was now reversed. There were no assigned points of withdrawal. The Communists might have broken through with their captured tanks, but they had no gasoline; and though they now had three airplanes on active commission, their pilots were inexperienced. At the beginning of the campaign the Red Army possessed 180,000 men under arms; by August 1934 there were less than one hundred thousand. The young Hunanese Hsiao K'eh broke through the ring with a column of about ten thousand men in August. There was still sporadic fighting, with the Communist forces withdrawing as well as they could toward Yutu on the Fukien border. From there, on the night of October 16, receiving news of Hsiao K'eh's successful escape and some not too accurate information about a weak point in the enemy lines, some ninety thousand of them, soon to be increased by another eight or nine thousand gathered from the neighborhood, set out on the Long March.

For years afterward the experience of the Fifth Annihilation Campaign remained a nightmare to the Red military command. For the first time they had seen how a modern army, under capable direction, equipped with mechanized units, could force its way into guerrilla strongholds. When he came to write *Strategic Problems*, Mao admitted quite frankly that appalling errors had been made. "The main error," he wrote, "is that we did not plan organically: we had not thought out the campaign. Elated by the victory at Hsingkuo, we regarded it as a triumph, but in effect it was a defeat, for it led us to unwise decisions. The enemy's supreme command was farsighted in its strategy: we thought only of what was under our nose. There are three essentials: an assurance of victory, an understanding of the campaign as a whole, a knowledge of the next strategic move." More bluntly, he wrote: "We panicked, and we fought stupidly."

THE LONG MARCH

THE STORY of the Long March already belongs to Chinese legend. The extraordinary adventure—a march of six thousand miles, continued against all odds and with an enemy hot on their heels— had the effect of placing the Chinese Communists on the path of the Japanese invasion. It gave authority to their rule; it provided a hard training ground for the future Red Army; and it settled once and for all Mao's dominance within the party, for the march was led by him and by Chu Teh, who regarded Mao as the guiding genius and for the most part bowed to Mao's decisions.

No complete and readable account of the Long March has yet been prepared. The Chinese Communists have published in two large volumes, printed in Yenan, a statistical survey of the battles they fought, the ammunition and prisoners captured, and the military strategies evolved. It includes maps and documents, most of them piously collected by Chu Teh, and the whole is printed on fraying brown paper in almost illegible type. More recently collections of essays and reminiscences about the Long March have appeared in China, many of them marked by hagiological fervor: in much the same way medieval monks wrote about the saints. By far the best account is given in Edgar Snow's *Red Star over China*, though it was written before the march was completed—more straggling columns reached northern Shensi after Snow had left. Snow wrote the stories of the survivors before their memories had dimmed. Arriving in Yenan ten years later, I was struck by the gradual decay of memory. They still told stories of the legendary Long March willingly enough; they remembered their long night marches, how hungry they were, and how close to extinction; they remembered sickness and despair; but often the details escaped them. The same incident, told by different people, became different incidents. The crossing of the Tatu River, told by three separate people, seemed to be three separate crossings, at different times and at different places, yet all three survivors had been within a few hundred yards of each other. The stories of the battles were even more difficult to piece together. "There were so very many battles," General P'eng Teh-huai told me. "Now, when I look back, it seems to be one enormous battle going on forever." Once, drawing the plan of a breakthrough in an encirclement campaign in Kweichow, he paused suddenly—he had made a mistake; the battle he had intended to describe occurred in Szechuan, several hundred miles away. So it was with all the commanders; they remembered small details and forgot the decisive events, and most of all they remembered the marshes and the snows, the strange landscape on the edge of Tibet where Lin Piao nearly perished and Mao was sick and only Chu Teh, gifted with amazing physical energy, seemed to be wholly and completely in command of himself.

For Mao the responsibility of the journey weighed heavily. He was the president of a provisional government on the march. During the last stages of the annihilation campaigns he deferred to the experience of the German Communist, Li Teh, but from the beginning he felt that positional warfare was wrong. He still believed that small compact groups of guerrillas could do as much harm as a division armed with automatic rifles.

At Kwangchang, on the Fukien-Kiangsi border, there had been the last shattering defeat, a defeat so terrible that when he came to describe the concluding stages of the Fifth Campaign in *Strategic Problems* he completely omitted any reference to this battle in which four thousand were killed and twenty thousand wounded, as though it was too painful to contemplate. Suddenly, there came the order, signed by Mao and Chu Teh, to abandon Juichin. Documents were destroyed. The machinery in the arsenal was taken apart and buried in the forests. Everything that could conceivably aid the Kuomintang was destroyed, and everything that could aid the Red Army on its march was placed on the backs of pack animals. Every man was ordered to take a rifle and fifteen chin of food. Two diversionary columns were set out, one under Fang Chih-min, with orders to establish itself in Yuying in the northeast of the province, and the other under Han Ying, with orders to hold out in the south along the mountains on the borders of Fukien, Kiangsi, and Chekiang. The first perished, and the second led an exhausting existence through years of guerrilla warfare in the south, the remnants of this army only reappearing in Shensi in 1938. Orders were given for all forces to concentrate at Yutu. There were skirmishes during the comparatively short journey from Juichin to Yutu, but the Red armies were helped by the rain and the moonless nights.

One of Mao's orderlies has left a description of him in the days just before the Long March. At the time Mao was suffering from fever, very pale, with enormous eyes. Doctors were unable to locate the seat of the fever, and wherever he went he was accompanied by a Red Cross nurse, a boy of seventeen who proved to be completely useless, for Mao paid no attention to him and continued to work as though he were well. As usual, he worked at night, poring endlessly over newspapers, books, and captured documents, marking important passages in red pencil. The Red Army was constantly on the move, and he traveled with it, but every night he would find somewhere to work, setting up a lamp and a table and then busying himself with the documents which poured out of the capacious knapsack he carried on his shoulders when on the march. The knapsack was divided into nine compartments: one for maps, another for newspapers, another for books, and so on. The knapsack he regarded as his most important possession, and he liked to have it in view. His other possessions were a sun helmet, a torn umbrella, two uniforms, one cotton sheet, two blankets, a lantern, a water jug, a special bowl to hold cakes of "three-layer rice," and a silver-gray woolen sweater. Possessing so little, he was able to move at a moment's notice.

Now, with their armies exhausted and the villagers no longer daring to help them for fear of immediate reprisals from the Kuomintang armies in the neighborhood, Chu Teh and Mao could reflect that they were once more in the same situation in which they had been on Chingkanshan. Without cannon, sometimes armed only with sabers, often barefoot, the soldiers marched to the point of concentration with little hope of any immediate respite, followed by a small army of sick and wounded men from the hospitals, for it was generally agreed that the sick and wounded would be treated unmercifully by the Kuomintang in their triumph. Those who survived the first month speak of the agony of wandering in the dark, in the rain, but it is possible that if there had not been this continuous rain which concealed their movements, the Kuomintang would have completely destroyed them.

Though the Red Army reached Yutu safely, it was soon forced to abandon the town, and there followed another march through hostile territory to the small town of Kaopilao. Winter was drawing on, the Kuomintang withdrew some of their forces, and soon Mao was ordering a general return to Yutu, a town large enough to be put in a state of defense, defended on one side by a river and with rolling plains on the other. Suddenly in October news reached Yutu that the Kuomintang was about to mount a still more powerful offensive. The time had come to break through the encirclement and if necessary abandon Kiangsi altogether.

The Long March began on the evening of October 16, 1934. Some eighty-five thousand soldiers set out on the march, and about thirty-five women. At this time Mao was ill and emaciated, still suffering from a fever that seemed incurable. Mao's orderly has left an account of the first hours of the march:

> Around five o'clock in the evening, Mao and about twenty others left Yutu by the North Gate, and then turned to the left towards the river, which was all yellow, roaring and foaming, as though calling on the armies to advance. Soon the sun set, and the gusts of bitter cold wind chilled us. The Chairman wore a gray cloth uniform and an eight-cornered military cap, with no overcoat. He walked with enormous strides along the riverbank.
>
> When we were some miles beyond Yutu, we saw flashing lights and heard strange sounds coming from the distance. Chuang

Fu-wu, the male nurse, was puzzled, and asked what was happening.

"They're our troops," the Chairman said.

I was puzzled, for I remembered I had not seen a single soldier on the road from Yutu, and how could so many soldiers have appeared from nowhere?

We found a bridge made of barges spanning the river, and the Red Army was crossing over, waving myriads of torches so that they resembled fire dragons. Their laughter mingled with songs and shouts, echoing backward and forward along the line.

"How is it there are so many?" I asked the Chairman.

"Oh, that's not many," he replied. "There are far, far more ahead of us."

So we walked over the floating bridge, crowded with cavalry and foot soldiers, porters and peasants who had come to say good-by. The Chairman would step aside to let them pass. At midnight some peasants shouted, "They are going to capture Kupo and Hsingtien soon!" and when daylight came the news was confirmed. We were very pleased, because both these towns had salt wells, and salt was lacking where we had come from. We had won the first victories of the Long March.*

Where were they going? No one knew. Years later, when Mao was asked what direction they had intended to take, he answered, "If you mean, did we have any exact plans, the answer is that we had none. We intended to break out of the encirclement and join up with the other soviets. Beyond that, there was only a very deliberate desire to put ourselves in a position where we could fight the Japanese." He had no idea, nor had anyone else, that they would find themselves close to the frontiers of Tibet within five months.

Hsiao K'eh had broken through, and they intended to follow him, and if possible consolidate all the separate soviets, none of them approaching the original Kiangsi soviet in size, for it was evident that these small soviets could no longer exist alone. The main objective was the largest of these soviets, in Szechuan, where Hsu Hsiang-ch'ien was in command of the Fourth Front Red Army consisting of around one hundred thousand trained soldiers. As Mao realized later, this was still another fantastic error; to march

* Memoirs of Colonel Chen Chang-feng (Peking, 1957), pp. 11–12.

so deliberately toward the largest remaining soviet camp was to invite the Kuomintang to straddle their path.

Other errors were committed. In their anxiety to retain as much as possible of their spoils, great quantities of food, ammunition, bank notes, and even silver bullion were being transported on pack animals, and this delayed their advance. It was a characteristic mistake; from the beginning, Mao had attached a great deal of importance to the spoils of war. Worse still, two columns followed the identical road taken by Hsiao K'eh without suspecting that the Kuomintang might have deliberately allowed Hsiao K'eh's escape in the hope of trapping larger columns; and the early days of the march, as they fought their way through the rings of blockhouses, were the most desperate and the ones in which they suffered their greatest losses. In the first three weeks twenty-five thousand men perished in the skirmishes around the blockhouses.

There was to be little rest for the men on the Long March as they skirted Hunan and Szechuan. Driving into Kweichow they met relentless opposition from the combined armies of the local warlord and from those sent down the Yangtse to Chungking by Chiang Kai-shek. Immense efforts were made to impede their progress. From Chungking, armies drove across the Szechuan border deep into Kweichow: an attempt was made to surround the Red forces with another ring of iron. The phrase "a ring of iron" recurs frequently in Chiang Kai-shek's manifestoes of that time. Hill forts were rapidly built, crossings were guarded, bombing planes were sent out. But the Communists were invisible from the air, because a low-lying cloud hovers over Kweichow for five months of the year, and the hill forts could be taken by assault.

A classic encounter occurred on the Wu River, where the Communists found themselves surrounded. They had already crossed the river, but the enemy lay on both banks, waiting to spring the trap. The Communists had a firm belief in the power of one man to win a battle. They sent a single soldier over at night after they had silenced the enemy guns with mortars. The solitary swimmer managed to capture one of the boats hidden against the shore, and this single boat was afterward sent backward and forward across the river crammed with Red soldiers until a beachhead was established. Later all the boats were captured.

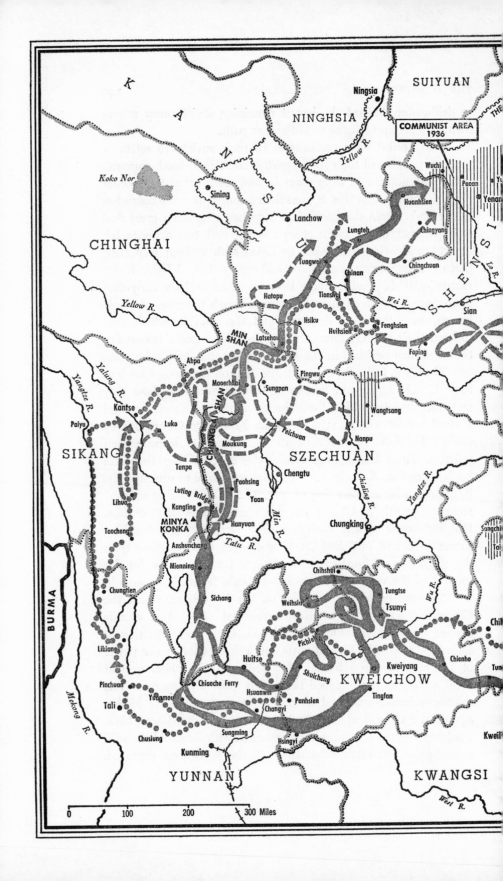

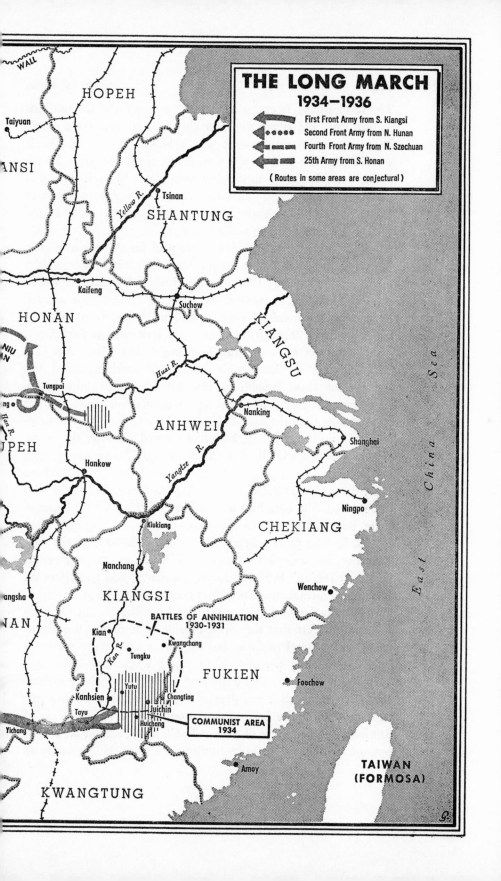

THE LONG MARCH
1934–1936

First Front Army from S. Kiangsi
Second Front Army from N. Hunan
Fourth Front Army from N. Szechuan
25th Army from S. Honan

(Routes in some areas are conjectural)

WALL

HOPEH

Taiyuan

ANSI

Yellow R.

Tsinan

SHANTUNG

Kaifeng

Suchow

HONAN

Huai R.

KIANGSU

NIU
AN

Tungpai

ng

Han R.

UPEH

ANHWEI

Nanking

Yangtze R.

Shanghai

Hankow

Kiukiang

Ningpo

CHEKIANG

Nanchang

Wenchow

angsha

KIANGSI

AN

Kian

BATTLES OF ANNIHILATION
1930-1931

Kwangchang

Kan R.

Tungku

Yutu

FUKIEN

Foochow

Kanhsien

Changting

Tayu

Juichin

COMMUNIST AREA
1934

Yichang

Huichang

Amoy

TAIWAN
(FORMOSA)

KWANGTUNG

East China Sea

The Kuomintang forces, who had not expected the Communists to turn back and attack the shore they had just left, were routed by a surprise maneuver—one which looked ludicrously simple when P'eng Teh-huai drew a map of the small campaign for me in the dusty loess soil outside his cave. It was by such ruses that they won their battles; and more and more they were forced to regard themselves as guerrilla forces, dedicated to ruses, to the endless game of cunning and surprise.

The successes in Kweichow were paid for at enormous cost. They were fifteen weeks in the province, with minor engagements taking place every day. The heavy cloud which hides Kweichow, as it hides Szechuan, in autumn and winter did not always succeed in keeping the bombers away. Occasionally, low-flying bombers did come down through the clouds and seek out the Red Army. Their casualties from air raids were slight, but Mao's wife, Ho Tzu-ch'un who was heavy with child, was seriously wounded during one of these bombings. Her wounds were almost fatal. Eighteen or twenty pieces of shrapnel entered her body. She was still suffering from the wounds long after the Chinese Communists settled in northern Shensi. Mao had married her after the execution of his first wife by Ho Chien in 1930. She was a Kiangsi girl, seventeen years younger than Mao, and she appears to have spent some time at the Normal College in Changsha, where Mao had studied. She bore him five children in seven years. Three of them were abandoned to the peasants they met on the Long March. In later years, when an effort was made to trace the children, they had completely disappeared. Mao was intensely moved by Ho Tzu-ch'un's fortitude during the march, and said afterward that the women showed far greater courage than the men.

The crossing of the dangerous Wu River showed the Communist commanders that they were capable of finding a way across almost any natural obstacle, but they were still at the mercy of events, wandering precariously in places where few advantages opened out to them. The important town of Tsunyi lay directly north of them, and it was decided to capture the town and perhaps make it it the base of operations against the province of Szechuan. Under cover of rain and mist they overran an enemy outpost in a village ten miles south of the town, killing nearly all the defenders. From the survivors they obtained a complete plan of the defenses of Tsunyi. At night, during heavy rain, a party of Red Army soldiers in borrowed Kuomintang uniforms crept up to the town, claiming to be survivors from the battle in the village and begging to be let in. A voice from the gate tower ordered the heavy wooden gates to be opened. It was a trick as old as China. Within ten minutes the Reds were in command of the gates, and the next morning the Red Army streamed into the town, the first large town to be captured by them on the march.

Here, at Tsunyi, was held a momentous meeting of the Political Bureau to decide the future course of the march. Strategy, tactics, the nature of command, the nature of their aims, all these were once more in the melting pot. Mao dominated the meeting. In his view they had reached a state of crisis: it was necessary to reconsider the whole basis of Chinese Communist philosophy. As he saw it, they were still dominated by the philosophy of Li Li-san, who had been deposed by Pavel Miff from the Central Executive in January 1931, though his uncanny influence could still be felt. Mao had a close acquaintance with Li Li-san. He had known him cursorily when they were youths together in Changsha, and he had come to know him intimately within the Chinese Communist secretariat.

Unlike Mao, whose romanticism was tempered by an astonishing regard for facts, Li Li-san was almost the pure romantic revolutionary. In March 1930 he had declared, "Prepare for the establishment of revolutionary power. When the revolutionary high wave arrives, ninety million can be organized in three days." In June 1930 he declared, "The aim of local uprisings is the capture of local cities. The perspective in view is convergence upon the central cities, so bringing about a victorious insurrection through the whole country." This declaration had even been adopted by the Political Bureau of the Chinese Communist party. It was as though Li Li-san suffered from an almost neurotic obsession with revolution in cities, an obsession which sprang perhaps from the fact that his major achievements had all taken place in cities. He had been a successful labor agitator, and had organized the anti-foreign campaign which broke out in Shanghai following the May Thirtieth Incident in 1925.

Against the desire to attack cities Mao now raised his voice. "There is no way to accomplish this," he pointed out, "with the resources we command. The desire to fight positional wars and to capture cities springs from the same adventurism. Our duty is to fight a protracted war, avoiding the enemy if possible, never engaging him unless it can be made certain in advance that the engagement is to our advantage." He attacked the policy which Li Li-san had encouraged with extraordinary invective. Li Li-san had desired to transform Communist-dominated trade unions into action committees. What was this but "the game of insurrection"? And surely the Long March, as it was being fought, savored of adventurism? He attacked all the principles by which Li Teh, the German military adviser, had fought, and proposed that thenceforward the column should be directed by Chu Teh and himself. He went over all the experiences of the annihilation campaigns in detail—it was through Li Li-sanism that the first campaign had failed in its main objective, and the fifth campaign had failed as the result of the same kind of adventurism. "Adventurism," he wrote later in *Strategic Problems*, "continued to arouse opposition against luring the enemy into deep penetration, but it ended in conservatism." The proper direction, he reminded, was an advance in the direction of the Tibetan tribesmen and the Mohammedans "until we hit a stone wall." He outlined the conditions of the advance. They were extremely simple. Once again the Communists must become "an army on the border," and the border this time was the border, not of provinces, but of China itself.

The argument was accepted, but the fighting went on. Chiang Kai-shek was determined to prevent the Red Army from escaping to Tibet, or to the borders of the Soviet Union. From Kunming, he himself directed operations, just as previously he had directed operations from Kweiyang. Mao determinedly opposed the idea of attacking the large cities, but he could not prevent the The Red Army, passing through Kweichow and Yunnan, took a The Red Army passing through Kweichow and Yunnan, took a good look at the two provincial capitals from the neighboring hills.

In Yunnan the Yangtse River is known as the Gold Sand River. It was necessary for the Red Army to cross the river to reach the uplands near Tibet. The Kuomintang removed all the ferryboats to the northern shore. The Communists made a forced march in three columns across the plain until they reached the river, while a fourth column was sent moving backward and forward between Kunming and the river to distract the enemy. The first column covered forty-five miles in a single day. They found a boat tethered on the south side of the river, and some of the men boarded it, disguised as civilians. The enemy was in no hurry. At the river crossing at Chouping, the Reds discovered a tax officer and explained that they were Kuomintang troops in disguise and wanted the boats sent over to the south bank, together with fuel and food. This daring group of soldiers found themselves invited to dinner with the local landlords; all the time, unknown to the landlords, Red Army troops were being ferried over to the north bank. The Red Army soldiers camped that night on the banks of the river, attended by the landlords, who solicitously provided for their comfort and offered them a feast. The next day at daybreak they climbed a mountain and were on their way toward Tibet when the landlords, who had begun to suspect these sunburned, hardened men, sent the min tuan, or local garrison troops, after them. These fired a few ineffectual shots, but they came nowhere near the Red Army forces, which had spent the night ferrying themselves over the river.

The pattern of their passage through Chouping was to be repeated. Ruse and cunning, exactly the same kind of ruse and cunning that was displayed by the heroes of All Men Are Brothers, now became the pattern of the Communist advance. Positional wars were to be avoided; food, if possible, was to be supplied by bowing landlords who complimented them on their achievements against the Reds!

Ten miles from Chouping lay Tungchow, guarded by two battalions of Kuomintang troops. They, too, were unaware of the Red advance. They were sleeping with their weapons scattered all around them when they were discovered. Their arms were captured, including some good machine guns. It was the Communists' easiest victory, and here they waited while their remaining troops, numbering now nearly sixty thousand, caught up with them. They had lost thirty thousand men on their march from Juichin, but most of the losses were replaced by new recruits.

They had held innumerable mass meetings, and on the march they practiced the same form of communism they had practiced in Kiangsi. The landlords were expropriated, the title deeds were destroyed, and the land was given to the villagers, together with arms with which to defend themselves. Here, too, for the first time they came in contact with tribal people, the Lolos and the Miaos, who lived among the mountains of Kweichow and Yunnan, in a primitive communism of their own. Some of these tribesmen they took with them; others were encouraged to fight against the Kuomintang—though they needed little enough encouragement.

In Yunnan, north of the Gold Sand River, the Red Army was generally a few days ahead of the most redoubtable of all the generals sent against them, Hsueh Yueh, the future victor at Changsha. Once a column of Szechuanese soldiers discovered their hiding place and attacked, but their morale failed at the moment of counterattack. The Chinese Communists afterward remembered with pleasure how the whole column suddenly began screaming to be allowed to surrender. Here, for the first time since they crossed Kweichow, they allowed themselves to rest. They would try to avoid forced marches with the enemy hot on their heels—one forced march had lasted two days and one night. Their enemies now were mountains, precipices, flooded rivers, marshes, and bitter snows.

The Red Army was approaching Tibetan territory. In this rugged landscape there were few trees, little vegetation, almost no houses, though here and there they came upon an immense gray, flat-roofed, fortress-like palace surrounded by stockades. Their food was running out, and now more than ever they depended upon their Lolo guides, who led them along the mountain trails to the defiles of the Tatu River.

It was May, and the river was in spate. They came to the small town of Anshunch'ang, which overhangs the river. Oddly enough, none of them knew until they came here that in this region a vast Taiping army had been crushed to extinction. Prince Shih Ta-k'ai, in command of the Taiping army, had waited for two days on the banks of the river to celebrate the birth of his child, and as a result of the delay had met defeat in the wilds above Mienninghsien, trapped in the gorges.

There was nothing to be done except to hurry, before the Kuomintang forces were able to encircle them. They found three boats and sent five hundred men over the river; then two of the boats sank, and it was decided not to send any more. At a conference at Anshunch'ang, Mao and Chu Teh worked out a plan of campaign. The men already on the other side of the river were ordered to continue the march to Lutingch'iao, and at the same time the major part of the Red Army would follow the trail along the gorges. It was hoped that those already on the other side would be able to reduce the regiment holding the bridge at Lutingch'iao before the main forces came up.

They had not reckoned, however, with the treacherous nature of the gorges. Astonishing luck had followed them. At Anshunch'ang they had captured the regimental commander at the bridgehead; he happened to be visiting his father-in-law. The maps, codes, and deployment orders of the Kuomintang forces in the neighborhood were captured with him. But though the maps were useful, and the codes might conceivably become useful later, and the deployment orders might be regarded as reasonably accurate, the main enemy remained: the rugged nature of the country through which they would have to pass. The trails along the cliffs were rarely more than five feet wide. A reckless company of Kuomintang troops concealed along the cliffs could have held them up indefinitely. The bridge at Lutingch'iao might already be destroyed. To surprise the enemy, they made forced night marches. There was no moon. They were compelled to light flares, and the news of their advance became known. Meanwhile, the men who had reached the north bank of the river were unaccountably delayed; the pathways scratched on the rock were often dangerous, so that tired men occasionally fell down the cliffs and disappeared in the river; and many of the pack animals had to be left in Anshunch'ang.

The sixty miles that separated Anshunch'ang from Lutingch'iao were more nightmarish than anything they had experienced during the Long March. For years afterward men talked of the cold nights, the darkness, the threat of the black river below, as they wound among these gorges where sometimes the cliffs were less than twenty feet apart.

But at Lutingch'iao, which means the "Town of the Iron Bridge," their luck held. Here in 1701 an iron bridge had been built under the orders of the Emperor Kang Hsi. Thirteen immense chains, each over three hundred feet long, made of charcoal-smelted iron, were secured to the cliffs. On nine of these loose planks were laid; the two chains at each side served as railings. Each link in the chain was as thick as a rice bowl. At the head of the bridge was a stone slab bearing the lines:

> Towering mountains flank the Lutingch'iao.
> Their summits rise a thousand li to the clouds.

Below the bridge were the roaring torrents cascading down from the gorges of the river's upper reaches, with ugly boulders rising from the river bed. The roar of the reddish water was deafening. Facing them lay the town of Luting, half on the shore and half spreading up the slope of the opposite mountain. It was a walled town, defended by two Kuomintang regiments. There were fortifications along the slopes, and machine-gun emplacements close to the bridge. When the Red Army arrived on the small cliff edge they found that the Kuomintang regiment on the south bank had already heard of their progress, and most of the planks had been removed. This was the only bridge lying on the frontier of Sikang and Szechuan. If they failed to capture the bridge, their only course would be to retire along the road they came by.

Once again a council of war was held. An attempt to cross the river by rafts and pontoons failed. At any moment they expected the Kuomintang to blow up the bridge, for nothing would have been simpler: a single stick of dynamite tossed at its moorings would have destroyed it. The bridge was three hundred feet above the level of the river; they heard the river booming below. All the fighting at the bridge occurred to the sound of the deafening roar of the river. They called for volunteers who would cross the bridge, making their way hand over hand, their only weapons hand grenades and pistols, for a rifle would have been useless. And the bellying of the iron chains as they hung over the middle of the river partly concealed the hundred volunteers who inched their way across, to the splutter of machine guns.

To divert attention from these volunteers, machine-gun fire was directed on the Kuomintang entrenchments from farther up the river. The small force which had already crossed over was nowhere in sight. One by one the soldiers making their way across the bridge fell down into the ravine, either because they were struck by machine-gun fire or because they were swept off by the wind. Nothing could be done for them.

In the end a solitary soldier climbed up on the planks on the farther side—the planks were already being drenched in kerosene, and the flames were rising—and by a lucky throw of a hand grenade put an end to the resistance at the bridgehead, though there was further resistance from the entrenchments behind. The passage of the one soldier had an electric effect. Fifteen or sixteen soldiers reached the burning planks. Almost at the same moment the advance guards of the five hundred who had taken ship across the river at Anshunch'ang came into sight, and shortly after their appearance the Kuomintang forces retired. A hundred Szechuanese soldiers surrendered and offered to join the Red Army. The planks, stored in the retrenchments, were put back on the bridge, and toward evening the whole of the Red Army had crossed the river. It was May 30, 1935.

The brilliant and carefully thought-out maneuver cost less than fifty lives, and of those only twelve perished by falling into the river. To make up for this loss, fifty soldiers were admitted into the Red Army ranks from among the villagers. "We were always at our best," said Mao later, "when we were faced with impossible odds. We knew that there was every reason to believe that we would fail; that was why we did not fail. Besides, the enemy thought we were trapped." He had watched the whole scene from the cliffs, with the Lolo chieftains at his side. Once they were over the bridge, there were no more decisions to be made: they would follow the mountain trails until they came out into the low-lying forests of western Szechuan. The maps, however, were sketchy, and none of them knew the dangers ahead.

They climbed the Ma An-shan Pass, ten thousand feet high and five thousand feet higher than Lutingch'iao. Here there were red rhododendrons and small waterfalls and charcoal-burners' huts;

and beyond Ma An-shan lay the terrible white mountain known as the Great Snow Mountain.

During the crossing of the Great Snow Mountain, Mao was sick and suffered from fever; during part of the journey he had to be carried. The hardships were beginning to tell. It was absolutely necessary that the mountain be crossed in a single morning, for by some freak of the weather tremendous winds occurred in the afternoons and at the same time the air pressure dropped alarmingly. But even during the mornings there was so little air that people could hardly breathe on these high mountain paths. Mao endured the journey better than Lin Piao, who suffered from a weak heart and was compelled to rest halfway up the mountain—a dangerous and wildly exciting three hours during which he suffered the full violence of a storm. At least half the pack animals perished on the heights, and some of those who remained were killed at night by whirling hailstones, an inch round and hard as rock.

On some Chinese maps the height of the Great Snow Mountain is given as 16,300 feet. Mao himself is inclined to believe, perhaps on insufficient evidence, that it is considerably higher. The prodigious height of these mountains—the Great Snow Mountain was the highest, but there were more to follow—was something he had never faced before. The mountains in Kiangsi, for example, are hardly more than hills, ranging up to two thousand feet. The prolonged marching through the snow mountains seriously weakened his army, and when at last his troops reached northwestern Szechuan, meeting the Fourth Front Red Army under Hsu Hsiang-ch'ien and Chang Kuo-t'ao at Tawei, they were prepared to enjoy a long rest. They were in a comparatively safe area at last. They were also well protected by their numbers, for Hsu Hsiang-ch'ien's army numbered about forty thousand men and there were about forty thousand survivors of the long ordeal over the mountains; moreover, the Communist troops from Szechuan were well armed.

The column under Mao rested for nearly a month. At the beginning of August, Mao decided that the time had come for the continuation of the march. News had come of the establishment of soviets in northern Shensi, and he was eager to establish a base there before winter. He had hoped to be there by the end of September, but had not reckoned with the dangers ahead.

There were many dangers. The Kuomintang troops were driving down on the Communist armies. It was high summer, with the rivers in flood. There was disagreement between Mao, the chairman of the Kiangsi soviets, and Chang Kuo-t'ao, chairman of the Honan-Hupeh-Anhwei soviets, which had achieved bases over large areas of northern Szechuan. The western route—the only one open to them—was unmapped, and ruled over by tribesmen far more suspicious than the Lolos of Yunnan. With Lin Piao, who was already being regarded as a stratagist of a high order, and P'eng Teh-huai, who now ranked immediately after Chu Teh, Mao set out with about thirty thousand men in the direction of the Grasslands, his numbers reduced as the result of severe, sporadic fighting in Szechuan.

The Great Snow Mountain, with its deceptively smooth slope, had been their introduction to their running battle with nature. There was more to come. In the Grasslands there was nothing but plain and swamp, the earth soft underfoot, few trees, the grass a foot high. By ill luck, August was a month of perpetual rain or fog. There was a thick haze over most of the swamp, and the mosquitoes were the size of horse-leeches. Nothing they had gone through up to this moment was quite as bad as the Grasslands. There were no houses or villages where they could pass the night. The tribesmen picked them off from well-concealed hiding places. It rained every night, making sleep impossible. The grass was too wet to burn to cook food, to dry clothing; and the few sticks of wood the soldiers were ordered to carry with them were used up in two days. No rice was available; they lived on green wheat which they carried in sausage-like bags over their shoulders. They dug up what seemed to be turnips, but these proved to be poisonous. The water made them ill. The winds buffeted them; hail-storms were followed by snow. Ropes were laid down to guide them across the marshlands, but the ropes vanished in the quick-sands. Men died of cold, thirst, starvation, drowning in quicksands. They lost their few remaining pack animals. A small column would be seen walking across a sea of thick, damp, foggy grasses, and then the whole column would disappear. Occasionally they came upon ancient forests, where there were layers of dead leaves beneath the trees. Here they could rest, search for mushrooms, and even light fires. But these were the lucky ones who were about to skirt the Grasslands. For the most part they struggled through the grass along trails which they had either to discover for themselves or which were pointed out to them by captured tribesmen. Sometimes these tribesmen led them straight into ambush, but more often they were won over by the diplomatic skill of Ho Lung and Mao.

Meanwhile, the columns were near starvation. Occasionally they had to fight for food, and sometimes a whole column would find itself engaged in a military operation where the total spoils consisted of a single sheep hidden among the reeds and grasses, defended by the Mantzus with poisoned arrows. The tribesmen hid their cattle well. Often the guerrillas were reduced to eating the roots of grasses and turnips, or chewing on hides.

People who went through the Long March still remember the Grasslands with horror—the long plains of black and yellow grass, the rain, the poisonous mud which made their legs swell with red blisters, the way the marshes would suddenly give place to slow-moving, nearly stagnant rivers, the mudholes, the ambuscades. At night it was deathly cold. They made shelters of clumps of grasses knotted together, but the cold penetrated. Worst of all, they had lost most of their medical supplies, and those who were ill were simply left behind—impossible to carry them on litters in a place where everyone was fighting for survival. The only treatment for infected sores was boiling water. Columns became lost or detached from one another. To collect the columns together, Chu Teh found it necessary to go three times across the Grasslands, spending an entire month walking among treacherous pathways, for the radios were out of order. When Mao was asked what he remembered most of the Grasslands, he said, "Just this: that Chu Teh crossed it three times, and I found the greatest difficulty in crossing it once."

During this stage Mao took little part in the military decisions. For the first time he was coming to grips with foreign relations. He met the tribal people and attempted, not too successfully, to barter with them. Unfortunately, the Red Army had almost nothing to offer them in exchange for their cattle and wheat except rifles, and these might be used against them. He found interpreters and did everything he could to bring them over to the Reds, but they were sullen toward the invaders. He feared the tribespeople, and half envied them. Quite naturally, without any preparation, as though by instinct, the Mantzus waged war against the Red columns in continual skirmishes which showed a surprising knowledge of the technique of guerrilla warfare. He confessed that he learned much from them, and he was especially impressed with their art of concealment.

The strain of the Long March was beginning to tell. Mao was very lean, with dark hollows under his eyes, and often ill. He missed his cigarettes, and most of all he missed the red Hunan peppers. He wore a faded blue uniform, carried no weapons, and there were usually books in his pocket—a copy of the monkey tale, *Journey to the West*, and the old dog-eared copy of *All Men Are Brothers*. The book *Journey to the West* described a pilgrimage by a learned monk through China, Tibet, and India; and what was surprising was the accuracy of the author of a medieval fairytale when it came to describing the borderlands of China and Tibet. Meanwhile he wrote poems. One of the longer poems was called "Grass." It appears in the collection of poems called *Wind Sand Poems*, which Mao collected together in Yenan, though nothing about the poem except the title is known.

The Long March was at last coming to an end, though a year was to elapse before the columns under Chu Teh and Hsu Hsiang-ch'ien, which had been left behind, were to arrive in northern Shensi. They had still to face short, sharp engagements with the Mohammedans who straddled their path in Kansu, but they were approaching territory where the Kuomintang forces were too far from their bases to offer effective opposition. Moreover, northern Shensi was part of the area which the "Christian General" Feng Yu-hsiang, owned as a kind of private reserve, and he was not unsympathetic to many of the Communist demands. He was not a Communist—he had executed Communists in the past—but he possessed a considerable knowledge of the peasantry, and he believed in the urgent necessity of agrarian reforms.

The columns under Mao had succeeded in forcing a passage through China. He had employed the characteristic "wide curve" he had used in the three annihilation campaigns. Success had been achieved at a frightful cost. A hundred thousand set out from Kiangsi. Fewer than twenty thousand remained, and many of these were recruits who joined the Red Army on the march. Many of the leaders were killed; those who survived bore traces of their sufferings for years afterward. In spite of the huge losses, Mao believed firmly that the expedition had proved the superiority of guerrilla tactics: the Red Army had shown the utmost strategical mobility. Above all, a legend had been created. Mao was perfectly conscious of the power of legends. In later years, when he came to examine the causes of the Long March, he came to the bitter conclusion that it was all entirely unnecessary. The Fifth Annihilation Campaign was itself ill-directed, and the Communists in Kiangsi should not have panicked so easily. There were at least two untried maneuvers which would have enabled them to escape the Kuomintang net and establish themselves in the region of Shanghai. He refused to regret the journey, just as he refused to regret his own inability to force the issue. "A revolution," he wrote, "does not march in a straight line. It wanders where it can, retreats before superior forces, advances wherever it has room to advance, and is possessed of enormous patience." When the Red Army reached Shensi, the surviving guerrillas could tell themselves that a revolutionary patience had won them all their battles.

Mao tends to be unrevealing about his personal life, and he generally dislikes to discuss himself, but on the subject of the Long March he has often talked at length. It was the time, he says, when he came to maturity. There were terrible battles, but he felt perpetually exhilarated. He had not thought he would survive, but at the same time he was perfectly aware, in an almost mystical way, that the Communists would develop bases in north China and demonstrate the authenticity of their experiment in battles against the Japanese. He says—there is no particular reason to disbelieve him—that he never faltered in this simple faith, and though he was conscious that the Kuomintang armies, which would also meet the Japanese, were being weakened by their wars against the Communists, he could see no other way out. The armies tested one another before being tested by the Japanese. Mao was also a little bewildered by his continuing good luck. He was never wounded. His health stood comparatively well the enormous strains of the journey, a fact which he attributed to his long walks in his youth. He observed, with a kind of ironic detachment, that it was possible to live on nothing except a furious hope. He took a deep interest in herbal medicine and began to propound theories which have something in common with psychosomatic medicine. He was delighted with the strange flora he came upon—the trees, the herbs, the grasses, the different uses to which they could be put. He prized his knowledge of new tobaccos. Most of all, he was astonished by the virgin quality of these unexplored lands on the frontiers of Tibet. He saw colors he had never seen before, mountains so preposterously grand that they resembled the feverish dreams of some Chinese painter, tribal people of whose existence he had been completely ignorant. Above all, having passed through so many provinces, he had come to know China.

In October 1935 Mao's column reached Pao An, and a year later most of the columns which had taken part in the Long March, and many others from various Red areas, came to join him. The march, with all its failings and miseries and splendors, had been successful.

Two months later, with pardonable pride, Mao declared:

The Long March is the first of its kind ever recorded in history. Since P'an Ku divided heaven from earth and the Three Sovereigns and the Five Emperors reigned, has there ever been in history a long march like ours? For twelve months we were under daily reconnaissance and bombing from the air by scores of planes; we were encircled, pursued, obstructed, and intercepted on the ground by a big force of several hundred thousand men; we encountered untold difficulties and great obstacles on the way, but by keeping our two feet going we swept across a distance of more than twenty thousand li through the length and breadth of eleven provinces. Has there ever in history been a long march like ours?

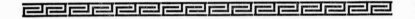

THE YEARS IN THE DESERT

"THE YEARS disappear like the jade birds who fly into the yellow hills," said the Chinese poet; and the small group of Communists living in northern Shensi might have disappeared among their loess hills if external events had not brought them once again into prominence. Gradually they built up their armies and joined forces with the small scattered Communist armies all over north China. They introduced village government and dispossessed the more exacting landlords; they coined money and set up small arsenals. But they were weakened by the Long March, and might have been erased altogether from the map of China if Chiang Kai-shek had foreseen the danger and swept the peasants with a program of social reform. Less than twenty thousand had arrived at this small outpost in the north. To anyone except a Communist it would have been inconceivable that an obscure walled village would soon rival Nanking as the center of imperial power. Yet it was so. From the mud huts and small caves of Pao An there came a continuous stream of commands, pronunciamentoes, and manifestoes destined to change the Chinese scene. Sooner than anyone could have foreseen, Pao An became a legend.

From the beginning Mao gave all the appearance of negligently doing nothing. He seemed, like the old Chinese sages, to be waiting on events. He spent the nights working; most of the day he slept. He lived in a cave. He smoked incessantly—homemade cigarettes or a yellow pipe with stringy, yellow, home-grown tobacco—and he read omnivorously. There were almost no government buildings or ministries: the affairs of state were conducted from small caves, among the walnut trees and the date palms. Chiang Kai-shek might have been excused when he said, "Now that they are sedentary, it will be easier to destroy them." Even some of the Communists took alarm. For the first time they were living beyond the reach of the Kuomintang, and safety seemed dangerous to men who had lived in danger nearly all their lives.

In the years that followed, Mao was to grow bored with Shensi. The high loess hills cut off the light of the sun; there was always the sensation of living at the bottom of a yellow valley. The land was poor, the nearby cities were under Kuomintang control, and in relation to the rest of China it was as though they were living in a remote village of Arkansas, their only means of communication with the outside world being a pedal-operated radio transmitter. Yet it was oddly satisfying. Mao's health had not been broken during the Long March, but he was slow to recover from some of its effects. He needed a rest to think out the next moves in the incalculable game of chess. Besides, legend demanded that the sage be silent and unmoving; then power would come to him of its own accord. Confucius said in the Analects, "To govern by means of virtue may be compared to the North Star, which remains steadfast and unmoving; all the stars are turned respectfully toward it." Simply by existing quietly in northern Shensi, he was acquiring power.

There were vast advantages in this extraordinary position, and not the least of them was that every move made by the Generalissimo only increased Mao's power. He had by now acquired a double eminence: he had shown at Tsunyi that his knowledge of tactics was superb, and throughout the Long March he had acted as political leader of the main column, and his policies had completely succeeded. Others coveted his eminence. Chang Kuo-t'ao, in particular, seems to have fought against him with some bitterness. He had been vice-chairman of the Kiangsi soviets, and later chairman of the Honan-Hupeh-Anhwei soviets, and regarded himself as at least the equal of Mao. During the summer of 1935 there were stormy discussions between Mao and Chang Kuo-t'ao concerning the bases of Chinese Communist operations. Chang Kuo-t'ao would have preferred to remain in Szechuan, where his personal power was established, and he offered to integrate the Kiangsi columns into his own army. Mao violently disagreed, pointing out that the Communist armies were still weak and un-proved—their battles against the Kuomintang had never been decisive, and it was absolutely necessary for the Communists to prove themselves by their actions. Soviets in northern Szechuan were inherently unstable. Tragic excesses had been committed by Chang Kuo-t'ao's army, and the peasants had been alienated. With some reluctance, faced with the determined opposition of Chu Teh and P'eng Teh-huai, Chang Kuo-t'ao signed an agreement to follow Mao's army to the northwestern areas of Kansu and Shensi.

When they met a year later at Pao An, Chang Kuo-t'ao assumed an attitude of intolerant opposition to the Communists who were already there. He accused them of adventurism, a charge which was greeted with distaste, for it was precisely Chang Kuo-t'ao's adventurism which Mao was fighting against. It was necessary, however, that he be treated with respect, and toward the end of 1936 he was sent in command of the Fourth Front Army to Kansu, to establish bases among the Mohammedans. Once again, as in Szechuan, tragic excesses were committed, and in a sudden rebellion in February 1937, the Fourth Front Red Army was attacked by Mohammedan tribesmen. Thereafter Chang Kuo-t'ao was in disgrace, and in 1938 he fled from the Soviet areas to Hankow, announcing that "no compromise is possible between the Kuomintang and Communist parties. An entirely new party must be formed." The Communists accused him of working for the Kuomintang secret police.

The defection of Chang Kuo-t'ao was not the first. Ch'en Tu-hsiu, who had led the new youth of China, had been drummed out of the party in 1927, to be arrested in 1932 by the Kuomin-

tang government and sentenced to thirteen years imprisonment—
in the eyes of the Kuomintang a comparatively light sentence,
since without Ch'en Tu-hsiu there might not have been a Communist party in China. He was released in the autumn of 1937
as the result of popular clamor for the release of all those who
had fought against the Japanese, either as intellectuals or as
soldiers. He died in Chungking in 1942. Mao's third adversary,
Li Li-san, disappeared to the Soviet Union, returning to Manchuria at the end of the war as General Lin Piao's political adviser and vice-chairman of the All-China Federation of Labor.

But on the whole defections were rare. The Chinese Communists were coming into their maturity. They had experienced
many of the possible forms which communism could undergo in
a country like China, and the experience of the Long March
had taught them to have faith in the simplest and most easily
manageable forms. More and more Mao came to personify the
peasant virtues of primitive communism. He believed that in some
remote era of China's past there had been a kind of primitive
communism; he also believed that feudalism came about as the
result of invasions of barbarian tribes. The Japanese were the
modern equivalent of the ancient barbarians, and he waited patiently for the moment when they would attack, convinced that
the choice of northern Shensi as a base was justified by the menace
of Japan. Not far away lay the Great Wall, and beyond that lay
the Ordos Desert, where, if necessary, they could go on still
another Long March, secure from any pursuers.

Meanwhile he devoted himself to a study of the peasantry,
and for some time he immersed himself in the study of a strange
language called Latinxua. Mass education had become, he believed, the key to the revolution. What could not be done with
an educated peasantry? Latinxua, which consisted of romanized
Chinese, and resembled the romanized languages introduced by
the French into Indochina and by the Russians into Siberia, might
provide a key, for it involved the learning of only twenty-six letters,
while the most elementary knowledge of Chinese was impossible
without the learning of at least a thousand characters. Newspapers
were printed in Latinxua; they were also printed in a Chinese

which deliberately used only the simplest words. He compared their successes. Somewhere, there may be still in existence letters written by Mao in that strange hybrid Latinxua, which he at one time embraced with the fervor of a new apostle. It was ugly and ungraceful: the horrible combination of consonants offended the eyes, and though Latinxua was never entirely abandoned—there are still newspapers printed in it—it gradually lost importance.

Meanwhile, the guerrilla armies which remained in central China were gradually growing more powerful, and Mao began to believe that if the Japanese did attack there would be two large centers of Communist resistance against them. There was still sporadic fighting against the Kuomintang. Telegrams were exchanged between Nanking and Pao An. By one of those arrangements which seemed strange to foreigners but had become accepted policy in Chinese civil wars, a telegraph office under Kuomintang jurisdiction was opened near Pao An, just as later a telegraph office was opened at Yenan. Increasingly, Mao assumed control of the organization of the peasantry, leaving the military decisions to Chu Teh. He traveled through the border regions, addressing the peasants. "We must hasten," he said. "Only with an awakened peasantry can we fight the Japanese."

By November 1936, Mao's suspicions that the Japanese were ready to launch their attack on China were being confirmed. Since the summer of 1935 he had believed that the attack would come, probably from the north, through Mongolia, and that it would be launched first through Communist territory. The Anti-Comintern Pact had been signed, suggesting that the Fascist powers were drawing more closely together.

In Mongolia itself strange events were taking place. On November 17, the Generalissimo flew to Taiyuan and interviewed Prince Ah, the vice-chairman of the Suiyuan-Mongolian Autonomy Council. It looked as though the Generalissimo were preparing to arrange that the forces in this half-Mongol province, where the lamas still ruled and bannermen still possessed power, would be thrown against the Reds.

Mao was not particularly disturbed by this development. He was more disturbed by the discovery that the Japanese were arming irregulars in Manchukuo and sending them across the border in disguise. There was a short, fierce battle at Pailing-miao, in northern Suiyuan, and afterward, in an abandoned lama temple, documentary evidence was found proving Japanese complicity. There were rumors that the Kwangtung army in Manchukuo was preparing to come over the border.

The atmosphere was ominous. Mao had expected war, but not in winter. Worse still, there came reports that the Generalissimo was preparing a last effort to sweep the Communist army from the face of the earth. He had sent Hu Tsung-nan's First Army against the Reds. It was severely defeated on November 21, with the capture of large supplies of ammunition. Stung by this defeat, was the Generalissimo about to make the long-promised "final and eternal liquidation"?

It seemed so. Calling upon his troops to prepare for a short but determined war against "the enemies in our midst," the Generalissimo flew to Sian, arriving there on December 7. He immediately set about preparing plans for a massive attack on the Communist strongholds. He wrote in his diary that "the bandit-suppression campaign has reached the stage when it will require only the last five minutes to achieve final success." The general order for mobilization against the Communists was to be issued on December 12. On December 11, the Young Marshal, Chang Hsüeh-liang, in command of the Tungpei forces, struck and ordered the arrest of the Generalissimo, his staff, and all the government officials, gendarmes, and special-service men loyal to him. If there had been no general order for mobilization, the Generalissimo might have been allowed to go free and nothing more would have been heard of what came to be known as the Sian Incident.

What had happened was very simple. Chang Hsüeh-liang was not prepared to attack the Communists. He had said as much in an interview with an American correspondent, Nym Wales, in October. His soldiers were largely Manchurians who were anxious to return home after driving the Japanese out of Manchuria. They had no particular quarrel with the Communists, who were now established in Yenan. It was four days later before the Young

Marshal sent an airplane to Yenan, with the request that Yenan send three responsible officials to take part in the trial of the Generalissimo.

The trial never took place. Chou En-lai, Yeh Chien-ying, and Po Ku flew to Sian. An immediate meeting of the Executive Committee of the Communist party was summoned in Yenan on December 15. Mao was chairman. He reviewed briefly all the information which had come by radio, and though the Moscow radio was to claim that all kinds of strange forces were at work, he guessed from the beginning that only Chang Hsüeh-liang was responsible for the arrest, and from that moment he gave it as his opinion that "it was pure mischief, and Chang Hsüeh-liang himself should be arrested."

No final decisions were made at the Yenan meeting, except one—that the Generalissimo's life and dignity should be spared, for otherwise a Japanese attack could be expected at any moment, or, worse still, Ho Ying-ching would assume command of the army and make a treacherous agreement with the enemy. The memory of the Ho-Umentzu agreement, by which Ho Ying-ching had agreed to a Chinese surrender along the Great Wall at the time of the Fifth Annihilation Campaign was still fresh in their minds.

Chou En-lai had three secret conferences with the Generalissimo, who deliberately treated the Communist general with the utmost disrespect. All these conferences, and many others, were referred back to Yenan. The Young Marshal had compiled eight demands to be made of the Generalissimo, who refused them all. For the Communists only one of these eight demands was important: the immediate cessation of the civil war. When this was agreed to, they urged that the Generalissimo be freed.

"Mao saw it all very simply and directly," Yang Shan-kun, the young Szechuanese chief of staff, told me later in Yenan. "He stripped the problem to its essentials, when we were all confused. The Young Marshal wanted the Generalissimo put on trial —a people's trial and a people's verdict—and this was the last thing Mao wanted. He wanted, and kept repeating that he wanted, the Generalissimo in command of all the Chinese forces. It was the only way he could see in which the Chinese would be able to oppose the Japanese successfully. He still thinks it was the only way. When all the reports were received from the delegates, he sent a strongly worded telegram saying that if necessary the Communists in Sian—many had been released from prison—should stage a coup, free the Generalissimo, and take him back secretly to Nanking. The Young Marshal wanted the Generalissimo sent to Yenan because he was afraid of the responsibility he had assumed. Mao absolutely refused. Under no condition did he want the Generalissimo in his own power, for the Japanese would have immediately suspected some kind of alliance between us and used this as an excuse for launching an attack, and Ho Ying-ching would have seized the opportunity of taking over power in Nanking. As soon as we knew that the Generalissimo loyally wanted to unite the Chinese against the Japanese, the die was cast. Even before that, we wanted him to return unharmed. At the final meeting of the Central Executive Committee there was only one dissenting vote: it came from Chang Kuo-t'ao, who later went over to the Kuomintang!"

Later conversations with Yang Shan-kun suggested a more complex interpretation of the event. At the back of Mao's decisions there was always the fear of Ho Ying-ching's treachery, but there were also other fears. In his annihilation campaigns Chiang Kai-shek had shown the greatest insensitivity to the losses of his armies. An immense army would be thrown against the enemy, and annihilated; immediately afterward, another immense army would be thrown into combat. He regarded China as an inexhaustible reservoir of men, and it occurred to Mao that the Generalissimo was quite capable of trying to solve his problems by setting the Tungpei and Hsipei armies against the Communists, and these would annihilate one another. "Mao believed that the real reason for the Generalissimo's visit to Sian was precisely what he said it was: he would order the Tungpei and Hsipei armies to launch a campaign against the Reds with the certain knowledge that we would destroy the Young Marshal's forces. After all, we had just defeated Hu Tsung-nan's army. And after we had destroyed the Young Marshal's army, the Generalissimo reasoned, we would be too weak to attack him for a little while. If this was the plan, and we had very good evidence of it, it was remarkably shortsighted. If we had been destroyed, the Japanese would have taken the opportunity to sweep through Shensi and Shansi."

By the end of 1936, the Generalissimo now safely in Nanking, Mao could reflect that the year had passed with an increase of power to the Communists. In the spring the Red armies had invaded Shansi, the "model" province of Marshal Yen Hsi-shan, returning with considerable supplies of captured equipment, and adding ten thousand highly trained troops from among the prisoners. The Generalissimo's threatened annihilation campaign had petered out, and the danger of civil war while the Japanese were preparing to launch an offensive against China no longer threatened.

There were other advantages. Mao had maintained his hold in Shensi for more than a year, and his armies, which numbered less than twenty thousand survivors in October 1935, numbered considerably more than one hundred thousand by December 1936. Moreover, he was no longer under the orders of the Comintern,* and he could use his own knowledge of the situation to determine what he came increasingly to call the "correct strategy." Directly or indirectly he now controlled vast areas of China. There was not only the border region in northern Shensi; there were other Red partisan areas in southern Shensi, another on the Fukien-Kiangsi border, another on the Shensi-Szechuan border, and still another on the Hunan-Hupeh-Kiangsi border. There were yet others in Anhwei and northeastern Kiangsi. All of these constituted redoubtable fighting forces, though the Kuomintang continued to consider them bandits. There were evidently some bandits among them—it has been calculated that there were twenty million bandits in China, people who live in the hills and prey on the villages. Various estimates of the forces under Chinese Communist control were published, but they differed widely and it is doubtful

* In a speech delivered on the disbandment of the Communist International in May 1943, Mao said: "Since its Seventh Congress in 1935, the Chinese Communists have received no assistance or advice from the Comintern." The Chinese Communists were first placed under the orders of the Comintern in 1923.

whether in 1936 they controlled more than a few million inhabitants. They were a force in being: they were not yet a force which had grown powerful enough to challenge the hegemony of the Kuomintang.

In December 1936 the Communist government moved from Pao An to Yenan. There were considerable advantages in the change. Yenan had long been a prefectural capital and one of the most important cities on the road from Sian to the Great Wall. Here, in 200 B.C., the Huns under Mao Tun had made a prodigious attack on the heart of the Chinese empire, retiring after capturing an immense quantity of spoils. The poet Tu Fu is supposed to have wandered here during his travels, for one of the city's suburbs bears his name. More important, historically, the capture of Yenan by Li Tzu-ching had led to the downfall of the last purely Chinese dynasty, for the Mings perished when Wu San-kuei invited the Manchus into the empire against Li Tzu-ching. Yenan had seen the beginning of the downfall of a great Chinese dynasty. Mao, who was passionately interested in history, began to believe that it might see the beginnings of a new kind of Chinese dynasty altogether. The choice of Yenan, not far from the burial place of the Yellow Emperor, was perfectly deliberate, and was based largely on its historical associations. There is one other reason for the choice which may have unconsciously influenced Mao. In *All Men Are Brothers* the city where much of the action takes place is also called Yenan, though it is another town altogether—in Shantung.

In the spring of 1937 Mao was largely concerned with the increasing menace of Japan and with efforts toward closer military liaison with the Kuomintang against the Japanese. On March 14, 1936, he had already declared his intentions. "It goes without saying," he wrote, "that we shall never allow Chiang Kai-shek to lay a finger on the Red Army. If his army will only cease hostilities against us, then we shall extend to him the hand of friendship again on the field of battle against the Japanese." He had repeated the offer in August 1936, with a plea for a united front against the common enemy, but it was only after the Sian Incident that he was assured of an end to the protracted civil war. At some time in the spring of 1937, and under conditions of some secrecy, a

closer liaison was established, with Chou En-lai as the official
Communist representative in Nanking. At this time four promises
were made to the Kuomintang. They were:

1. The Communists propose to abandon the agrarian revolution they
   have practiced in the past.
2. They promise not to overthrow the Kuomintang by force.
3. They promise to reorganize the Soviet government in the border
   region as a democratic local government.
4. They agree to reorganize the Red Army as a national revolutionary
   army.*

The consequences of the new agreement were far-reaching.
They prepared the way for a decisive change in Communist-Kuo-
mintang relations. The first promise was perhaps the easiest to accomplish. Experience in Yenan and Pao An had proved that a
moderate socialist party, retaining many of the landowners in
possession, was a perfectly "correct" policy in wartime; and Mao's
own view of the rich farmers had changed remarkably since the
time of the Kiangsi soviets. The second promise implied a recip-
rocal agreement on the part of the Kuomintang not to attempt to
destroy the Chinese Communists. The third was carried out with
a great display of elections and balloting. The fourth led eventually
to the formation of the Eighth Route Army; already, on August
10, 1936, Mao had announced that "the Workers' and Peasants'
Government" had been renamed "the Peoples' Government," and
"the Workers' and Peasants' Army" had been renamed "the
Peoples' Red Army." The changes in the names were significant

---

* Gunther Stein, The Challenge of Red China (New York, 1945), p. 114.
These four promises were recited by Mao to Gunther Stein. The official China
Handbook 1937–1945 (New York, 1947), p. 67, gives the Kuomintang version of the agreement:
1. The Chinese Communist Party shall struggle for the realization of the
   Three Principles of the People.
2. They will abandon the policy of overthrowing the Kuomintang regime,
   give up the Communist movement and discard the policy of confiscating
   land by force.
3. They will dissolve the present Soviet organization and by carrying into
   practice the principles of democracy, they will help to bring about the
   political unity of the whole nation.
4. They will disband the Red Army.
   It is clear that the official version of the "four promises" published by
the Kuomintang is weighted against the Chinese Communists and includes
matter which the Chinese Communists were incapable of accepting.

of the changing atmosphere of the times. It was proposed that the "four promises" should officially be made public on July 15, 1937. Suddenly, early on the morning of July 7, there came the Japanese attack on the Marco Polo Bridge. The disastrous Sino-Japanese War had begun in earnest. It was not until September 22, ten weeks after the beginning of the war, that the Chinese Communists published their version of the agreement with the Kuomintang. In it they expressed willingness to fight for the realization of the Three Principles of the People and pledged themselves to renounce the policies of insurrection, and land-confiscation. They did not pledge themselves to abandon their army.

The war, long foreseen by Chiang Kai-shek and by Mao, came unexpectedly. It was thought that the Japanese might invade China in August or September. It is possible that even the Japanese were unaware of the implications of the incident at the Marco Polo Bridge. The Communist forces were mobilized, and with Chou En-lai directing their mobilization from Nanking, there seemed to be every possibility of a close liaison between the two armies. The Red Army became officially the Eighth Route Army—the Pa lu chün—and out of the scattered guerrilla forces in central China the New Fourth Army was brought into existence. In Hopeh, P'eng Teh-huei met his old adversary, Wei Li-huang, and for a brief space their armies were joined.

By 1939 it was clear that the Japanese could advance little farther, and that Chiang Kai-shek, with his policy of vacillation, was incapable of making up his mind on the proper method of attack. He distrusted the guerrillas. He had no desire to fight positional wars. Behind the Ichang gorges, in the mountainous and thickly wooded areas of Szechuan, he felt secure; and this fatal sense of security prevented him from organizing his large armies on any firm basis. Factions broke out within the Kuomintang. It was the period when Chen Li-fu began to exert a strange domination over the Kuomintang. The landowners of Szechuan threatened trouble. When winter came at the end of 1939, Chiang Kai-shek was organizing security under the heavy protecting clouds that covered Szechuan.

Security, as so often in China, involved a balance of forces.

There existed, even during the period of the Sino-Japanese War, semiprivate armies, only theoretically under the control of the Kuomintang. In Yunnan, General Lung Yun ("Cloud Dragon") behaved like an independent satrap. The Kwangsi generals retained their armies near the capital in Kweilin. Most of these generals were fighting for position and power, and their loyalty depended upon the armaments and money they received from the central treasury.

Chiang Kai-shek, confused by conflicting loyalties and obsessed by an ancient hatred for the Chinese Communists, determined that at least one of the conflicting factors in the struggle for power should be eliminated. In December 1940 he ordered the New Fourth Army to cross the Yangtse. The order was carried out. By early January, most of the army, except for some headquarters and combat troops, had crossed over. Passing through a long mountainous defile on their way to the river, these were suddenly attacked by some eighty thousand troops operating under the orders of General Ku Chu-tung, commander of the Third War Zone, and General Shankuan Yun-hsiang. Both these generals had fought in the annihilation campaigns in Kiangsi on the side of the Kuomintang. It is possible, but only just possible, that they acted in defiance of the orders of the Generalissimo. For eight days there was a massacre. The headquarters staff and some five thousand combat troops were cut down. Han Ying, once vice-chairman of the Kiangsi soviets, was killed. General Yeh Ting was captured. Fewer than two thousand escaped.

It was a sign of the times. From this moment onward there was distrust and suspicion on both sides. The Communists observed that the attack was entirely treacherous and against all the accepted canons of war. General Yeh Ting had sent a message to the Kuomintang commander, reminding him that they had been cadets at the Whampoa Academy together: then why the attack? Invited to visit the Kuomintang headquarters under a safe conduct, he was immediately put in irons. For the next five years messages were to be exchanged constantly between the Kuomintang and the Communists, but no one could ever tell whether these messages meant anything at all.

FIVE BOOKS

DURING THE COURSE of the anti-Japanese war, Mao's authority in the Communist areas remained unchanged: he was the theoretician of the Communist revolt. His speeches and reports were usually recognized as final. There were party discussions; there were elections; there were continual conferences at Yenan; but the main brunt of working out essential strategies had been left, as though by common accord, to him. He invented slogans, and he was constantly called upon for advice.

In 1940, northern Shensi suffered from a drought, and he began a campaign for self-sufficiency in food. Soldiers, sent out to till the land, complained of difficulties. He wrote back: "Remember you work for the people. Enlist their enthusiasm. Learn from their experience, and develop mutual benefit." The last phrase was purely Confucian. The slogan, "Move your own hands," and the later one, "Move your bottoms over"—referring to intellectuals who sat away from the peasants—were, however, his own. For long periods during the war he was concerned with discovering the theoretical solutions, while Chu Teh and P'eng Teh-huai were left in complete charge of the army.

During this period he wrote a number of short books. They were written with grace and learning and a hard-bitten power. In the early guerrilla campaigns he seemed to order his columns as though he were ordering a dance. His arguments in the books have something of the same effect. He often writes in apothegms. He frequently quotes the classics, and sometimes when he ridicules them, he gives the impression of a man who protests too much.

These books are major sources for an understanding of the Chinese Communist revolution. Logical, complex, deliberately designed for the widest possible audience, they occasionally show signs of being written with some difficulty, against the grain, each word chipped off the chestbone. These signs of strain arise, perhaps, from the fact that he uses Chinese proverbs, classical allusions, and quotations from Marxist literature; and the algebraic Marxist symbols mingle uneasily with the grace of Confucius and the rough common sense of the peasants. There are elements in his style which derive from Confucius and Han Yu and from the great Chinese novels, but he has also been influenced by the spare ironical prose of the story-writer Lu Hsün. Mao has been a journalist: sometimes he writes as a journalist. He is a poet: sometimes he is not always free from demagoguery. He is a general: he will sometimes write as though each word is being sharpened for battle. He reads voluminously—he said once that he counted a day wasted if he had not fought a battle or read sixty pages—and sometimes he gives the impression of desiring to throw pell-mell into his own prose everything he has ever read.

His five major works are all short and could be bound together to make a single 300-page book, though another 300 pages of notes would probably be necessary if they appeared in an English edition. Though most of his works have been translated in full, they are surprisingly little known. It is doubtful whether they have been read by the foreign secretaries most concerned. They are important books, because they reveal his mind and the temper of the Chinese revolution he led; and it would be a pity if their continued neglect led us to underestimate the quality of his thought. The five major books are, *On a Prolonged War; The*

New Democracy; The Strategic Problems of China's Revolutionary Wars; The Chinese Revolution and the Communist Party of China; and Coalition Government. In the pages that follow his main conclusions are outlined and many of the more illuminating passages quoted.

On a Prolonged War

Like most of Mao's published work, the book was originally a series of lectures. They were delivered before the Yenan Association for the Study of the Anti-Japanese War, between May 26 and June 3, 1938. They were later published in Chieh-fang (Liberation) in July, where they occupy only thirty-nine pages.

On a Prolonged War was an attempt to grapple with the problem of the war, and to discover its main outlines: how it should be fought, how long it would last, the circumstances of final victory. Methodically, Mao examined the stages the war would pass through.

The first stage was described as Japan's geographical advance and China's defensive retreat. The enemy would occupy all the large cities and lines of communication east of a front which links Canton, Hankow, and Lanchow. To bite off so large a portion of China would involve, of course, inevitable strains on Japan's economy, but at the cost of fifty divisions, amounting to a million and a half men, and an expenditure of ten billion yen, and after a campaign lasting eighteen to twenty-four months, Mao believed, the Japanese would succeed in their purpose.

In fact the Japanese campaign did come to a standstill within eighteen months, did cost ten billion yen, and did involve an army numbering more than a million. The Japanese did not, however, succeed in all their objectives: they occupied only two-thirds of the area they had intended to occupy.

The second stage of the war would be one of stalemate and watchful sparring, of indecisive conflicts and a kind of shadow play, prolonged in time but short in maneuver—the graceless heaving of two giants who, though wrestling furiously, give the impression of simply standing against each other. During this time the Chinese might be expected to summon up their forces and mobilize on all levels, while the Japanese would weaken; and as the international situation grew more favorable to the Chinese, the Japanese rear would be placed increasingly in jeopardy. Upheavals in the homeland, the determined opposition of guerrillas operating behind the Japanese lines, short, sharp attacks at critical points along the front would force the Japanese to retire, or else they would be driven to wild excesses. Whatever happened, if China could endure a prolonged war, and if she was sufficiently mobilized, the destruction of the Japanese army became certain. "China will beat the nose and pull the tail," forcing the Japanese to fight in two directions, on two fronts.

The third stage would be that of the counteroffensive and the final Japanese collapse as a result of defeat in China, economic exhaustion, revolution, and internal pressures—a collapse which might appear quite suddenly and unexpectedly. In this final stage, mobile war would give way to positional war, and guerrilla warfare would lose its importance.

The thesis is simple, but it is most revealing. Mao contended rightly that war must be considered in terms of its inevitable stages. There are progressions and retrogressions; the ultimate solutions are discovered when nothing is apparently happening at all, during those periods of stalemate, wavering, and defection. The simplest, or two-stage kind of war occurred in 1904, when a Japanese offensive was followed by a Russian retreat. The war in China was clearly comparable with the Napoleonic invasion of Russia. There was Napoleon's offensive, a short period of stalemate, and a Russian counteroffensive. In China the period of stalemate would, for various reasons, become almost unbearably long, but its very length must be regarded as part of the price of victory.

Again and again, using the three simple stages the war must take, Mao analyzed the situation, now in terms of military strategy, now in terms of tactics, now in terms of resources. He worked out the relative importance of mobile, positional, and guerrilla warfare during the three stages. "In the first period," he wrote, "mobile warfare will be primary, but afterward positional warfare will assume the primacy. Guerrilla warfare will tend to become far less important than before, though both of the other tactics will be assisted by it." In the second stage, "China will advance increasingly in bureaucratic and military power, and there will be a general mobilization of people and their culture. Guerrilla warfare will expand. In the economic field, there will be a process of expansion in small industries and considerable agricultural expansion. There will be an increase in international aid. There will be great changes."

The casual analysis of the stages assumes something of the form of prophecy. It is as though Mao were saying: "Tomorrow will be fine, the day afterward windy." Even the expression, "There will be great changes," seems to go back to the Confucian *Book of Changes*, which is concerned with just such political prophecies. Actually, Mao was outlining a rigid scheme which would embrace all the conceivable possibilities of the war according to very simple laws. He is not primarily concerned with guerrilla warfare, as so many have thought. He regards it as auxiliary to the war of movement. Mobile war is the aim, but guerrilla warfare is a fundamental device to be employed relentlessly on every occasion where it can be justified. There are even moments when he seems appalled by the temptations of guerrilla war. "Guerrilla war," he wrote, "is fundamental to us, but there must be no slackening of mobile war." And again: "In the area as a whole a mobile war is primary, guerrilla war secondary; in the area considered as small parts, guerrilla war is primary, mobile war secondary." It is a typically Chinese statement, but the force of it can be realized only when we consider how vast were the temptations to fight a ceaseless guerrilla war against the Japanese.

As early as the summer of 1938 Mao examined the Japanese mistakes. He assumed that they would continue to make the same mistakes throughout the whole invasion. He found five major mistakes: (1) They mobilized too slowly because they underestimated Chinese resistance. (2) They failed to concentrate their main strength on one objective, but dissipated their forces. (3) Except in relatively small areas, they were incapable of coordinating their forces. (4) They failed to follow up. (5) They failed to take prisoners, in contradistinction to the Chinese Communists, who attempted, not always very successfully, to capture rather than kill the Japanese. A captured Japanese could be used against the enemy.

He was equally critical of the mistakes of the Chinese. They, too, failed to mobilize sufficiently. He said: "We are weak because there was no general mobilization of the political consciousness of the people before the war." The Chinese were, in fact, too passive, but "passivity is fatal to us; our task is to make the enemy passive." Against passivity, he inveighed passionately. Only a deep, serious political consciousness had power to change the situation for the Chinese. "The nation's internal political progress is inseparable from a determined waging of the war. The greater our political progress, the greater our ability for determined resistance; the greater our determined resistance, the greater our ability to progress politically." Here he was saying exactly the same thing three times, but each time with a different inflection and a different accent. Passivity was one kind of weakness; there remained others. There was the inevitable weakness of the Chinese compelled to wage war against a highly industrialized enemy. Under some conditions, China could not possibly win. One of these conditions was the absence of outside aid, and he particularly mentioned Great Britain, France, and America as possible allies. He wrote:

> Since our own strength of itself will still remain insufficient, we shall have to depend upon aid from abroad and on internal changes in the enemy's country. If not, we cannot be victorious. It is for this reason that we stress the importance of Chinese propaganda abroad and our work in foreign relations.

He was writing with the long view. In 1938 there was comparatively little belief that foreign aid would be forthcoming. The powers seemed to be disposed to welcome Japan as the arbiter of China. Yet he was completely convinced that after a long war China would emerge victorious. "Those who believe we can win a speedy victory are as incorrect as those who say we cannot win."

Not all the book is written with this professional air. There are moments when a hard passion breaks through, when the horror of the invasion is allowed to penetrate the bleak schematization of a threefold war. Referring to a prince of the Spring and Autumn Period, and equating his hatred of the four feudal virtues with his hatred of Japan, he wrote:

> We are not Sung Jang-kung. We do not want the stupid, piglike *jen, i, tao,* and *te.* We want to take the enemy's eyes and ears and seal them as completely as possible. We want to make them blind and deaf; we want to take out the hearts of their officers; we want to throw them into utter confusion, driving them mad.

A great deal of material that appeared in *On a Prolonged War* appeared in Mao's report to the Sixth Plenum of the Chinese Communist party delivered on October 12, 1938. The report bore the title *The New Stage,* and though it dealt with an infinity of other problems, it was mainly concerned with the fact that the anti-Japanese war had already reached the stage of stalemate. The time had come, according to Mao, for the complete mobilization of China's resources. He quoted widely from the previous book, and *The New Stage* is admittedly indebted to *On a Prolonged War.* This long speech, written very carefully, with a multitude of subheadings and paragraph titles, is less convincing than it might have been. It is a deliberate propaganda speech, without grace, and almost excessively repetitious, and it is surprisingly full of blandishments to the Kuomintang. Mao quoted with approval Chiang Kai-shek's message to the people: "The center of gravity of China's ultimate victory does not lie in Nanking or any other large city. It lies in the stout hearts of the people all over the country." He paid tribute to the Kuomintang, calling it "the party of the brilliant revolution," and he set forth a program for the numerical strength of each: the Kuomintang should have a membership of five million, while the Communist party should reasonably limit itself to a membership of one million. Following the party line, he demanded that the united front be continued. "There are no real differences between us, for we too desire that the Three Principles of the People be put into operation." As though answering the perpetual question raised within the ranks of the Kuomintang concerning the theory of the class struggle, he said in a revealing paragraph: "We do not deny the existence of the class struggle, but the struggle itself can be adjusted for the sake of our national unity against the enemy. There can be formulated a proper policy of the relations between the classes which will be acceptable to all classes." It is doubtful whether he believed a new orientation could come about during the stress of war, but the hope remained. The class struggle, as he said again and again in his articles and books written in wartime, is the first casualty of the war.

The New Stage is most revealing when it continues the arguments of On a Prolonged War. For the first time there appears the casual statement, later to assume tremendous implications, "The villages and the countryside will defeat the cities and the towns." Here, too, Mao brought his mind to bear on the larger perspectives of a peasant revolt. There were only a few conditions which could bring about a large-scale peasant revolt. "It would be impossible, for example, to imagine a peasant revolt in modern England, France, the United States, Germany, Italy, or Japan being maintained for any length of time; nor is a peasant revolt possible in a small semicolony. It is only because China is a vast semicolony, with untapped resources of its own, that the peasant revolt can be brought about." He was talking of the peasant revolt against the Japanese invaders, but there is more than a hint of perpetual revolt—the revolt that continues until in the end the Kuomintang surrenders its powers.

Mao's concern through much of his life has been to discover the relationship between Chinese and Western civilization, and in The New Stage he stated his final opinion categorically:

> The idea of "unconditional westernization" is a wrong one. China had suffered greatly by blindly absorbing foreign materials. Chinese Communists should never break this rule, even in the application of Marxism. We must unify appropriately the general truth of Marxism and the concrete practice of the Chinese revolution, i.e., we must adopt the national form before we can find Marxism useful, and we should never subjectively or mechanically apply it.

Dry, precise, logical, rarely very penetrating, *The New Stage* is a rough sketch for the far more powerful *The New Democracy* written a year later.

The New Democracy

With *The New Democracy*, which Mao published on January 19, 1940, the stage was set for a possible compromise with the Kuomintang. It was written hurriedly and first delivered as a speech lasting eight hours. It has a number of minor inaccuracies, and like *The New Stage* it is almost excessively repetitious; but it represented a hard-headed and practical program of reform and a new approach to the problem which had obsessed the Chinese Communists from the beginning: under what conditions would communism develop in China? The situation had changed since the Kiangsi soviets. The Communists were no longer a small harassed force fleeing from the Kuomintang. Steadily, with extraordinary patience, they were gathering together a vast army in the north and they were perfectly aware of their power. What was necessary was to develop a program which would not exasperate liberal sentiment within the Kuomintang. But at the same time the Communists had no intention of retreating from their advanced positions. To solve the problem, Mao invented an entirely new political category, "the new democracy," which differed from all other democracies, not by its newness, but by the fact that it represented the discovery that there might reasonably be an interim stage between feudal China and a purely socialist China. "The first stage," he wrote, "is new democracy, the second is socialism. But the duration of the first stage will be rather long. It certainly cannot be completed in a morning and an evening, for we are not visionaries: we cannot divorce ourselves from the reality of the situation."

Mao never made clear the exact length or the exact kind of development he proposed for "the new democracy." It manifestly represented a period of political experiment, and Mao probably derived his new insistence on "gradualism" from the British Fabians. The theory on which the Chinese Communists reposed was no longer the expropriation of the landlords, the commune, the sudden flash of a proclaimed dictatorship. He was feeling his way cautiously. The Nazi-Soviet Pact had occurred just before the book was written. The Kuomintang was sending out feelers toward the Communists, and there existed passages in Sun Yat-sen's *Three Principles of the People* which were evidently acceptable to the Communists. If a compromise could be effected, it could be arranged on the basis of a gradual transfer of power.

Once again, Mao reposed his faith entirely on the peasantry. "The war of resistance," he wrote, "is really a peasants' war. Everything we use in resistance, everything we live on is really given to us by the peasants." Elsewhere, he amended the statement to include the workers, the intelligentsia, and the petty bourgeoisie. As for the class of people he described as the "national bourgeoisie," the upper middle-class supporters of Chiang Kai-shek's regime, he was prepared to accept that they possessed a revolutionary quality but held that they were also innately treacherous. "They are revolutionaries, but they are also prepared to compromise," he wrote. "They have a dual nature and belong to both camps at the same time." In this, at least, there was a remarkably accurate diagnosis of a whole class, which supported Chiang Kai-shek but drove him almost insane because he knew its support might be withdrawn at any moment.

Basically, *The New Democracy* remains a Marxist-Leninist textbook written to support the thesis of revolution by gradualness. Mao inveighs against those who desire the socialist dictatorship immediately. Such miracles, he says, are eminently desirable, but they are clearly unobtainable:

> If we say that of the two revolutionary stages, the first is the prerequisite for the second, and that the two must be consecutive without allowing any stage of bourgeois dictatorship to intervene, then this is correct. But if we say that the democratic revolution does not have its own definite task or its own definite time, but can tackle other tasks, such as those of socialism, which in fact can only be brought about at another time, and if we heap all these tasks together with the democratic tasks and attempt to carry them out simultaneously—that is "trying to do everything

at once." Such an attempt would be clearly utopian, and will be rejected by all true revolutionaries.

Though the statement could hardly be more repetitious and shows clearly that it is a part of a speech, yet it conveys exactly what Mao intended to convey. The time for socialism was not yet. There were possibilities of canalizing Communist doctrine with the doctrine of Sun Yat-sen. There were tasks which could be called "democratic," and these had to be confronted before the tasks which could be called "socialistic." Eventually, when the Communists had taken power, "new democracy" came to mean something which could hardly be distinguished from "socialism"; but neither Mao nor Chiang Kai-shek could have foreseen the swift defeat of the Kuomintang in 1949.

The New Democracy leaves many questions unanswered. It could hardly do otherwise, for the political configuration of China was still fluid. Except in one particular, The New Democracy avoided dogma, but that one particular was fraught with alarming consequences. Having traced the changes in the character of the revolution from the May Fourth Movement, he insisted that the revolutionary front could only be understood as part of the world proletarian socialist revolution:

> With all the imperialist countries as her enemies, China cannot obtain independence without the aid of the one socialist country and the international proletariat. The world now lives in an era of revolution and war, a new era, where capitalism is definitely dying and socialism is beginning to flourish. In the international environment of the middle of the twentieth century, there are only two ways open to all decent people in the colonies and semicolonies. They must either go over to the side of the imperialist front and take part in the world counter-revolution, or come to the side of the anti-imperialist front and take part in the world revolution. They must choose between these two. There is no other way.

The implications of his later journey to Moscow were thus stated quite clearly in a pamphlet issued ten years previously. Here for the first time Mao introduced a completely dogmatic theme.

The world was divided into black and white. There were no half-lights. Only the Soviet Union, which had given almost no assistance to the Chinese Communists and had indeed interfered gratuitously with their development, was to be relied upon. That other democratic and near-socialist states would emerge among those whom Mao professed to call imperialist did not occur to him; that even America with its TVA and New Deal was gradually progressing toward a welfare state apparently had no meaning for him. For once he was content to rely on dogma, on the inevitability of an exclusive alliance between China and the Soviet Union. "The whole world now looks upon communism as its savior," he wrote, "and so does China." He had listened to the radio and studied the textbooks. He did not know that over large sections of the world there was bitter disappointment over the course the Russian revolution had taken, and for once he found himself talking of matters of which he had no direct knowledge.

Except for the reference to the Soviet Union and the almost casual manner in which he dismissed all other alliances, The New Democracy did prepare an intelligible blueprint for the future. He insisted upon a poised, scientific attitude and deliberately set himself against arrogant theorizing. He summed up most of his past revolutionary experience when he wrote:

> A scientific attitude should be one that seeks the truth in concrete facts, and problems can never be solved with the arrogant attitude of considering oneself always right or of acting with self-assumed authority. The catastrophe facing our nation is so grave that only a scientific attitude and a spirit of responsibility can lead us along the road of liberation. There is only one truth. This truth is determined, not by subjective boasting, but by objective practice. Only the revolutionary practice of millions of people can be taken as the gauge for measuring truth.

Here, as elsewhere, he is dogged by ambiguities, for there is arrogance in his statement that "there is only one truth," and he is not altogether free of "subjective boasting." But on the whole the book is unusually humble, and it lacks altogether the wildly unrealistic approach of the Generalissimo's China's Destiny. The similarities between the doctrine announced in The New Democracy and Sun Yat-sen's *Three Principles of the People* are amazing. Mao accepts all of Sun Yat-sen's theses, with four qualifications. First, he insists on the eight-hour day. Second, he refuses to accept Sun Yat-sen's philosophy of history. Third, he sees no hope that the revolution can be established "in a single throw." Finally, he says that there will be a difference in the thoroughness of the execution of the revolutionary policies: the Communists have the habit of thoroughness. With this oblique reference to future wars and past campaigns, he dismisses the *The Principles of the People* only to include them within the orbit of his own *New Democracy*.

Whatever its defects, *The New Democracy* was appropriate to its times, and Mao's brief analysis of the forces at work commanded the respect of Chinese students, especially those who found *China's Destiny* indigestible. He claimed with some truth that the bourgeoisie unites with the workers and the peasants to oppose the external enemy, only to combine with the external enemy when the workers and peasants appear as an emerging force. Something like this happened in France, when it became clear that Weygand preferred German military occupation to a revolution of the workers and peasants. In China, there was always the danger that Chiang Kai-shek would make peace with the Japanese in order to crush the Communists. Unfortunately, as so often in Communist literature, the simple theory assumes the character of an axiom, and the fact that it is no more than a theory is conveniently forgotten; for the truth is that people are so complex that they can never be divided into these simple categories, and those who subscribe to these theories are culpable before history.

In one of the more engaging passages of *The New Democracy*, Mao appealed for an ever increasing absorption of the culture of foreign nations. China, he said, must never remain static. It must learn from all nations, from all cultural movements. In a curiously involved passage, he suggested that learning introduced from abroad must be regarded as food, "which is first chewed, and then introduced into the stomach and intestines for digestion, where saliva, pepsin, and other secretions of the organs separate it into essence and residue, and so the essence becomes our nourishment and the residue is passed out of the body altogether."

Just as Marx, in the *Communist Manifesto*, praised the bourgeoisie for its great triumphs, so Mao praised the feudal empires of China "which created such brilliant cultures in ancient times." He went out of his way to praise the great writer Lu Hsün as "the bravest, firmest, truest, most correct, and most zealous of our national heroes," forgetting that there were others who deserved the honor more. But his greatest praise is reserved for the peasants, "who are our all."

The Chinese Revolution and the Communist Party of China

Written shortly after *The New Democracy*—the actual writing of it took place in November 1939—the three lectures which made up *The Chinese Revolution and the Communist Party of China* attempted to provide a theoretical basis for the "new democratic revolution." *The New Democracy* deals with practical affairs. *The Chinese Revolution* is almost wholly devoted to theory of a kind which is peculiarly Chinese, for it is based on premises which have little enough to do with historical fact, and a great deal with the ethos of the Chinese nation. It is a strangely unequal work. A list of uprisings and an examination of class categories will be followed by a burst of passionate poetic prose. There are constant hints of the ancestral greatness of the Chinese and the coming proletarian empire, and there is a complete absence of the blandishments to the Kuomintang which characterize *The New Stage*. In its own way the work is comparable to some of the works of Lenin during the early stages of the Russian revolution, and it possesses an authority which places it among the most important documents Mao has published. The Chinese Communists themselves recognize its authority; they place it highest among his works. Yet it is a work which is fundamentally visionary—a sociologist trained in Western sociology could hardly be expected to recognize the peculiar resonance it possesses for the Chinese. It is important, also, to remember that it was written when the coastal cities were occupied by the Japanese and the wartime capital had been moved to Chungking.

The work begins with a vision of the ancient, classless China which existed before the feudal empire was established:

China has gone through thousands of years of primitive communist society, equal and classless. Afterward, there was a collapse of this primitive, classless society, and the era of class distinction began. First there was a society based on serfdom, and from this arose feudalism. The process has lasted five thousand years.

No evidence is brought forward to prove the existence of an ancient communistic society three thousand years B.C., nor is there any reason why he should bring forward such evidence. It is a statement which belongs to Chinese beliefs, to the legends which became crystallized in Chu Yuan's story of the Peach Blossom Fountain, with the vision of a white or yellow-haired people who live in a state of pure anarchism, every man ruling himself within the village community. The omission of supporting evidence for the existence of such a classless society is less important than the omission of reasons for its collapse. He adduces none, and we are left to wonder how it is that feudalism develops. Why did these peasants assent to become serfs? Did the collapse occur as a result of inherent weaknesses within the archaic society? What impulses brought about the victory of feudalism? It is easier, and more necessary to his present purpose, to discuss the characteristics of feudalism, and so he continues with a brief examination of these characteristics. Curiously enough, he omits here any reference to the possibility that feudalism arose as the result of the invasions of barbarian tribes. It arose, in Mao's view, simply and solely to perfect the machinery of exploitation. "Let us examine," he says, "the economy of feudalism. It was clearly a self-sufficient economy with the peasants producing their own food and making most of the articles they used with their own hands. But while the emperor, the nobles, and the landlords owned most of the land, the peasants owned little or none. They used their own tools to plough the land, and to their overlords they were compelled to present forty, fifty, sixty, or even seventy per cent of the crop. And not only did the emperor, the nobles, and the landlords live upon the exploited peasants, but the government monopolized by the land-owning class compelled the peasants to support a vast bureaucracy, an army which suppressed the peasants, making them pay tribute and taxes and conscripting their labor." It is a familiar picture, and if it is perhaps excessively simple, the general outlines are probably correct. At this point, following the classic argument of Sun Yat-sen, Mao explains how the feudal society broke down under the impact of the West:

> But we must recognize that China is no longer a feudal society. Since the Opium War of 1840, Chinese society has gradually become semicolonial and semifeudal, and since Mukden it has become (as the result of Japanese occupation) colonial, semicolonial, and semifeudal. The invasion of foreign capital broke up the economy of Chinese society by destroying the self-sufficient natural economy of town and rural handicrafts, substituting a commodity economy. The destruction of the previous economy created markets for capitalistic commodities, while the widespread bankruptcy of the peasants and handicraftsmen enabled the capitalists to exploit cheap labor.

What is to be done? Clearly, he says, the battle is engaged for the subjection of foreign capital to Chinese needs, the capitalists must no longer possess the authority they possessed in the past, and the aims of the Chinese revolution must be reconsidered in the light of the most urgent demands. But it is not essentially against capitalism that Chinese communism must wage war: there are more important enemies. The argument of *The New Democracy* is repeated with some significant changes, and remembering the recent defection of Wang Ching-wei to the Japanese, he enlarges upon the roles of the various classes in a long paragraph which successfully summarizes his position. It is written in the dry, algebraic formulas of communist theory, but it is so important that it should be quoted in full:

> Since our present Chinese society is still colonial, semicolonial, and semifeudal, the chief enemies of the Chinese revolution are still the imperialists and the semifeudal forces. Since the task of the Chinese revolution is to carry out national and democratic revolutions to overthrow these two enemies, and since the forces

which will overthrow them are sometimes still joined by the national bourgeoisie and by part of the upper bourgeoisie, even though the upper bourgeoisie has betrayed the revolution and joined the enemy, yet the dagger of the revolution should not be directed against capitalism and the private property of the capitalists, but against imperialist and feudal monopolies. Therefore the nature of the Chinese revolution at its present stage is not that of proletarian socialism, but of bourgeois democracy. But the present Chinese bourgeois revolution is not the old and ordinary kind of bourgeois revolution, for this kind of revolution is already out of date. No, on the contrary, it is a new and special kind of bourgeois democratic revolution. This kind of revolution is developing in China, and in all the other colonial and semicolonial countries, and we call this kind of revolution the New Democratic Revolution.

This new kind of New Democratic Revolution is a part of the world proletariat socialist revolution, which resolutely fights against imperialism, i.e., international capitalism. Politically, it is formed by several revolutionary classes which unite together to form a revolutionary democratic dictatorship over the imperialists, traitors, and reactionaries, and to oppose the transformation of Chinese society into a society of bourgeois dictatorship. Economically, it strives to nationalize all large capital interests, and all the large enterprises of the imperialists, traitors, and reactionaries, to divide up the large estates and to distribute them among the peasantry, at the same time helping middle and small private industries, while making no attempt to abolish the economy of rich farmers. Consequently, while this new kind of democratic revolution clears the way for capitalism, yet in another sense it is also creating a precedent for socialism.

The argument, which has the appearance of being ambivalent, stressing the necessity of capitalism at the same time that it stresses the necessity of a socialist dictatorship, is not new: it is one which Mao had acknowledged almost from the time when the Communist government was established in Yenan. It differs completely from the classic Stalinist argument, and there is no sign of the acceptance of capitalism in the speeches he made when he was chairman of the Kiangsi soviets. He says further: "It may be ex-

pected that a form of capitalism will survive as an inevitable result
of the New Democratic Revolution in an economically backward
country like China."

But the force of *The Chinese Revolution and the Communist
Party of China* lies less in its theoretical aspects than in its affirmation of revolutionary values. The Chinese revolution is set against
the long history of China. Mao shows a fierce pride in Chinese
inventive genius, recalling that papermaking was invented 1700
years ago, while printing from wooden blocks was invented 1200
years ago. He ranges across the centuries for examples of Chinese
peasant revolts and introduces long lists of the more successful
revolts which accomplished the overthrow of dynasties. The real
meat of the work, however, occurs in three long paragraphs buried
in the middle, where in a kind of poetic prose, each paragraph
beginning with an affirmation of danger, and ending with an
affirmation of the "correct" policy to be pursued, he announces
the revolution. It is in such passages, which marry revolutionary
logic with poetry, that he most clearly reveals himself, and they
should be studied carefully by those who attempt to come to
grips with the man. He begins casually enough with a statement
that the main enemies are the imperialist powers (meaning Japan),
the semifeudal forces (meaning the bureaucrats and the landlords
on the side of the Kuomintang), and the upper bourgeoisie who
have betrayed the people by collaborating with the imperialists
(meaning Wang Ching-wei and the class he represents). Then
he continues:

> Faced with such enemies, the prolonged and bloody state of the
> Chinese revolution becomes inevitable. Because our enemies are
> so powerful, our revolutionary forces can only be strengthened
> and accumulated over a long period of time, so that it may
> become an invincible force in achieving ultimate victory over
> our enemies. And while these enemies ferociously suppress the
> Chinese revolution, our revolutionary force must be persistent
> and strong in guarding its own camp and defeating the enemy.
> It is incorrect to imagine that our revolutionary strength will
> quickly become overwhelming or that the Chinese revolution will
> succeed easily.

Faced with such enemies, it is clear that the method to be adopted and the predominant pattern of the Chinese revolution cannot be peaceful. Success can be achieved only through armed struggle. Our enemies do not allow the Chinese people to carry out peaceful activities or to possess any political freedom. Stalin has rightly said: "The special feature of the Chinese revolution is the revolt of the armed masses against the armed reactionaries." It is incorrect to ignore the principles of armed struggle, revolutionary wars, guerrilla warfare, and political work in the army.

Faced with such enemies, questions arise concerning the special revolutionary bases. The great imperialist powers and their reactionary allied armies in China have always indefinitely occupied the important Chinese cities. If the revolutionary force refuses to compromise with foreign imperialism and its servile underlings, but contrarily, struggles to the very end, and if the revolutionary force is to accumulate and nurture its own strength and avoid fighting decisive battles with powerful enemies when its own strength is not yet ascertained, then it must turn the backward remote areas into progressive, strong bases, making them great military, political, economic, and cultural revolutionary strongholds. Then, from these strongholds, the revolutionary force can start to drive out those malicious enemies who are based upon the large cities and who encroach upon the villages. Also, from these strongholds, the revolutionary force may, through prolonged struggle, gradually achieve total success. Under such conditions, and because of the unbalanced nature of Chinese economic development (the rural economy is not entirely dependent upon the urban economy), and because of the vastness of China's territory (there are immense spaces for the revolutionary forces to fall back on), and because of the disunity and conflict existing within the anti-revolutionary camp, and because the main force of the Chinese revolution, which is the Chinese peasantry, is under the leadership of the Communist party, so there arises the great possibility that the Chinese revolution will succeed first and foremost in the countryside. Thus the revolution is driven to its conclusion within a totally unbalanced atmosphere which increases our difficulties and causes the prolongation of the revolution. Thus, too, we are enabled to understand why it is that these prolonged revolutionary struggles, starting out from such special strongholds, are composed chiefly of peasant guerrilla wars under the leadership of the Communist party. It is incorrect to ignore the principle of making and establishing revolutionary bases in the countryside, and it is equally incorrect to ignore the need for strenuous work among the peasants, and the need for guerrila wars.

What he is doing in such passages is ascribing logic to a state of affairs which had come about as a result of the failure of the Kiangsi soviets. He passionately defends the existence of the border government, and he has no illusions about the struggle with the right wing of the Kuomintang, whatever he may say at other times, for the trap is sprung in the opening words of the extraordinary panegyric of revolution: "Faced with such enemies, the prolonged and bloody state of the Chinese revolution becomes inevitable."

The Strategic Problems of China's Revolutionary Wars

In February 1941, almost immediately after the New Fourth Army Incident, Strategic Problems was published in Yenan in a small volume of fifty pages printed on thick brown paper. In many ways it was the most revealing of the five books which Mao published in the space of three years. Intended as the first volume of a general survey of guerrilla war, Mao's book is concerned to discover the fundamentals of guerrilla warfare, and how a small force can destroy a greater. "There are," he explains, "no mysteries whatsoever in the strategy of defeating superior forces. This is how it is done. In this way, and only in this way, can our armed revolutionary forces succeed in destroying an enemy twenty times our number."

There was nothing secret in Strategic Problems. Copies of it were received in Kuomintang headquarters in Chungking, and presumably, for the book was issued as a textbook for the Red Army, copies fell into the hands of the Japanese. What was ominous both for the Kuomintang and for the Japanese was that Mao considered that the Red Army had reached a position where it no longer needed to conceal its methods. He explains almost casually all the tricks of the guerrilla trade, admits his mistakes, describes with his own maps the various phases of the five annihilation campaigns waged against the Red Army on the borders of Kiangsi and Fukien, enlarges on "centripetal withdrawal" and "defensive retreats," and explains the conditions under which small armies can break through an encirclement. The writing is unusually close-knit, and large parts of the book appear to have been written as early as 1936. Often, the book is more significant for its omissions than for what it includes. Mao shows no indication of having read deeply in military books by European writers. For the most part his sources are Sun Wu, the ancient military commentator who appears to have lived about 500 B.C., *The Spring and Autumn Annals*, which may have been compiled by Confucius and which certainly relate to battles of the sixth century B.C., and the novel *All Men Are Brothers*. Also, it is clear that he had made a special study of the military campaigns of the Han dynasty. He praises the Russians for avoiding a positional war with Napoleon in 1812 at Moscow, and he twice praises the French for their strategic withdrawal on August 21, 1914. For the rest, there is a careful discussion of all the innumerable forms of guerrilla campaigns. Combat disposition, command, camouflage, concentration, deployment, night fighting, anti-aircraft defense, ambush, feints, and the various types of encounters and operations are all passed under review. He explains that the whole purpose of guerrilla war is the capture of spoils. Guerrillas are not interested in a war of attrition; they are interested in mobility, the quick thrust, disguise, the physical annihilation of enemy troops. The temptation to engage in a war of attrition must be avoided at all costs. "While such a game of 'matching pearls' is nothing between two dragon gods of the seas," he writes, remembering a fairytale written by Prince Huai Nan-tzu, "it is ridiculous for a beggar to match pearls with a dragon god." In *Strategic Problems* the ancient past continually obtrudes, and he discusses at length a battle between the states of Lu and Ch'i which occurred in 684 B.C. It is one of the merits of the book, and one of the peculiar distinctions of Mao, that the discussion of this ancient battle becomes entirely relevant to the war against the Kuomintang or the Japanese.

There are moments during his recital of military problems when Mao seems to delight in the inevitable contradictions of guerrilla warfare. "Our strategy is one against ten, while our tactic is ten against one—such contradictions provide the laws by which we overcome the enemy." Or again: "A revolution or a revolutionary war is on the offensive, yet it has its defensive and retreat. To defend in order to attack, to retreat in order to advance, to take a flanking position in order to take a frontal position, and to follow a corkscrew path in order to go directly to the objective— these are inevitable phenomena in the developments of all events, and why should we suppose that military events are otherwise?" He can also be brutally humorous, as when he writes: "A communist war which lasts ten years may be surprising to other countries, but for us this is only the preface. The introduction and the preliminary remarks have been written, but there remain many delightful paragraphs for the future." The concluding remarks show a characteristic effrontery:

> Now that we have reached a stable period, and can now make our own ammunition and our own guns, we are in danger of depending on our own resources. Such an attitude is unwise. We should not depend upon our own war industry, but on that of the imperialists and our enemy at home. We have a claim on the output of the arsenals of London and Hanyang, to be delivered by the enemy's transport corps. This is not a joke, but the truth. *Where the Red Army was able to provide a limited quantity of good ammunition, producing it in its own arsenals, it scored the least victories.**

But though a constant, unrelenting effrontery was demanded of the Red commanders, and he insists that guerrilla war is fought for the sake of spoils—the American government might have sent less ammunition to Chiang Kai-shek if it had known how ardently the Communists in Yenan were waiting for the moment

* He is referring to the situation during the Fifth Annihilation Campaign when the Reds possessed a large arsenal at Juichin.

when they could capture it and turn it against their enemy—the study of strategic problems is not always pitched to this high, romantic key. Guerrilla warfare introduced peculiarly difficult tactical problems. The Red armies were forever faced with encirclement. Even when the Kuomintang armies were not immediately encircling them, they were still conscious of being distantly encircled by the huge weight of Kuomintang power. Mao never underestimated their power, nor their capacity to recover from the blows inflicted upon them. In all his accounts of his battles he shows little respect for Chiang Kai-shek, but he not infrequently shows respect for some of the Kuomintang commanders. "There were a few men among them," he said, "who knew our minds, and how we were fighting. If there had been more, we would not have won so often or so easily."

Mao learned the rules of guerrilla warfare in a hard school. It was a very primitive kind of war, and the tactics he employed were not unlike those of the heroes of the medieval romances. He liked to tell the story of Sung Chiang, one of the heroes of *All Men Are Brothers*, who launched three attacks on Chu village and was twice defeated because he failed to make a complete reconnaissance in depth. Before his final attack he had mapped out all the roads, the sunken lanes, and the bridges, broken the alliance between Chu and the neighboring villages, and his own soldiers in disguise were being infiltrated into the enemy camp. Some light on this kind of war is thrown by T. E. Lawrence, who fought a similar guerrilla campaign against the Turks, and who wrote in his classic account of the Arab revolt:

> It seemed to me proven that our rebellion had an unassailable base, guarded not only from attack, but from the fear of attack. It had a sophisticated alien enemy, disposed as an army of occupation in an area greater than could be dominated effectively from fortified posts. It had a friendly population, of which some two in the hundred were active, and the rest quietly sympathetic to the point of not betraying the movements of the minority. The active rebels had the virtues of secrecy and self-control, and the qualities of speed, endurance and independence of arteries of supply. They had technical equipment enough to paralyse the

enemy's communications. A province would be won when we had taught the civilians in it to die for our ideal of freedom. The presence of the enemy was secondary. Final victory seemed certain, if the war lasted long enough for us to work it out.*

If the war lasted long enough . . . Exactly the same problem faced the Chinese Communists, who confessed openly that only a long war could bring them to power.

One day, at the guerrilla base on Chingkanshan, some peasants had asked the question, "How long can the red flag wave?" Mao answered, "As long as there is space to move in." In *Strategic Problems* he turns the statement into poetry: "No one need worry about whether there is enough room to move around in. In our country, 'when night falls in the west, the day breaks in the east; when light recedes from the south, the north is bright.'" Other things beside time and space conspired to help the Communists. The land is incredibly mountainous, with the result that most modern implements of war are hopelessly ineffective. In mountain defiles it is difficult to make use of cannon, and still more difficult to use tanks; and though airplanes took a heavy toll in the fourth and fifth campaigns, it was only because they were unexpected and because the Red armies allowed themselves to be caught in the open. Afterward, they developed a simple method of "scattering," and airplanes rarely troubled them, even during the Long March. A hundred other things came to their defense. The very nature of Chinese civilization, its furious contrasts, the divisions between the people, between the provinces, between the warlords, all these supplied the inevitable basis for revolution. Mao was, of course, perfectly conscious of these contrasts, and he ranges through them at some length when he comes to discuss the characteristics of the revolutionary war. It was a consideration of these contrasts which led him, after the Sixth Congress of the Chinese Communist party, in 1928, to decide that the conquest of China was possible once the Red Army possessed a convenient base of operations. He wrote:

* T. E. Lawrence, *Seven Pillars of Wisdom* (New York: Doubleday, Doran and Company, 1935), p. 196.

If we analyze the question, we see that throughout China there exists an uneven political and economic development, and this is indicated by the coexistence of a frail capitalist economy and a predominant semifeudal economy; a few seemingly modern industrial and commercial cities and boundless expanses of rural districts in medieval stagnation; of several million industrial workers and hundreds of millions of peasants living under a decaying regime; of great warlords administering the central government, and lesser warlords administering the provinces; of a regular army and a variegated collection of local armies; of great steamship lines, motor roads, and railways, together with field trails and wheelbarrow paths such that even a pedestrian has difficulty walking on them.

For hundreds of generations the Chinese had celebrated the "golden mean," but he could see no evidence of it anywhere; and the absence of a tolerable median civilization made revolutionary warfare only the more possible.

Coalition Government

For some years Mao had been watching the growing dogmatism within the party. Dogmatic himself, he recognized the danger signs. He had fought against dogma at the Tsunyi conference, and even before. Now, as the war came to an end, he was conscious that the time had come to restate the case for the Communists in the light of all the experience the party had undergone. On April 24, 1945, he called the Seventh Congress of the Chinese Communist party into existence at Yenan, and on that spring day, while Chu Teh presented a report on the battles in the liberated area, Mao proclaimed that the Chinese Communists had fought the Kuomintang too long. It was time for a marriage.

He began by announcing that a compromise was entirely possible; that the Kuomintang and the Communist Party could exist together; that a single government composed of members of both parties might work reasonably well. The statement seems to have been made with intense conviction. The Japanese were reeling under American attacks, the war against Germany was over, and the time had come to formulate a convincing blueprint for the future. He distrusted the Kuomintang, and was prepared to fight it if necessary. At the same time he was prepared to envisage a period of relative calm, and even of co-operation between the two parties; and it is probable that at this time he underestimated the corruption which already existed within the Kuomintang ranks.

Coalition Government is the most carefully constructed of all Mao's published political writings. It breathes a kind of confidence which is not always present in his works. He called for reforms within the Kuomintang, but he also called for reforms within the Communist party; and he insisted on a "bedrock," absolute reliance on the demands of the people. Again and again he says, "The people must rule. There is no rule without the people. We must find what the people want, and then satisfy them." The implications are clear. The Kuomintang has not interested itself in the demands of the peasants, and just as long as it refuses to interest itself in those demands it will fail. He wrote:

> Our starting point is to serve the Chinese people earnestly and wholeheartedly, and never to be severed from the people; to set out always from the point of view of serving the people's interests, not serving the interests of a small group or oneself; to give equal responsibility to the people and the guiding organization. Experience during the last twenty years has taught us that all tasks, policies, and methods that were correct corresponded to the demands of the people at that definite time and place, and all that were incorrect were separate from the people's will.

The principle of reliance upon the popular will was one which was rarely, if ever, followed by the Kuomintang, which operated as though the people were simple counters to be moved at will. The war had made the Kuomintang more authoritative than ever, demanding from the people sacrifices so great that they were already in a state of passive noncooperation over large areas of Nationalist China. In return for their sacrifices they were offered nothing but the continuing corruption of the high officials. It was as simple as that, and among these simplicities Mao knew himself at home. The Kuomintang government no longer led. The

Communists had not yet begun to lead. The leadership must come, if it was to come at all, from "the broad masses of the people." To prove that popular will may sometimes be in advance of the government, Mao wrote:

Our comrades must not think that what is unintelligible to us is also unintelligible to the masses. Very often the masses stride ahead of us and want urgently to advance forward, while our comrades do not act as leaders of the broad masses, but on the contrary reflect the opinion of some backward interests. Every comrade should be made to comprehend that the highest criterion of all our statements and activities is whether they correspond to the highest interests of the broadest masses, and whether they are supported by the broadest masses. Every comrade should be taught to comprehend that as long as we rely on the people, firmly believing in the infinite creative power of the people, then we may be able to overcome all difficulties, no matter how serious they are, and no enemy will be able to overwhelm us, but will be overwhelmed by us.

This was not essentially the policy pursued in the early days of the Communist revolution in China. It was a policy hammered out of the war against the Japanese, out of the extraordinary conditions in north China, and out of a clear understanding of the error committed by the Kuomintang, an error that was finally to destroy them.

Though, technically, *Coalition Government* constitutes an appeal for a government of the Communists and the Kuomintang, it is also an attempt to analyze the basis of any government in terms of the popular will: the absolute primacy of the popular will is accepted. But here a doubt arises. There is never any attempt to analyze the nature of the popular will. What does it consist of? On what forces does it rely? How does it express itself? To some extent, of course, it expresses itself in the ballot box. It also expresses itself in the deliberations of the village councils, in the opinions seeping up through the ranks of the army, in the resolutions of county governments, in the overt signs of change which appear in the political atmosphere of our time. "The main task of the leader," Mao wrote elsewhere, "is to keep his ears to the ground." It was in this way that he understood "the popular will," but there was always the danger that "the popular will" might be another name for the incantatory editorials of the *Liberation Daily*. It was a danger he faced, though he did not always face it squarely, and it is significant that he demanded "equal responsibility for the people and the guiding organization," in the same breath in which he demanded the primacy of "the popular will."

The appeal for the coalition government had already appeared in *New Democracy*. In the new book the argument was reinforced and given weight by the successes of the Communist armies in North China. Here, too, Mao defined more clearly than elsewhere his attitude to investment capital. He insisted that capital was not in itself an issue: there were some forms of capital that were perfectly acceptable, for the need had never been greater. "To develop industry," he wrote, "enormous capital is required. Where will it come from? It can come from only two sources: the capital accumulated by the Chinese people themselves and from foreign loans, and we shall welcome all foreign investments as long as they obey the laws of China and are advantageous to our economy." This was not a sop to the capitalists, but a statement of simple truth. Wrecked by war, China could hardly expect to survive without enormous capital investment from abroad. But he refused, with considerable bitterness, to accept a state of affairs by which China would become a semicolony at the mercy of foreign capital:

> Some people refuse to understand why the Chinese Communists do not fear capitalism, but on the contrary develop it as much as possible. Our answer is simple: we have to replace foreign imperialist and native feudalist oppression with capitalist development because this is the inevitable course of our economy, and because the capitalist class is benefitted as well as the proletariat. What is superfluous today is foreign imperialism and native feudalism, not native capitalism. On the contrary, our capitalism is indeed too little.

There was nothing original in this complaint: it had been made repeatedly by Sun Yat-sen. What was new, and strange, and encouraging was that Mao seemed to have worked out an answer to the pressing question: how shall we have peace? Capital would provisionally remain; the Kuomintang capitalists would have some of their powers clipped away; but the need for capital was so great that he seemed prepared to accept an interval of "new democracy by means of a coalition government," where power centered in an elective assembly and the Communists would be represented for the first time in the legal government. There is no reason to believe that *Coalition Government* is a dishonest document. For ten years the Communists had been gathering power to themselves by default of their enemies, the Japanese and the Kuomintang. The time had come for a careful evaluation of policies. Eventually, the Communists believed, they would take over power peacefully, either by sapping at the foundations of Kuomintang rule or by providing that their own policies answered more closely the needs of the people. Though civil war was conceivable, the Communists hoped to avoid it, and *Coalition Government* suggested a possible alternative to war.

With the publication of *Coalition Government*, the die was cast. Mao made it perfectly clear that the Communists were no longer to be treated as bandits. They would fight back against any further annihilation campaigns. The alternatives were coalition or war; and though the first was preferable, there was no reason to believe that their armies would be unable to fight. The Communists were not prepared to accept isolation, and they refused to be swallowed up within the Kuomintang. The Kuomintang was therefore placed in a dilemma: it must either accept coalition, or be faced with a war even more heart-rending than the campaigns fought in the early thirties. Unfortunately for the Kuomintang the Communists had assured themselves of victory if war broke out by possessing a social program superior to their enemies', and nothing in all Chiang Kai-shek's writings speaks with so much assurance as Mao, when he said:

> People must understand that no matter how tortuous the path may be, the independence and liberation of the Chinese people will be realized, and the time for it is already at hand. The great aspirations of countless martyrs during the last hundred years must be fulfilled by our generation. Whoever desires to prevent these aspirations from being translated into fact, that man will fail.

THE STORM BREAKS

WITH THE END of the war against Japan, the Chinese Communists were solidly entrenched behind Japanese lines. Unknown to the foreign press, they had fought a series of hard campaigns. They had taken part, with Lin Piao as commander, in the first engagement of consequence between the Chinese and the Japanese at Pinghsinkuan. They had destroyed railroads and coal mines under Japanese occupation, and combined with General Wei Li-huang, who fought against them in the annihilation campaigns, in the battle of Chekuo. In 1940 there occurred the "Hundred Regiment Campaign," which came to an end, after four months of bitter fighting, in December. Almost immediately afterward occurred the New Fourth Army Incident, and the Chinese Communists were compelled to secure their flank against the Kuomintang. They continued, however, to fight the Japanese, and an endless war taking place in hundreds of separate areas, a war fought in tunnels underground and in forests and in the outskirts of cities and in the plains, drained the Japanese of their strength, so that the Tokyo radio clamored for some way of preventing the continual bloodletting. Openly, the Tokyo radio proclaimed that the main enemy in China was the Chinese Red Army. It was hardly an exaggeration, for the Kuomintang had lost its offensive. By early 1945 the Kuomintang government no longer possessed the power or the authority for the counterattack, and less than a hundred miles of railway remained in its hands.

While the Kuomintang waited for the war to end, the Chinese Communists were busy extending the areas under their rule and removing them from the rule of the Japanese. Their guerrilla wars went on. To the Americans who flew to Yenan and established the Yenan Observation Group, they provided admirable intelligence. Radios were sent to them. Special apparatus was flown in. It was observed that the Red Army was a fighting force, trained to guerrilla warfare on a scale unsuspected before. It was also observed that Mao and Chu Teh possessed an authority over their troops denied to Chiang Kai-shek.

As the war came to a close, Mao and Chu Teh were openly preparing to exert the authority of the Yenan government to the uttermost. Mao had no knowledge of Russian intentions: the occupation of Manchuria was clearly decided upon at the last moment. He thought the war in the Pacific would end with an American thrust against Japan and the southeast coast of China. He had considerable admiration for the Americans who visited Yenan, and showed it in countless ways to the military officers who came to stay at Whittlesey Hall on the south bank of the Yen River. At the same time he was perfectly aware that the Kuomintang-Communist negotiations, which continued throughout the war, had ended in complete failure. What was to be done?

In an address, "Our Task in 1945," delivered before the People's Congress of the Shen-Kan-Ning Border Region, on December 15, 1944, Mao outlined the main strategy. The Americans had reached Leyte and might at any moment land on the Chinese coast. The Japanese had just driven a continental line through China which joined Tokyo to Singapore. The war was still in a state of stalemate. He still hoped for an all-out offensive by the Chinese armies, but it was clear that no political basis for such an offensive existed until a coalition government had taken power, or until the people, like the French *maquis*, rose in a *levée en masse*.

The specific problems facing the Chinese Communists, said Mao, were fifteen in number. The first was the expansion of the liberated areas by continued calculated attacks on weak enemy-held garrisons. The second involved attacks on their battle fronts. The third involved the training of the self-defense corps and the people's militia, and in discussing the training of the self-defense corps he returned, as he was to do again, to the necessity of expanding the liberated areas:

> Except in some areas where it is impossible to expand further, we must try our best to expand. Among the ninety million liberated people every man and woman citizen, except the old, young, and sick, must be organized into self-defense corps, while never giving up their production at home; and they must do this to defend their homes and villages, and to help the army. . . . Of our ninety million people, at leave five per cent, that is four and a half million, should join the people's militia. This means that the present people's militia must be doubled.

It was still, of course, guerrilla war. Mao pointedly remarked that the chief weapon of the people's militia must remain the land mine, which was often no more than a stone hollowed out to contain gunpowder. The fourth objective—the most ominous for the Kuomintang and for the Japanese—was the training of a regular army on modern principles, which presumably meant an army trained to fight positional wars. The fifth objective was economic: the new areas must be supported by the old. The sixth involved the Red Army itself: he demanded the utmost solidarity between the officers and the soldiers. He admitted that there were still "militaristic" habits among the officers, who sometimes neglected the soldiers when they were ill, deprived them of their food, and punished them arbitrarily, insulting and shooting deserters. "All these," Mao commented, "are utterly bad habits, and must be rooted out relentlessly." He ordered every unit to launch a "support-officer-love-soldier" movement, based upon adequate political training. The soldiers must keep the trust of their commanders, and the defects and mistakes of both should be publicly explained and swiftly corrected.

So far Mao had dealt largely with the state of the Communist military forces in relation to the enemy. Many of the remaining proposals were devoted to internal politics. The seventh concerned a "support-government-love-people" movement. The eighth demanded that all those who held posts under the government work for a coalition government. The ninth asked for a careful examination of the problems of rent reduction—rent must be reduced in the newly liberated areas, for it was only by reducing rent that the peasants in the new areas would be made to rally round the Yenan government.

The tenth proposal concerned production and mutual aid groups. "The people must have sufficient food and clothing to acquire a surplus. Our slogan should be 'three years' cultivation, one year's surplus,' for within a few years we must strive to be completely, or at least nearly, self-sufficient. To this end, division of profits to private persons according to the quality of their work can and should be put into practice."

The eleventh proposal concerned intellectual and cultural work among the peasants. Culture he defined as art, newspapers, schools, and public health. A vast effort must be made to raise the standard of education. "Tyrants," he said, "feed on the ignorance of the people, but we rely on the intelligence of the people." The sly challenge to Chiang Kai-shek was followed by another, for he carefully pointed out in the twelfth proposal the necessity of the widest possible expression of popular elections.

The thirteenth proposal involved the education of cadres, or government personnel. He did not have a very high opinion of them and thought their inefficiency due to lack of education. He continued the charge in the fourteenth proposal, which attacked the dogmatism and pride of these same officials. "There are cadres which hate to hear criticism, delight only in praise, and never receive suggestions from the people, because the people are afraid to offer them, and are afraid of being humiliated or retaliated against." He proposed to wage a pitiless war against these cadres and he ordered that no one should be punished for speaking out:

Anyone, as long as he is not an enemy and does not attack with malicious intent, should be allowed to speak, and it does not matter if he is wrong. It is the duty of the leaders of all ranks to listen to others. The following principles should be observed: First, say what is on your mind and without reservation. Second, the speaker is not to be blamed, while the listener should take notice. If the principle that the speaker is not to be blamed— this is a real and not fictitious principle—is lacking, then the full effect of the principle cannot be obtained.

The fifteenth and last proposal introduced once again the necessity of a coalition government. "We must think of all the ways and means which will help to promote the establishment of such a government. One way is to continue negotiations with the Kuomintang; another way is to urge the entire population to demand a coalition; and there may be other ways." On this note the speech to the border government comes to an end.

The speech has been quoted at length because it conveys the thoughts going through Mao's mind toward the end of the war. The civil war was still far away. The Japanese war could be expected to last at least another year. The Chinese Communists were still concerned with an immense number of small-scale operations. Shortly afterward, on April 24, 1945, during the Seventh Congress of the Chinese Communist party, held at Yenan, Mao made his report "On Coalition Government," and here he was elected chairman of the Central Committee. It was an odd title, for he had been in fact if not in name chairman ever since the Tsunyi conference, and even in Kiangsi he had been addressed by this title.

When the Japanese government accepted terms of unconditional surrender five days after the dropping of the first atomic bomb, the position of the Chinese Communists suddenly changed. The dynamics of their expansion demanded a race to the coast between the Communists and the Kuomintang. Chu Teh, as commander-in-chief of the Red Army, issued an order to the guerrilla forces beseiging Japanese-occupied cities to advance and accept the enemy's surrender, an order immediately countermanded by Chiang Kai-shek. By August 15, Chu Teh and Mao were urging that the United States cease lend-lease aid to the Kuomintang, who might use the guns, airplanes, and ammunition shipped into China against the Communists. It was a reasonable request; it was not followed, and the guns, airplanes, and ammunition eventually fell into the hands of the Chinese Communists.

By the end of August the danger of civil war was imminent. Chiang Kai-shek may have hoped that he could launch an immediate "annihilation campaign" with American military support, but there was popular clamor for a meeting between the two adversaries in a final effort to solve outstanding problems. The initiative had passed into the hands of Chiang Kai-shek. He dispatched a telegram to Mao, humbly requesting a meeting in Chungking. Mao answered: "My humble self is most willing to come to Chungking to discuss peace and national reconstruction with you." The letter was signed "Your younger brother." For the first time in eighteen years the two adversaries met face to face.

It was an unhappy meeting. It was the first time Mao had flown in an airplane. The Americans had guaranteed his safety, but he could not avoid wondering at the prospects ahead: he distrusted Chiang Kai-shek too firmly to believe in the proffered good intentions. They drank toasts, commended each other in public. There were long conferences and strange, tortured interviews between them. Both were ill at ease. Chiang was politely cold, Mao warmly ironical. But gradually a basis of agreement was discovered. There would be a termination of "the period of tutelage," all political parties would receive equal rights, a People's Consultative Council would be assembled, and there would be popular suffrage. The agreement, which Chou En-lai and Wang Jo-fei signed on behalf of the Communists, was completed on October 10, and on the next day Mao flew back to Yenan. He was not convinced of the Generalissimo's good intentions. He still hoped for peace, but he saw little sign of it. No final decisions had been made about the status of the Eighth Route Army or the New Fourth Army, and the question of the Chinese Communist authority to accept the Japanese surrenders was still unsolved. Bitterness against Chiang Kai-shek had increased. "He treated me like a peasant." Mao said afterward. The wound had not healed; it had only opened wider.

At this point American intervention in Chinese problems became a factor of considerable importance. General Hurley, working sometimes heroically and sometimes with an incredible lack of knowledge of the Chinese mind, attempted to grapple with the problem. He had visited Yenan. For a brief while he had been accepted by the Chinese Communists as an earnest mediator, in spite of his strange habit of breaking out with Indian war cries at inopportune moments. But when United States forces landed at Tientsin in September and established themselves in Chinwangtao and Peking on the pretext that they had come to guard the railways, it became clear that the American government was firmly resolved to protect the Kuomintang against the Communists. "On the one hand," exclaimed Chou En-lai, "we see American ammunition fired at Communist troops, while on the other hand the Americans are trying to bring about peace." The tragic ambivalence, which is visible in so much of American foreign policy, was now at work. In despair of understanding the forces unleashed by the dubious peace, General Hurley resigned.

With the increase of American intervention, the forces making for civil war also increased. On November 15, the United States government declared its intention to continue lend-lease aid to the Kuomintang government amounting to $777,638,292 up to June 30, 1947. A few days previously Chu Teh had protested to General Wedemeyer, who commanded the United States forces in China, against continued American intervention in Chinese affairs. The reply was unfavorable to the Communists. The Communists believed that the crisis had come, and in December the evacuation of Yenan began. Kalgan, which had been captured in August, became the industrial capital of the Communist empire; and though Mao and Chu Teh remained in Yenan and continued to rule from there, the greater part of the administrative offices, the university, the art academy, the military college, and the medical college made their way toward the Yellow River. Caravans of mules, ponies, and donkeys laden with books, beds, office files, and food wandered among the yellow hills of Shensi. For the second time since the Kiangsi soviets the government was on the march.

In the early days of 1946 there was a breathing spell. General George Marshall had been sent to replace General Hurley. He was a man of an entirely different caliber. He made a serious effort to understand the opposing camps. He visited Yenan and commented favorably upon the Communists' social policies, and he detested the servility of most of the Kuomintang officers he met. Urbane, polished, sensitive to social forces, he refused to accept the claims of either side in the quarrel, his preferences remaining with the liberal groups in the center, though for the most part these had long ago despaired of the reactionary policies of the Kuomintang.

There was sufficient evidence to show that the reaction was in full swing. On February 22 the Kuomintang secret police raided the Communist newspaper offices in Chungking, reducing them to debris. The political programs of the People's Consultative Assembly were deliberately sabotaged by Chiang Kai-shek, who kept urging Kuomintang members to carry out "a decisive campaign" against the Communists. Increasingly, on the radios of both sides there was to be heard only violent vituperation.

The Communists had more cause for their invective than the Kuomintang. Their armies were being attacked by Kuomintang troops armed with the latest American equipment, and a military advisory group of high American officers was established under the name of MAGIC (Military Advisory Group in China) in Kuomintang headquarters. There were battles outside Changchun, and a serious engagement, which reportedly cost one hundred thousand lives, at Shihpingchieh. The Communists possessed three ports, Weihaiwei, Chefoo, and Lungkow. Through all other ports military aid to support the Kuomintang was arriving in huge quantities. It seemed, as summer came on, that civil war would be inevitable, and not even the diplomacy of General Marshall could prevent it. The Communists had reported earlier that a million Kuomintang regular troops were being transferred for an offensive against their own areas, while seven Kuomintang armies were being transported to Manchuria by United States airplanes and warships. Suddenly, at the beginning of June, the tension quietened. A truce was announced. And to make sure that the truce was effective, General Marshall organized truce teams consisting of Americans, Kuomintang, and Communist officers. A hush came over China. It was as though quite suddenly history had grown silent and was holding its breath.

During the truce I flew from Peking to Yenan, determined to see Mao and to try to fathom the sources of Communist power in China. I was also anxious to discover more of Mao's poetry, for some poems of his were known to exist, and one of them had been printed in *Ta Kung Pao* in Chungking. I half expected to find a large, thriving city and had not guessed that I would find only a beautiful valley with the winter wheat growing on the loess hills. The beauty of the valley mocked the tragic summer. There was no great arsenal of power; instead, there were yellow hills, a few houses, a market place, a sluggish blue river, a crumbling old pagoda, date palms and apple orchards set in a strange, wild, desolate valley thick with dust, everything yellow except for the gay blankets covering the entrances to the caves. Yenan suggested the famous story of the Peach Blossom Fountain, which lies beyond the cliffs at the other end of the world.

There was no sign of Mao. There were rumors that he had suffered a kind of stroke a few months earlier when twelve of his closest friends, including Yeh Ting and Wang Jo-fei, had been killed in an air accident as they returned from a conference in Chungking. There was time enough to take stock of Yenan. I spent an evening and half a night with Chu Teh in his garden among the date palms, while the wolves howled outside in the moonless valley. P'eng Teh-huai talked of his campaigns. Ma Hei-teh talked of the cave hospital. Yang Shan-kun talked about the Sian Incident. There were *yang-k'o* dances, and an admirable performance of the "Yellow River Cantata," and long walks in the valley, which had been inhabited since the birth of China. The printing presses were in the caves beside the river: thousands of sculptured buddhas gazed down on the small rotary presses, many of the statues dissolving in the steam. I remember once coming upon a boy resting his foot idly on the head of a sculptured prince of the T'ang dynasty so fresh and so delicately carved that even now, though the head had lain beside the road for countless years, the closed eyes seemed about to open; and there was something in the expression and the curling hair which showed the influence of Alexander's voyages.

Mao remained invisible. There were unaccountable difficulties in seeing him. They said he saw no one, he was displeased with foreigners, they even hinted that he refused to see any foreigners again. It sounded possible. From conversation with the people in Yenan, it became clear that there was a kind of remoteness about him. Intangible and aloof, from a small house in the shadow of the mountains, not far from the radio transmitter which derived its electricity from a foot pedal, carefully tending a small garden of tobacco plants and tomatoes, he spent the nights pondering over the telegrams received from all parts of China, and every decision he made had incalculable consequences. The truce teams were marching out from Peking; there was the possibility of peace, but the final conclusions were known only to a few men in Nanking and Yenan.

Mao had not entirely disappeared. Once I caught a glimpse of him in a jeep—a cloud of dust, a red, sunburned face peering through, then the dust swallowed him. There was only time enough to observe that he looked amazingly fit and well, and the stories of the nervous prostration were probably unfounded. A few days later I saw him at a play. He sat directly in front of me, his face illuminated by the blinding blue light of the stage, a ruddy face which reflected almost childishly all the passing emotions of the actors. The play was a morality, based on one of the innumerable incidents in the novel All Men Are Brothers. There was the heavy, leonine head, with blue-black hair, very thick, muscular shoulders, a long, smooth forehead, the spectacles glinting and the hands braced against the knees. One can tell more about a man from the way he enjoys drama than from observing him elsewhere. What was strange was that he was wholly feminine, reflected all the gestures of the actors, pursed his lips when they were roaring with anger, and gently waved his arms when the firecrackers exploded; and he glowed with the wildest joy when the armies of stage peasants, in beautiful embroidered costumes, at last overthrew their feudal lords in still more beautifully embroidered costumes. It was a medieval morality, and Mao enjoyed its medieval gusto. The peasant heroes wore the finest silks, the finest dragon-painted gowns; some of the evil princes wore ugly red and black masks which gave them the appearance of tigers.

It was all impenitently romantic, with the fierce romanticism of the Chinese—that race which is permanently sustained by romanticism—and with the last flutes and the last drumbeats, while the saltpeter flames of the burning castles filled the stage, Mao clapped and cheered as Americans clap and cheer at a football game.

The play concerned the victory of armed peasants over their feudal lords, one of those legendary victories which occurred two thousand years ago; yet the same play, against the background of the whole of modern China, was being played elsewhere, far from Yenan, in a thousand hamlets and a million villages. I think it was at this moment, while we were all scrambling out of the theater, that I realized fully how certain the Chinese Communists were of their eventual victory. In the end the captains with their nodding plumes, their crowns of emeralds, their robes of flowing jade and red-gold watered silk stood out among the broken towers, and without the least shock one realized that at the core of the Chinese Communists there was the sense of a known victory. They knew that because they had the unnumbered peasants at their side, the diadems and the crowns would fall to them. Mao disappeared down the dark road, a half-smiling figure with heavy shoulders, a shadow against the starlight.

I began to think that this was the last I would ever see of him. He appeared at night and slept by day; he had the scholar's desire for solitude, and he was content to calculate and pore over the reports coming into this half-deserted village by radio and messenger. I would leave Yenan and never see him face to face. Meanwhile the winter wheat grew wild on the loess mountains, and sometimes, visiting an old ruin or coming down from a cliff dwelling, I would see in the dust a rider of the Eighth Route Army racing toward Chu Teh's date garden, and it was pleasant to see the Persian roses on the saddlecloth.

But if it was impossible to see Mao, it was at least possible to see his friends. Men spoke of him, as they spoke of all legends, quietly, without emphasis, relating how he had gone among the peasants of Hunan with no weapons, wearing a drab white cotton coat and white trousers, and the famous sun helmet, lean and youthful-looking. They had known him when he was in command of a peasant army less than a hundred strong; and now this solitary man possessed armies greater than any possessed by Napoleon, and seemed unaware of his great possessions. A man who could organize the Chinese peasants in this fashion is not to be despised. With his Hunanese fire, his addiction to scholarship, and his passion for the *lao pai hsing*, the peasants with their hundred names, he represented the potentiality of the people in much the same way that Leonardo da Vinci represented the potentiality of art. It was not only that he was new, but he possessed the flair for discovering unsuspected newness everywhere—it was he, and he almost alone, who had brought this movement into being, and at the same time his decisions were the result of popular forces he could hardly control. He guided and was guided, imitating in himself the classic theorem of Aristotle that freedom "is to govern and to be governed." He led the way—the way which had been made possible by the emergence of consciousness among the Chinese peasants.

For it had come at last, this last and greatest revolt from the heart of Asia. Colonialism, imperialism, exploitation—those tarnished words were losing their meaning, or rather they were slips of burning paper and the flames were biting the edges. We had thought too long that nations were permanent, and when we thought of the West as in decline, we imagined that it was declining from its own weakness and not from the strength of others. There were places in China where the West was not important. In the whole of Yenan only the printing presses, two jeeps, the radio, and the sculptured head of a T'ang dynasty prince showed the influence of the West. On the walls of the huts of the Communist generals there were no maps of America or Europe; they were content with China, content with the Chinese peasant.

I confess I preferred it like this. The scented valley, steaming with the summer sun and crowned with mountains of winter wheat, showed the beginnings of a new civilization. In the same way, on the shores of the Euphrates, below Mount Hymettus, and on the seven hills of Rome, and around the Ile de la Cité, new civilizations had sprung from a single thesis; and now, while civilizations fade or gather strength by desperate missions, we must set ourselves more than ever to understand how the seed dies and is born again in a flowering tree.

So I thought, wandering in Yenan, perplexed by the figure of Mao, who seemed even then to be destined to fulfill the role assumed by the Chinese emperors. Though I heard the legends concerning him, the essential man escaped, as perhaps he will escape all historians in the future. I came to believe, on those days when the sunsets were bursts of gold on golden mountains, that I would see only the ancient Shensi earth, the solitary peasants, the generals in the caves, and once again, for already it had become like the phrase of Vinteuil, the haggard rider coming through the dust with the blaze of a scarlet saddlecloth, a gun on his shoulder, and, in his saddlebag, reports from the hundreds of scattered armies directed from a cave.

One evening, just before the airplane was due to arrive from Peking, a message came from Yang Shan-kun, the chief of staff, to say that Mao was giving a small party. The day had been cloudy. Now the clouds lifted, and the violence of the sunset saturated in sand only increased the sense of violence which had been present all day. During the afternoon I had ridden in one of the two jeeps to the cave-hospital. On the way back we had stopped at the cave-university, and when the jeep turned up a steep incline, we climbed out, for the sand was slippery. A moment later, the jeep with its driver slipped over the edge of a small cliff. There were some black pigs in a sty at the bottom of a thirty-foot drop. The driver was still in the jeep. When we ran down he was not dead as we had expected, but covered in blood and oil, and groaning, and the jeep had broken the back of one of the pigs, which was screaming. It was some time before a peasant brought a knife and skewered its throat. The jeep axle was bent, probably broken. In the capital of the Chinese Communist empire, there now remained exactly one jeep.

I remember that I was almost afraid Mao would turn on me and say I was responsible for destroying half of his remaining vehicles. But nothing of the kind happened.

It was growing dark, and in the little enclosure of the "Foreign Office" the Chief of Staff was playing with his children among the wilting tomato plants. There was a high wall. An armed guard at the wicker gate was picking his nose and gazing down at the river and the plain. Beyond the tomatoes lay a small bare room with a stamped earth floor, three yellow homemade chairs, and a vast map of China disintegrating with age; and beyond a curtain dinner was being prepared with a clatter of bowls and chopsticks. There was P'eng Teh-huai, vice-commander-in-chief of the border regions, thickset, with the face of an angry Buddha; there were some secretaries and soldiers in dusty gray uniforms; and there was a Chinese-American major who alone represented a foreign power.

Then Mao came into the room. He came so quietly that we were hardly aware of his presence. He wore a thick brown Sun Yat-sen uniform which seemed to have been woven of goats' hair, and as he stood beside the towering P'eng Teh-huai he looked slighter and smaller than I had imagined him. I had suspected he was changeable when I saw him at the theater; now, once again, he assumed the appropriate disguise. There is hardly a photograph of him which resembles any other photograph, so strangely and so suddenly does he change. Today, he looked like a surprisingly young student, a candidate for a doctorate, and perhaps he played for his college: the shoulders were very heavy. The hair was very sleek and long, the eyes large, the lips pursed, and he had no mannerisms. There was about him a kind of quietness such as you will find among people who have lived much alone. But this quietness was delusory. It was true enough, and almost tangible, but it went oddly with the young student who seemed to be, not the giver of the party and the equal of emperors, but a young man who had strayed by accident from a university campus. He was fifty-three and looked twenty.

Unaccountably, the room filled up. His wife came in, wearing black slacks and a sweater, and she said "Nin hao?" in greeting, with a classical Pekingese accent, and suddenly you realized that her long face possessed more beauty and expression than the face of the considerably more famous Mme. Chiang Kai-shek; also, she brought with her the scent of the flowers she had been gathering in the uplands. Chu Teh came in, limping a little, for the water in Yenan has a strange effect on the bones of the legs—I observed twenty to thirty peasants who limped in the same way. He had the face of a wise peasant and smiled broadly. God knows how many other generals there were at this time. It was like the opening scene of Tolstoy's *War and Peace:* you were continually expecting the princes and generals to enter, forgetting that they had entered a few minutes ago, disguised as university students and peasants.

The major-domo—a soldier in a faded gray tunic, wearing rice-straw sandals—announced that dinner was ready in the room behind the faded curtain. We sat down to the blackwood tables piled high with chicken soup, huge loaves of soft white unleavened bread, sweet rice, millet, and tomatoes which glowed like small fires in the darkening room. Behind us there were photographs on the wall of Mao, Chu Teh, Attlee, Truman, Stalin, and Chiang Kai-shek. All the photographs were thick with dust.

Mao began speaking in a surprisingly low voice, smiling at Chu Teh, whose harsher voice growled in reply. One by one the people in the room seemed to disappear in the thick wheeling shadows, until the electric light from the American generator on the other side of the river clicked on, blinding us all in its yellow glare. The sun sets quickly in north China. There is a final flash of sunset some minutes after the sun has gone down, then the valley is given over to the landscapes of the moon. Wolves howled, and sometimes, through the thin walls, we heard the gun butt of a soldier, or a distant command.

In embroidered blue gowns, two old scholars were sitting at the table. One of them had been Mao's teacher years before. This small man, whose forehead resembled a brown egg and whose eyes resembled black coals, with a small threadbare beard, was at least seventy: delicate, precise, attentive, speaking with a soft Peking drawl. He looked as though he belonged to a different race altogether. He had come in the same airplane that brought me to Yenan, and when we fell into air pockets over the Shensi mountains, he continued to fan himself as though nothing so irresponsible as an airplane would deflect him from the purpose of traveling in comfort. Now he asked Mao questions about the Long March, and shook his head in wonder. "Yes, yes, a strange journey—and the airplanes, what about the airplanes?" "We were afraid at first," Mao answered. "Then they no longer frightened us at all." Chu Teh was drinking an eggcupful of rice wine. P'eng Teh-huai was eating cheese curd—he was still troubled by ulcers. The American major began to take photographs by flashbulb. Mao went on talking about the Long March, lost among his own legends, his voice rising and becoming gradually more animated, losing its feminine quality, his long fingers making expressive gestures over the salad bowl.

"And what was the strangest thing of all?" The old professor leaned forward, expectancy written all over the thin delicate face.

Mao thought for a moment. "I suppose it was the fish," he said. "We came to places where so few people had been before that if you waded into the river, the fish would leap into your hands."

I said, with the hope of bringing him away from fish, "Lao Tzu was of the opinion that government should be as easy as the cooking of little fish. Do you agree?"

He answered, "There should be no government—the people should rule themselves."

A little later he returned to the Long March. "There will be many Long Marches in the future."

"So the war goes on?"

"It must, unless the Kuomintang allows the people to rule." It was a strange statement, the first intimation that the peace talks were breaking down. Something in the way he said the words sounded like doom. A week earlier, talking to Chu Teh, it seemed that a vast hope of peace ruled in Yenan, that all problems might be solved, that soon enough there would be a coalition government, a government of the talents.

After dinner, when the generals and professors had departed and the last flashbulb had exploded, I was left alone with him. He smiled, pushed his hands through his thick hair and sat down astraddle a small blackwood chair. I asked whether it would be possible to see more of his poems and told him how well "The

Snow" had been received in the south. Previously I had asked Yang Shan-kun to make inquiries about them.

"I have been thinking," he answered, "and I have decided not to give them to you. They are ma-ma-hu-hu—so stupid. I only write poetry to amuse myself. Would you like me to write a poem on your visit to Yenan?"

"Yes, please."

"I shall see if I have time." After a while he said, "We are fighting tremendous battles now—it is not the time to write poetry." He was talking, I imagine, of battles which take place in the minds of people, for it was still the period of truce.

He talked about his poem called "The Snow." "Yes, it's a good poem. I wrote it in the airplane. It was the first time I had ever been in an airplane. I was astonished by the beauty of my country from the air—and there were other things."

"What other things?"

"So many. You must remember when the poem was written. It was when there was so much hope in the air, when we trusted the Generalissimo." A moment later he said, "My poems are so stupid—you mustn't take them seriously."

The light had gone out. A servant brought a rapeseed oil lamp, and in this light his face seemed to shine blood-red, heavy and drawn. I don't know why, but I had a feeling we were engaged in a kind of duel. He asked about the health of Wen Yi-tuo and Chang Shih-jo, two professors I knew in Kunming. "They are good men. If you see them, tell them how much we admire them." Then he asked about university life in the south, how the students lived, whether I thought they would be returning to Peking immediately, and then, because the conversation was running into generalities, I said something about the failure of the Spanish Republic in the civil war as it fought against the massed artillery of the Germans. I had been there. Once in the distance I had seen the guns. The Kuomintang possessed heavy artillery: could the Chinese Communists fight against such heavy weapons?

The softness of the face turned to darkness. Even in the blood-red light of the lamp (there were some chemicals in the

oil which turned the flame scarlet), he resembled a student, with
the gentleness of a student, but now the voice changed timbre,
and there was a kind of inflexible sadness in the gaunt features:
the lines had grown hard, and it was like a face of lead, as heavy
as lead. He said, "Spain is not China. There were only eight million people fighting against Franco, but the Chinese liberated
area numbers a population of one hundred and thirty million. The
Spanish Republic fought for three years. We have fought for
twenty-one years. But from the beginning up to now we have
desired peace and we do not want this war to be prolonged."

He went on: "There are some people abroad who are helping
the Kuomintang to fight with their offer of ammunition. These
supplies should be stopped, and the democratic people of other
countries should oppose the sending of ammunition to the Kuomintang. There are people abroad who do not want and do not
approve of democracy in this country. These people are acting
with the consonance of the reactionaries in China. Let them know
that whatever happens, if we are faced with mechanized war, we
shall fight on if necessary with our hands and feet." At that
moment he made a violent gesture, throwing out his clenched
hands and feet, scowling at the invisible enemies across the seas
who were responsible for the killing of his soldiers. Then he grew
very quiet and said, "Have you any criticisms?"

"About what?"

"About Yenan."

I said there were two. In all the government offices I had
seen there were maps of China, but no maps of the world; and
the Yenan radio was still behaving with an extraordinary violence,
the same kind of violence which had long ago betrayed the Kuomintang broadcasts from Nanking. "Why do you curse one another in a period of armistice?"

He said, "About the maps—we shall learn in time. Remember
we are learning all the time. About the radio—it is mostly for
internal consumption. Also, we have to scream at them because
they scream at us. They are entirely hateful. That's why we are
fighting. We can't have this endless corruption and the killing
of soldiers who have surrendered." The last accusation had been

made with great bitterness by Chu Teh. The Communists said
they captured as many prisoners as possible, for they could use
them; and there were sufficient reports that the Kuomintang
simply murdered prisoners out of hand. It was this which hurt
most.

I asked when there would be peace, for it was clear that the
armistice could only survive by a miracle.

"When the people rule," he answered. "The people who are
fighting against us don't want to realize democracy at all."

The duel became more intense later. "There seems," I said,
"to be one—and only one—solution for the problem of civil war."
This was that the leaders should retire from the scene. They were
encrusted with legends. Mao himself, Chu Teh, P'eng Teh-huai
had almost ceased to be human beings. They were regarded with
the awe generally reserved for gods. It was the same with Chiang
Kai-shek and his immediate entourage. "The best, surely, is a
government of the ordinary talents, without geniuses." I spoke
of how in ancient Greece as soon as politicians became too
popular they were exiled. Chu Teh had been responsive to the
argument, saying with a kind of peasant gravity, "Perhaps you are
right. If it would help China, and if legends are dangerous, I am
prepared to go." He had, I learned later, discussed the strange
suggestion with Mao by telephone. Now Mao answered quickly
and almost angrily, "I am no one. Why should I go? What can
one man do? If the Generalissimo died, it would make no difference: the rotten social system would go on." Being the poli-
tician he is, he could hardly have given any other answer.

It was the end of the road. The theory of "no one," which
lies deep in Chinese history, had him in its toils. He asked about
England, saying first (which pleased me) that he had read some
of her poets in translation. I said there was a social revolution in
England on a scale never achieved before, and it seemed to me
that Chinese communism and English socialism had something in
common: certainly the program announced in *The New Stage*
and *Coalition Government* did not differ widely from English
practice. The English were nationalizing their heavy industries,
and there were vast programs of social reform.

"Yes," he answered, "but they are taking over the heavy industries only because they can then put into operation a firmer export drive."

"Is that the only reason?"

"Of course. They are not truly socialist."

I insisted that they were, for the announced aim of the English Socialists was to share the wealth of the country more equitably—"the share-wealth party" is also the name of the Chinese Communists.

"If they are really socialists," he went on, "how do you explain their foreign policy? They are still imperialists. They will never let India free."

I said they would, sooner than he believed.

He looked incredulous, almost as though he were talking to an ignorant child, and changed the subject of conversation to pronunciation, asking how the word "India" was pronounced and repeating it several times. I had observed that he listened intently to the translator, but he also listened to my words, and he was evidently comparing them. He knew much more English than he was prepared to admit. He said, "There is one good thing about the English—they are not helping to extend the war in China. We shall remember that." He spoke fiercely against the French in Indochina and the Dutch in Indonesia, and all the time there was that heavy, moody look on his face, such a look as I had seen in Spain when General Modesto complained about the German guns. The rapeseed oil lamp was gutting, throwing up hard little sparks of silvery flame. He was looking tired. He was a man who threw his whole energy into conversation, unconscious of anything else, unconscious even of the soldier with the dispatch case who had come in some moments before. Now he read the dispatches quickly; then he said, "Have you any more questions to ask? I'm tired."

"One more. How long would it take for the Chinese Communists to conquer China if the armistice breaks down."

"A year and a half."

He said this very simply and slowly, but with absolute conviction. Occasionally he had used the word "correct," and it was clear that he regarded this judgment as a "correct" summary. Then he rose, standing like a great bear in the lamplight, and when making a handshake he lifted his elbow high, as though to avoid the impact of a Western handgrasp. I asked once more about the poems. He smiled, and said, "We shall see about them." I saw him wandering up the road, the heavy shoulders, the blue-black, glossy hair, a bowed figure whose shoulders seemed to be streaming with blood from the blood-red lamp of the soldier who walked behind him in the night.

I did not see him again until the day I flew back to Peking. The sky was gray. The whole of Yenan was a gray puddle, the rain falling in torrents. He came to the airfield, wearing a drab blue cotton coat, blue trousers, a woolen scarf tied around his throat, and a workman's cap on his head. He looked almost unrecognizable. He was hardly distinguishable from the peasants on the field. He said, "I have come to see you safely off." He laughed and joked.

I asked for the last time about the poems and told him I had found two more to add to the collection.

"That makes how many?"

"Three."

He laughed again, the rain coursing down his face. "How did you get them?"

"The editor of Liberation Daily gave them to me." The propeller was revolving. "No poems?"

"No more for a little while."

As the airplane streaked over the airfield in the pounding rain to rise above the dark pagoda and the river now flowing in torrents, Mao disappeared among the small knot of peasants on the field. Four hours later we were flying over the gold roofs of Peking.

The truce was still on. There was time to examine the poems, and put together whatever else could be learned about Mao and the arts.

THE POETRY OF MAO TSE-TUNG

WE UNDERSTAND men best through their poetry and their sensitivity to the arts; and of everything that Mao has written, nothing is more revealing than his poems and his attitude toward the developing culture of China.

Those who are close to him say that they can never remember a time when he did not write poetry. He wrote verses as a boy, and kept on writing poems throughout the revolutionary wars. At meetings of the soviet government in Yenan, he would write poems as other men wrote "doodles," and after the meeting was over there was always a rush to pick up the poems he had thrown haphazardly on the floor. What is curious about these poems is that they are written in the strict meters of classical Chinese prosody. There are no innovations, no experiments. His classical mind seems to recoil from the dangerous temptations of free verse. Publicly, he inveighs against all poetry which does not possess a social content and is not written according to the modern idiom. Privately, he is the master of a kind of classical verse which will probably remain, because it possesses qualities

229

free verse can never acquire, and because it is perfectly possible, as he had proved, to write classical poetry with modern feeling, in the same way that it is possible to write sonnets with modern feeling. Speaking in May 1942, he declared, "Our primary duty is, not 'to add flowers to the embroidery,' but 'to send coal to the snowbound.'" Art must be placed wholly at the service of the revolution; it can have no other purpose than to extol and educate the peasants and the workers. In effect, he was stating once again the necessity of socialist realism.

It is doubtful, however, whether Mao entirely believes that art is a state weapon and nothing more. Like hundreds of thousands of Chinese, he is known to admire the Ch'ing dynasty novel, *The Dream of the Red Chamber*, which describes the innumerable love affairs of a young aristocrat who eventually becomes a Buddhist monk—a book written with a superb delicacy and understanding of the movements of the human heart. Man is not wholly a political animal. In birth, childhood, marriage, and death he removes himself almost entirely from the political arena. Mao is half prepared to accept a divergence between art and politics, but he insists that there must be a synthesis between motive and effect, and the motive can only be political. There are even moments when he gives the impression of believing that all the art of China, except the songs of the peasants and the works of a few recent proletarian writers, are nothing more than bourgeois propaganda. It is a strange and probably untenable position, for his own poetry has been deeply influenced by a T'ang dynasty poet who celebrated the imperial splendors of a decadent court.

Ts'en Ts'an, one of the major poets of the reign of the Emperor Su Tsung, was born about A.D. 720 in the province of Ho-nei. He was the friend of the greatest of all Chinese poets, Tu Fu, who called him his "younger brother," and who accompanied him on many journeys. He climbed high in court circles, becoming censor and eventually governor of Chiachou. There was no evidence that he was ever a soldier, yet he described battles, usually battles which had occurred hundreds of years previously in the Han dynasty, with a remarkable sense of movement. He was one of the very rare Chinese poets who rejoiced in the poetry of war. The two poems which are his chief claim to fame are concerned with the pleasures of hunting down the enemy in winter. In these frozen, romantic landscapes, to the sound of the jingling of coats of mail, the poet is perfectly at home. Because Mao's furious imagination is also at home in them—he quotes from them often, and he echoes them in his own poems—they should be given here in full. The first describes a visit to a general commanding a frontier post near Kokonor. It was from this poem that Mao quoted to Edgar Snow the phrase about the trees of Peking resembling "ten thousand peach trees blossoming." The second describes the preparations for an advance by the same general against the Huns.

A POEM OF FAREWELL

The north wind sweeps over the land, twisting and breaking off
*   the hoary grass:*
The barbarian weather brings the fluttering snow of early August.
As though overnight a small wind came to make thousands of
*   peach trees blossom.*
These snowflakes slip through pearl curtains and wet the screens,
The fox fur no longer warm and the silk coverlet too thin,
Benumbed with cold, the general can hardly draw his hornbow.
But the border guards must still wear their freezing armor,
And icy pillars a thousand feet high pile on the northern ocean,
While overcast clouds hang curdled for ten thousand li.
Amid the booming of pipes and the squeaking of flutes,
The orderlies drink a toast in honor of the returning guest.
The evening snow whirls thick on the gates of the camp,
And the wind fails to move the frozen red flag.
Then, at the north gate of Lun-tai, I bade you farewell,
You who will go on the drifts of snow of Tien Shan.
I lost sight of you when you turned beyond the cliff,
Leaving only the footprints of your horse behind.

HORSEMEN OF THE GREAT SZECHUAN ROAD

Behold, the horsemen are galloping along the Szechuan road
*   beside the snow-white sea,*
Sand stretches like prairie grass, so vast, and the yellowness meets
*   the sky.*
Here at Lun-tai, in late autumn, the wind howls at night.

A riverbed of broken stones as large as kettledrums
Is thrown up by the wind, and everywhere the air is full of stones.
The Huns pasture their fat horses on the yellow grass.
Westward among the gold hills smoke and dust are flying.
The Han general collects his forces against the western enemy.
All night he has not removed his coat of mail.
All night the army marches, weapons touching,
The wind's muzzle is a knife slashing the sky.
The manes of the horses are icicles, strings of cash turned to ice,
Five-petal flowers among the smoke clouds of sweat.
In the tent the general dips his pen in ice.
Ah, if the Huns heard of it would not their courage fail?
We—we know that they have no love for our short swords.
We—we know that the army awaits tidings of victory.

Mao's own poetry reflects a similar excitement, a similar atmosphere, and similar assurance of victory. There is nothing ambiguous in the poetry of Ts'en Ts'an, and there is a complete absence of the self-pity which occasionally characterizes Tu Fu. It is poetry direct and swift as an icicle.

Of the collection of about seventy poems brought together in Yenan under the title Wind Sand Poems (Feng Chien Tze) very little is known except that it includes a long poem called "Grass," written in memory of the journey through the Grasslands, and a poem on his dead wife. Only a few copies of this book were made and given to his intimates.

While I was in Yenan, only three of Mao's poems were available. The first was written when the Long March was coming to an end.

LIUPENG MOUNTAIN
The sky is high, the clouds are winnowing,
I gaze southwards at the wild geese disappearing over the horizon.
I count on my fingers, a distance of twenty thousand li.
I say we are not heroes if we do not reach the Great Wall.
Standing on the highest peak of Six Mountains,
The red flag streaming in the west wind,
Today with a long rope in my hand,
I wonder how soon before we can bind up the monster.

Mao had been careful to explain that by "monster" he did not mean Chiang Kai-shek only. "I meant all the evils—the Japanese, the Kuomintang, the terrible social system." Nor should the red flag be taken to mean only the Communist flag, for here there is a deliberate confusion between the red flag and the red banner carried by the ancient Chinese generals. Mao delighted in such confusions in the same way that T'ang dynasty poets would deliberately write poems about the border warfare of their time, while pretending to be writing about wars a thousand years earlier.

The second poem appears to have been written in a mood of tranquil rejoicing some time after the Red Army was settled in Shensi.

THE LONG MARCH

No one in the Red Army fears the hardships of the Long March.
We looked lightly on the thousand peaks and the ten thousand rivers.
The Five Mountains rose and fell like rippling waves,
The Wu Meng mountains were no more than small green pebbles.
Warm were the sheer precipices when Gold Sand River dashed into them,
Gold were the iron-chained bridges over the Tatu River.
Delighting in the thousand snowy folds of the Min Mountains,
The last pass vanquished, the Three Armies smiled.

The geography of the Long March provides the necessary commentary on the names of the mountains and rivers in the poem; it is unnecessary to discuss them here. What is remarkable is the use of phrases like "the Three Armies"—the number of armies possessed by the Chou dynasty emperors, the traditional poetic name for the armies of the empire. In fact, at least four armies had taken part in the Long March. The third and fourth lines of the poem are almost contemptuously traditional. The poetic imagination, so carefully based on archaic sources, rises slowly, and it is only in the last four lines that we are made conscious of the poet's imaginative powers.

The significance of this poem lies in its desperate invocation

of the whole of the long epic march across China. Mao is talking
of great spaces and deliberately employing the corpus of Chinese
legends. They hover like enormous statues seen through the mists—
his poems seem nearer because the legends are farther away—
there is depth and a kind of permanence in the juxtaposition of the
legendary past and the present. Then, too, he uses numbers as the
mystics use them. By being mathematically inexact, the poem
acquires an emotional accuracy; the strict verse form gives it sub-
stance; rhyme is a prison, but the poet needs to imprison his imagination for fear that he will spill himself grotesquely through
all the countries of the mind. In Chinese, too, a phrase like "the
Red Army" has connotations which are completely absent in the
English. In Chinese, as in Russian, red is the adjective for spring,
courage, the beauty and health of adolescence, without any connotations of communism.*

In "The Snow," written in August 1945, while flying in an
airplane between Yenan and Chungking, at a time when there
seemed to be some hope that the Kuomintang and the Communists would form a truce, he wrote the most famous of all his
poems. It shows signs of having been written under the strain of
intense excitement. But Mao says he simply wrote the poem to
while away the time, and to give a present to a friend he had
not seen since 1927, who would be waiting at the airport. The
friend allowed a copy of the poem to pass into the hands of the
editor of Ta Kung Pao, and from that moment hundreds of

* Red is the proverbial color of joy in China. It is also the color which represents great dignity. The face of an emperor or a sacred personage is painted
red on the Chinese stage but so too is the face of the heroine. Red was the
imperial color of the Chou dynasty. It is also the color associated with sex;
the famous novel, The Dream of the Red Chamber, immediately suggests to
a Chinese by its title a dream of sexual devotions. Usually, death is denoted
by white, but the death of an old man who has many descendants is always
celebrated with red. Oddly enough, red sometimes signifies death. On the
Chinese stage death is denoted by a red flag or a red cloth thrown over the
face. The particular value attached to the name "the Red Army" by the
Chinese is something which should have been studied and elucidated. The
Kuomintang armies never had a name comparable to this; and though it was
Chiang Kai-shek who ordered that the Communist army be called the Eighth
Route Army, his own armies never acquired the peculiar luster which the
Communists succeeded in shedding over this name.

Chinese, particularly in the universities, came to feel a real respect for Mao as a poet. The poem attempts something which had rarely, if ever, been attempted before. With a full consciousness of the whole weight of Chinese history, and of his own position in it, Mao tried to write a poem which would embrace the whole of Chinese legend and Chinese history in a moment of time:

THE SNOW
In this north country in the flaming wind
A thousand acres are enclosed in ice,
And ten thousand acres in whirling snow.
Behold both sides of the Great Wall—
There is only a vast desolation left.
On the upper and lower reaches of the Yellow River
Only a great tumbling of waves.
The silver serpents are dancing on the mountains,
The winter elephants career on the plains:
We desire to compare our height with the skies.

O wait for the pure sky!
See how charming is the earth
Like a red-faced girl clothed in white!
Such is the charm of these mountains and rivers
Calling innumerable heroes to vie with each other in pursuing
*   her.*

The Emperors Shih Huang and Wu Ti were hardly lettered,
The Emperors T'ai Tsung and T'sai Tsu were barely chivalrous,
For a whole generation Genghis Khan was a favorite of Heaven,
But he knew only how to bend his bow at the eagles.
All have passed away—only today are there men of great feeling.

What is surprising is that the poem is almost a love poem addressed to the Chinese earth, and there is even a hint of sexuality in the description of the "red-faced girl clothed in white," for everything about the description is ambiguous, and the lines could be translated in many different ways. There is a further hint of sexuality in "the silver serpents dancing on the mountains," for the serpent has an obvious sexual meaning in Chinese, though here they may well be the mountains themselves or the smoke wreaths seen from the airplane. As often happens in Chinese poetry, there are varying depths of meaning yet these different meanings meet at a point of fusion, and the implication is clear— there is a compact with the past for the sake of a future inheritance, and a proud belief that the time has come when the Chinese will be masters of their own land. What is certain is that Mao deliberately attempted a poem which invokes the whole past history of his country, all its legends and all its landscapes, a poem comparable in its intensity with Hölderlin's "Patmos," where the whole of European history and legend is placed in the fire of poetry, seen through the flames and made to glow permanently in a moment of time. The poem is an astonishing achievement, for in the shortest number of words he produced the most complete picture of the Chinese scene, and the method was peculiarly his own; for the poet built up slowly the vivid portrait he desired to convey, and crowned it in the last line of all, and this method is something altogether new in Chinese poetry, which knows few climaxes comparable to these.

There are probably deep-seated reasons for his refusal to publish the romantically entitled *Wind Sand Poems*. He knows, as all Chinese poets do, how much of a man's character is revealed in his poetry. He has always been secretive, always a little apart, exalted above the crowd. His insistence that the modern artist must mingle with the crowd and derive his roots from the broad masses of the people is perhaps only a measure of his own conscious distance from people. Though he talks with everyone quietly and naturally, no one is ever for a moment forgetful of that distance which always arises between those who have never wielded authority and those who wield it daily.

Those who were interested in discovering the springs of Mao's character gradually accustomed themselves to the thought that no more of his poems would be printed in his lifetime. He had stated publicly that he regarded all experiments in the ancient Chinese verse forms as doomed to failure; he had given his benediction to the new forms; and he seemed in no mood to permit the publication of his occasional verses. Quite suddenly, in January 1957, he relented to the extent of permitting eighteen of his poems to be published in the magazine, Poetry, edited by his friend Tsang Keh-chia, and a year later one more poem appeared in the same magazine. The first group of poems included the three I have already quoted. Many of the poems consist of short verses written during the Long March, but the collection includes three new poems of quite extraordinary power: "Changsha," which is full of memories of his schooldays, "Kunlung Mountain," a lyrical fragment conveying a benevolent salute to Europe and America, and "Swimming," written after he had accomplished his long-cherished ambition of swimming the Yangtse river.

Mao seems to have sent these poems to the editor of Poetry with some misgivings. In an introductory note he warned against any attempt to overvalue the poems and in the typical Chinese style he begged the editor to correct their faults:

> I have always been reluctant to have these poems published formally, because they represent an antique style, and I am afraid they might mislead the younger generation. Also, there is a lack of sufficiently poetical flavor, and they are altogether ordinary. But since you believe they are worthy of publication, and you have offered to correct the faults of these old pieces, I will do as you wish.
>
> Poetry is an excellent magazine. I hope it will grow and prosper. Poems should, of course, be principally written in the new forms. It does no harm to write a little in the old style, as long as it is not set as an example for the young. This ancient style puts fences around the imagination, and it is not easy to learn. All my remarks are offered only as advice.

The mood of most of these new poems is quietly meditative. Occasionally, as in the poems written during the civil war, he strikes a note of defiance at the enemy. In "Changsha" he lashes out at the ancient feudal rulers in a line which translated literally reads: *Dung ancient days ten thousand household lords*. As always in his verses he writes with full command of the precise, graphic quality of the Chinese language, which permits the poet to emphasize the vivid appearances of things. The fourth line of "The Pavilion of the Yellow Crane" reads in a literal translation: *Snake tortoise grip great river*. He is speaking about high and strangely shaped rocks, and to the Chinese imagination such shorthand effects are almost commonplace, for their romanticism belongs to the Chinese landscape.

Indeed, the most remarkable thing about these poems is their romantic feeling. When Mao says, "Could I but lean on Heaven and draw my precious sword . . . ," he is speaking in the style of the ancient heroes, perfectly aware that he is borrowing from a culture and a way of thought which is remote from the present time. That solid heaven, made of glittering blue rock, exists in the imaginations of nearly all Chinese poets, who are often tempted to compare themselves with legendary mountains or lakes lost in far wildernesses. There are echoes of Taoist belief in the gods and goddesses who preside over his poems. What is new is the essential toughness behind the romantic imagery. The swords are real swords, the black dragons are seen in their modern context, and the spirits of the hills—those commonplaces of ancient Chinese poetry—are suddenly confronted in "Swimming" with the modern hydro-electric plants, huge dams, and engineering works on the banks of the Yangtse. Mao makes no attempt to hide his affection for the ancient legends.

Here are translations of all the new poems which were published in *Poetry*. They are placed in chronological order.

CHANGSHA

Standing alone in the chill autumn,
The Hsiang river flowing northward,
On the shores of Orange Island,
I see the ten thousand hills all crimson
And the forests all stained with red.

The immense river is a transparent green,
And a hundred boats are racing by.
The eagles strike against the sky,
The fish swim in the shallows;
In the freezing air all creatures strive for freedom.

Alone in the desolate vastness,
I ask of the ageless earth:

"Who is the ruler of the universe?"
I remember a hundred friends coming here
During the crowded, eventful years:
All of them young and upright,
Gleaming with brilliance,
True to the scholar's spirit.

I remember how vivid they were
As they gazed upon rivers and mountains:
The Chinese earth gave strength to their words,
And they regarded as dung the ancient feudal lords.

Do you remember
How in midstream we struck out at the water,
And the waves dashed against the speeding ships?

THE PAVILION OF THE YELLOW CRANE

Nine immense rivers flow through China,
A single deepcut railroad threads north and south.
Blue smoke and rain shroud the heavens:
Stones, snakes and tortoises grip the great river.

Where have the yellow cranes flown?
Only the haunts of the wayfarers remain.
I lift my winecup and drink to the roaring river.
My heart is as full as the rising waters.

CHINKAN MOUNTAIN*

The hills below are thick with banners.
On the hilltops drums and bugles sound.
Ringed round by a thousand of the enemy,
We are standfast and do not move.

Already we have built a strong bulwark:
The will of the people will build a fortress.
From Huangyangchieh† comes the thunder of guns,
And the enemy fled during the night.

---

* Chinkan Mountain lies on the border of Kiangsi and Fukien.
† At Huangyangchieh, at the foot of the mountain, the Red Army trapped
a Kuomintang force in 1928.

NEW YEAR'S DAY

Ninghua! Chingliu! Kueihua!*

The narrow pathways, the deep woods, the moss slippery.

Where shall we go today?
Straight to the foot of the Wuyi mountains,
To the mountains, the foot of the mountains.
The red banners will unfurl like a scroll!

HUICHANG†

The dawn is beginning to break.
Do not say we are marching early.
Wandering over these green hills, we have not grown old.
The landscape is good for the eyes.

Outside Huichang the high mountains rise,
Range after range stretching to the eastern ocean.
Our soldiers look south toward Kwangtung.
So green, so fertile, and so far away!

TAPOTEH‡

Red, orange, yellow, green, blue, indigo, violet.
Who in the sky is dancing, waving this ribbon of color?
After the rain the setting sun returns,
Line after line, the hills and the pass are blue!

Once there raged a desperate battle here,
And the village walls were pierced with bullet-holes.
They are a decoration, and today
The hills shine more splendidly.

THE LOUSHAN PASS^a

Cold is the west wind!
The wild geese cry in the frosty morning moonlight.
O the frosty morning moonlight!
The ringing of the horses' hooves.
And the sobbing of trumpets!

* The names of three counties in Fukien province.
† A town in Kiangsi where the Red Army set up a revolutionary base.
‡ A district near Juichin within the Kiangsi revolutionary base.
^a A pass in Kweichow, which the Red Army crossed in January 1935.

Do not say the Pass is guarded with iron.
Today we shall leap over the summit.
O we shall go leaping!
The dark green mountains are like the sea,
And the dying sun like blood.

THREE SHORT POEMS
Mountains!
No whips, speeding horses, no way to alight.
I turn in astonishment
And see the heavens four feet away.*

Above the Bare Skull mountains,
Below Eight Precious Hills,
Heaven is three foot three inches away.
Men on foot must bow their heads,
And horsemen must alight from their saddles.

Mountains!
Seas boiling and heaving, waves tumbling.
We march as furiously
As ten thousand horses plunging into battle!

Mountains!
They pierce the blue heavens, the peaks unbent.
Should the heavens fall,
We shall build pillars for the sky.

KUNLUNG MOUNTAINS†
Rising straight into the air above the earth,
Lofty Kunlung, mistress of the world's joys.
The three million jade dragons are soaring.‡

---

* More accurately: "three feet three inches." Mao quotes from a folk song in a northern dialect.
† The Kunlung mountains are the abode of the blessed, believed to be some-where in Tibet.
‡ Mao adds a note to explain the three million jade dragons: "There is an old saying: 'Three milion jade dragons are fighting, their broken scales flying all over the sky.' Originally this referred to flying snow, but I have used it here to describe the snowy mountains. One summer, when I was standing on the Min mountains, I saw them arranged as though they were dancing, shining with a dazzling whiteness. There was a saying among the people that the Monkey King passed by, and that was why they were all on fire. Then

All the heavens are transpierced with frost.
Snow melting in summer,
And the rivers brimming over.
Men may become fishes and tortoises.
Who will judge us over a thousand autumns?
Who will confer punishments and favors?

I say to the high mountains:
"Why so high? Why so much snow?"
Could I but lean on heaven and draw my precious sword,
And cut you in three pieces,
I would send one to Europe,
The second I would give to America,
The third I would keep for China.
So there would be a great peace on earth,
For all the world would share in your warmth and cold.

A POEM FOR LIU YA-TZU*
Remembering when we sipped tea by the Kwangtung lake,
And again when we exchanged verses at Chungking, the leaves
    yellowing,
After thirty-one years I return to my home,
And read your wonderful verses at the season of falling flowers.
Take care not to grieve too much.
Gaze with a broad view at the world around you.
Do not say the Kunming Lake† is shallow.

The waters here are better for fishing than the Fuchung river.[a]

---

with his palm-leaf fan he quenched the flames, and the mountains turned
white." The Monkey King is the chief character of the novel Hsi Yu Chi,
or The Journey to the West.
* Liu Ya-tzu was an old friend who hesitated to come to Peking when the
Communists took power.
** The Kunming Lake is in the Summer Palace in Peking.
*** A river near Hangchow in Chekiang province. The reference is to Yen
Kuan who during the Later Han dynasty preferred fishing in the Fuchung
river to attending the Emperor at the capital.

ANOTHER POEM FOR LIU YA-TZU*

Long was the night, slow the coming of the red dawn.
For a hundred years the devil-monsters whirled in a dance,
And there was no coming together of the myriad people.
Now the cock crows, dawn breaks over the world,
And from a thousand places arises a swelling music.
Never were poets so inspired!

PEITAHO†

The heavy rains fall over the northern land,
The white breakers leap to the sky.
Of the fishing-boats from Chinwantao
None can be seen on the ocean.
Where have they gone?

For over a thousand years
The Emperor Wu of Wei flicked his whip.
Only The Tung Lin Mountain Stone remains.‡
Now though the autumn winds blow mournfully,
All the world is changed!

SWIMMING^a

Barely have I drunk the waters of Changsha,
Now I am eating fish in Wuchang.
I swim across the great Yangtse river,
And see the sky of Chu unfolding before me.
I care not whether the wind blows or rain falls.
This is better than idly strolling in a courtyard.
Today I am free!
Confucius stood by the water, saying:
"All Nature is flowing away."

---

* Mao added a note: "While we were watching performances during the
national celebrations in 1950, Mr. Liu Ya-tzu composed an impromptu poem
to the melody Wan Hsi Sha, and I replied with another poem employing the
same rhyme scheme."
† A seaside resort near Chinwantao, in Hopei province.
‡ The Tung Lin Mountain Stone was a ballad sung in commemoration of
the Emperor Wu of Wei (222–256 A.D.).
a Written in May 1956, after swimming across the Yangtse River from
Wuchang to Hankow.

The masts are swaying,
The Tortoise and the Snake are silent.
Great achievements rise before my eyes.
A bridge will join north and south,
Making a pathway over sky and waters.

To the west we shall build stone walls
To hold back Wushan's clouds and rain.
And the narrow gorges will form a smooth lake.
The mountain goddess, if she is still there,
Will see the world all changed.

THE IMMORTALS
A POEM FOR MADAME LI SHU-YI
I lost my proud poplar, you lost your willow.
Poplar and willow soar high into the heavens.
Wu Kang, asked what he has to offer,
Presents them with the wine of cassia.

The lonely goddess of the moon spreads her sleeves,
And dances for these happy souls in an endless sky.
Of a sudden comes word of the Tiger's defeat,
And they break into a flood of tears.*

This poem, written in 1957 and published in *Poetry* in January 1958, is perhaps the most profoundly personal of all Mao's poems, for it commemorates the death of his wife at the hands of the Hunanese warlord Ho Chien as much as it commemorates the husband of Madam Li Shu-yi, who was killed during the early years of fighting with the Kuomintang. Mao employs all the resources of Chinese mythology to paint the blessed abode of the dead, and the last lines refer to the tears of joy shed by them at the news that the enemy had been vanquished. Yet the poem has a brittle beauty. One could imagine an exactly similar poem writ-

* The poem properly demands a commentary much longer than the poem itself. The maiden name of Mao's wife was Yang Kai-hui—yang means "poplar." Madame Li's husband's name was Liu Chih-hsun—liu means "willow." According to the legend Wu Kang was a prisoner of the moon, condemned to cut down the cassia tree. Every time he raised the ax the tree became whole again. Chang O, who stole the elixir of immortality, became the moon's lonely goddess.

ten by a Chinese poet two thousand years ago. What is astonishing is that Mao should have written a poem so saturated with mythology. It is as though he felt that to express great grief no other images were appropriate.

Mao's poems express the quality of the man—romantic, fiercely proud, learned in ancient mythologies, happy to feel the wind and sun on his face, in love with life. Many of the verses end with a quick stab of anger, a sudden explosion of hate. There is no feeling for ordinary people. He sees armies on the march, endless journeys, dawns and sunsets. The forces of nature occupy the foreground, and he is continually measuring himself against them. The poems would be almost inhuman if it were not that we are made aware of a powerful, stocky, supremely intelligent man hurling himself into storms and tempests with a superb abandon.

Mao is intensely aware that his poetry breaks all the canons of Communist poetry. He has never written poems about "the broad masses of the people," while constantly demanding such poems from Chinese poets. In his speeches on art and literature he is always urging the necessity of writing for the masses, and for the masses alone. For years he fed his spirit on the romantic novels, The Dream of the Red Chamber and All Men Are Brothers, but he demands that the Chinese novelists write stories about co-operatives and communes. Fadeyev's The Nineteen was held up as a universal model. It is a novel concerning a small band of anonymous guerrillas; there are no persons.

Though he has had an enormous influence on the developing culture of China, there are odd gaps in Mao's understanding of the arts. He is insensitive to music, and showed little interest in the amazing sculptures to be found in the neighborhood of Yenan. There were hundreds of beautiful stone Buddhas in the cave-temples. He allowed them to melt away in the steam from the printing presses installed in the caves, though it would have been a simple matter to direct the steam outside. Passionately excited by China's past glory, he thought of this glory in terms of poetry, history, philosophy, and the four or five great novels which are among the major glories of Chinese culture. Sculpture and painting are largely outside the range of his sensitivity.

Mao's public views on art conform to the strict Communist pattern. The only art which can be tolerated is that which actively supports the Communist revolution. His attitude toward art was expressed in a lecture delivered in Yenan in 1942:

> The love that we writers and artists with our intellectual background bear for the proletariat stems from the fact that society has forced on us the same destiny it has forced on the proletariat. Nowhere in the world does love exist without reason nor does hate exist without reason. As for love of mankind, there has been no such all-embracing love since the human race was divided into classes. The ruling classes have preached universal love, as did Tolstoy. But no one has ever been able to practice it because it cannot be attained in a class society.
>
> A true love of mankind is attainable, but only in the future when class distinctions will have been eliminated throughout the world. Classes serve to divide society: when classes have been eliminated, society will be united again. At that time the love of mankind will flourish, but it cannot flourish now. Today we cannot love the Fascists nor can we love our enemies. We cannot love all that is evil and ugly in the world. We must aim to eliminate them.*

According to this view all literature must be made to serve the class struggle, and there can be no place for poetry or novels which exalt the individual. Literature must be a hammer to split the head of the bourgeoisie wide open. In this pitiless view of art there is no place for romantic fiction like *The Dream of the Red Chamber*. Also there is very little place for the romantic poetry of Mao Tse-tung.

No one would claim for Mao's poems that they are among the best produced in modern China. For himself he claims only that he writes as best he can, attempting to fuse a modern spirit into an ancient and difficult idiom, in the twilight between a

---

* Mao Tse-tung, *Problems of Art and Literature* (New York: International Publishers, 1950), pp. 39–40.

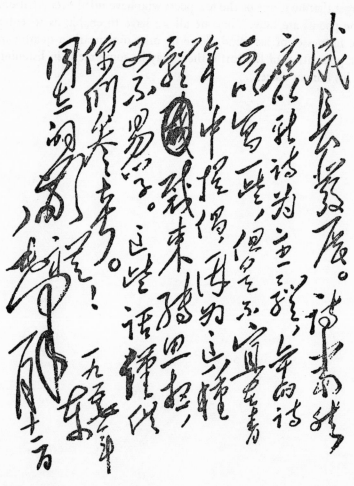

Closing page of a letter from Mao Tse-tung to the editor of Poetry. His signature appears at lower left.

dead culture and another still unborn. We see a brilliant, romantic, and penetrating mind at work, steeped in the past and fiercely aware of the present, and as we read the poems we may easily forget that he is one of the few poets who have ruled over a nation. The poems are here. They are all we have to enable us to enter the fastnesses of his mind. Since he rules over nearly a quarter of the population of the earth, there may be some merit in listening to his human voice.

THE CONQUEST OF CHINA

WHEN THE JAPANESE war with China was coming to an end in 1945, Generalissimo Chiang Kai-shek delivered a broadcast speech to the nation in which he made extraordinary claims for the party he represented. "The Kuomintang," he said, "is the historical party of national revolution. It overthrew the Manchu dynasty. It destroyed Yuan Shih-kai, who wanted to be emperor. It utterly defeated the militarists who followed Yuan Shih-kai. It brought about national unification. It achieved the removal of the unequal treaties. It led the country in the eight-year-old struggle with the Japanese. Finally, it is the party of liberation and progress."

If any one of these statements had been entirely correct, it is probable that the Kuomintang would have retained its power. Unfortunately, none of them was correct. The Kuomintang did not overthrow the Manchus, or Yuan Shih-kai, or the militarists who followed. All these had been overthrown by popular movements which the Kuomintang had followed rather than led. The removal of the unequal treaties was a bribe offered by Great

249

Britain and America to keep the Kuomintang from making a separate peace with Japan. Nor had the Kuomintang led the nation throughout its eight-year-old war with Japan, for after the third battle of Changsha, early in 1942, the Kuomintang completely failed to resist the enemy. As war progressed it had become so reactionary and corrupt that any talk of liberation and progress was merely ironical. By the end of the war the Kuomintang was an overripe fruit on a tree, waiting to be plucked by the Communists.

Chiang Kai-shek's speech, delivered on a sweltering August day in Chungking, shortly before victory was announced, was more interesting for its omissions than for its claims. It is noteworthy that most of the claims related to military successes. He did not claim that he had freed the peasants from excessive taxation or improved their social welfare, and he made no reference to the perplexing increase in the number of the Chinese Communists. He had decided long before the end of the war to press on with his war against the Communists, and in an incautious moment he had addressed his generals to the effect that "now at last the time has come to destroy the Communists root and branch." He had hoped to accomplish the conquest of China by the end of 1946. If he had read the minutes of the Seventh Congress of the Chinese Communist party held in April 1945, the first since 1928 to be held on Chinese soil, he might have paused. In 1937 there were two million people in an area of thirty thousand square miles living under Communist rule. In 1945 there were ninety-five million people in an area of three hundred thousand square miles.

Chiang Kai-shek did not pause. There were reconnaissance flights over Yenan by Kuomintang planes even during the June truce. In the first week of July, Yenan was raided in earnest by six P-47's and a B-24 Liberator. It was a month of grim fighting. During the truce the armies had been held to their fixed positions; now, like huge shadows racing across a sunlit landscape, they met and grappled, flung themselves upon one another in Manchuria, Kiangsu, and Anhwei, and General Marshall in despair could say, "We have done our best. There is almost nothing left that can be done." Now, as in 1919, when the Chinese students rose against the Treaty of Versailles, most of the blame was laid at the door of the Americans. Their popularity had once been great; now, when their popularity was in decline, they failed to take any remedial measures. Something was lacking, some fatal flaw was at work. Perhaps the reasons were not far to seek. It was simply that America had failed to assume its historical task, had failed to lead the Asiatic revolt. Too many of the soldiers and officers sent to China were ignorant of social forces. Coming from an artificial, complex, and industrial civilization, they had little but contempt for the slow-moving Chinese peasants, and they could not understand how these same peasants in battle captured so much American equipment. July was a month of horror. Slowly, dramatically, it announced the opening of an Attic tragedy.

All through his active life Chiang Kai-shek had been concerned to safeguard his rear. While the fighting between the Communist and Kuomintang armies continued, he struck out against the liberal elements in the country. Within a few days of each other Li Kung-po and Wen Yi-tuo were killed. Li Kung-po had been one of the famous "Seven Gentlemen" who stood out against Japanese demands in Shanghai in 1936, and had been imprisoned for his pains. Wen Yi-tuo, a professor of classics at Lienta University in Kunming, a poet and a born leader, had been elected to the Consultative Assembly which was to be held in Nanking in August. Others, like Kuo Mo-jo, had been attacked shortly before. Once again there was the promise of a reign of terror. When the Communists suggested that the only solution was the withdrawal by both sides to the lines held in January, Chiang Kai-shek answered with the oft-repeated claim that he was determined to smash the Communists within five months. The war was gathering momentum, and by January 1947 both Mao and Chiang Kai-shek declared that there was no hope of further mediation; the war must be fought out to a solution.

The solution came much sooner than anyone had expected. From Nanking came orders that Yenan must be occupied. It was thought that the occupation of the Communist capital would demonstrate Kuomintang power to lay the Communist ghost. In fact, the ghost was never more alive. Yenan was occupied. Mao and Chu Teh simply saddled their ponies and wandered toward the Great Wall, to find a harbor later in the obscure railway center of Shihchiachuang. At the end of June the Red Army crossed the Yellow River, and in September new Communist laws concerning agrarian policy were passed. They had been written by Mao. Deliberately, as in his speech of December 15, 1944, he restated Communist policy toward the rich peasants. There was to be no feverish expropriation. "The peasant unions shall expropriate surplus animals, agricultural implements, houses, grain, and other property of the rich peasants. These shall be distributed to the peasants who are lacking and to other poor people, and *furthermore an equal share shall be distributed to the landlords.*" It was a policy long hammered out in Yenan, and it was to remain when the Communists had achieved power. Meanwhile, the Kuomintang wall was crumbling as though it was made of soft sand. By December, Mao could say, "Comrades, the turning point has come."

It had come, indeed. No power on earth could now stop the flood. There was hardly any need to direct the war. Manchuria, once occupied by the Russians—who had played a devious game of removing industries existing there to Siberia while assisting the Chinese Communists by giving them captured Japanese rifles and machine guns—had become an arsenal; and Lin Piao's victories had become examples to be taught in textbooks.

Once again, for the third time, Mao retired almost completely from the military direction of the Red armies. He was concerned with the political atmosphere, with a thousand problems of agrarian reform. At the Seventh Congress he had said: "Those comrades who have made mistakes, no matter how devious, grievous, and costly, if they admit their mistakes honestly and if they have analyzed their mistakes and learned from them, are better leaders than men who are untried." He was in a mood to forgive. The agrarian reforms were meeting unexpected obstacles. Minor cadres exceeded their powers. They had to be corrected, taught humility toward the people, shown that the revolution could only succeed, the armies could only make headway if there was cooperation between the Red Army and the peasants. Again and again through his speeches of this year there are these simple, almost childlike warnings against pride, against exceeding "the proper attitude toward the peasants, which should always be one of brotherhood."

Yenan was recaptured a year after the Kuomintang drove down the empty valley. By June 1948 Mao was claiming that during the second year of the Liberation War—it had begun, according to the Communists, in July 1946—they had annihilated 1,520,000 Kuomintang troops and enlarged the liberated areas to nearly a quarter of the total area of China.

A People's Assembly was convened in Shihchiachuang. Once again, as previously in April, Mao was more concerned with the agrarian revolution than with the inevitable progress of the war. He had said in April:

> We spend altogether too much time in seeking out the hidden wealth of the landlords. No, comrades, this is not the way. In this the masses are wrong. All the correct opinions of the masses we must carry out loyally, but sometimes they are incorrect. You must understand that some of the middle peasants must be allowed to obtain more land than the average of the poor peasants generally. We do not advocate absolute egalitarianism. Our aim is only to destroy feudal exploitation, and we must place special attention on the middle peasants, we must allow them to work freely. The whole area where agrarian reform is possible cannot exceed eight per cent of the rural communities, or ten per cent of the rural population. In the old and in the semiliberated areas this figure may be reduced even further. We must remember, comrades, that the development of agricultural production is also the most important aim of the agrarian revolution, and as long as the middle peasants, the independent laborers, the professional men, and the peasants who have newly acquired riches do not engage in exploitation, or engage only slightly in exploitation, then they must be allowed their freedom.

Much had happened since the Autumn Harvest Uprising in 1927. Squarely, Mao placed himself on the side of the middle peasants against the rest.

But a new enemy was taking the place of the Kuomintang. Mao's armies fought with captured American equipment. Huge spoils had been gathered, but bitterness remained. He thundered against what he called American imperialism, and he saw no excuse for the American blunder in supporting the one party in China which opposed revolution. On November 7, 1948, he placed American imperialism before the Kuomintang as the main enemy of the Chinese Communists. He said, "The particular task of the Chinese Communists is to unite all revolutionary forces within the whole country, to drive out American imperialism, overthrow the reactionary rule of the Kuomintang, and establish a unified democratic people's republic in alliance with the Soviet Union."

Now, as winter came on and the Red armies came in sight of Peking and fought into the outskirts of Changchun, the whole theory upon which Chinese Communism reposed was due for change. Soon they would occupy immense cities. The order went out for an entirely new orientation, a shift from a rural, agrarian revolution to an urban, industrial revolution. "The war of resistance is really a peasant war," Mao had said in 1942. Now he said, "We have it in our hands to use all the resources of industry."

There occurred in 1949 a repetition of the revolution of 1911, when thousands of Manchus simply surrendered to the revolutionary armies without putting up a fight. This time it was the Kuomintang generals, long displeased with Chiang Kai-shek's organization of the war, who for the most part went over and calmly accepted the new dispensation. There was, however, one essential difference between the Manchus and the Kuomintang generals. The Manchus had possessed only cumbrous nineteenth-century weapons. The Kuomintang generals possessed the most modern equipment from America, and the spoils which the Chinese Communists had been waiting for were vastly more powerful than they had ever dared to hope.

During 1949, the Kuomintang lost its initiative beyond recovery. No one any longer believed in the star of Chiang Kai-shek. The dynamic which had brought the Kuomintang to power in the Northern March of 1927 had at last perished. Without loyal soldiers, without a strategy of defense, without will power, and without any sustaining belief in its own mission, it was slowly dying. A peripatetic government remained, continuing to exist like the branches of a fallen oak which put forth shreds of green without knowing that the tree is dead. The tree was hollow and diseased, and few people in China could regret its passing.

The astonishing victories of 1949 were not wholly or essentially due to the brilliant military strategy of the Communists. Chiang Kai-shek defeated himself. His battle plans were unrealistic, and like Hitler he was disposed to order that towns should be held "to the last man," regardless of what the military situation demanded. As usual, he paid little attention to his foreign military advisers. He conceived an immense plan of defense in depth, and it was characteristic of him that he should resurrect the same strategy of retreat he had employed against the Japanese. He even thought he could hold his line indefinitely beyond the Ichang gorges, basing his command once again in Chungking. He never knew which way the wind would turn, and desperately attempted to retrieve a situation already lost.

One by one the provincial capitals fell. In the middle of January, Tientsin fell, to be followed a fortnight later, after prolonged negotiations, by Peking. Nanking fell on April 23. On the next day, five hundred miles away, fell Taiyuan, the capital of Shansi province. Hangchow fell a week later, to be followed in a few days by Hankow, Wuchang, and Hanyang, the three conjoined cities which had seen the birth of the 1911 revolution. Sian, the capital of Shensi, fell almost immediately afterward. The breathless pace continued. In five days toward the end of May, Nanchang, which had seen the birth of the Red Army, and Shanghai, which had been the greatest industrial center of the whole of China, surrendered with only token fighting.

After the fall of Tsingtao, early in June, Chiang Kai-shek began to regroup his forces, and there were signs that he intended to launch a counteroffensive, but the desultory fighting in the summer ended only with retreats, which the Generalissimo excused on the ground that he was once more buying time in exchange for space. In August, Fukien was overrun, and Lanchow, the capital of Kansu, at the other extremity of China, fell a few days after the capture of Fuchow. Sinkiang province surrendered in September, while most of Kwangtung, including Canton, was

in the hands of the Communists by October. Kweiyang, the
capital of Kweichow, and Kweilin, the capital of Kwangsi, fell in
November, and on the last day of the same month fell the provisional capital, Chungking, though Chengtu was not to fall for
nearly a month. Yunnan, Sikang, and Szechuan followed.

The series of uninterrupted victories reads like a Napoleonic
battle roll. The "soft underbelly" of south China split open, and
generals who had sworn to die in defense of the Kuomintang saved
their lives by leading their own troops to join the Red Army.
Cheng Ch'en and Chen Ming-jen, who had fought against the
Red Army in the annihilation campaigns, offered to lead their
forces against Chiang Kai-shek. The redoubtable Ma Hung-kuei,
whom they had fought in the northwest, rode up to a Red outpost
and surrendered almost as though he were making a journey to
his private hunting fields and desired to be accompanied by his
new-found friends. General Lu Han, the Lolo tribesman who had
shared the rule over Yunnan with his half-brother for twenty
years, surrendered almost as casually.

Almost alone the Kwangsi generals, who had possessed vast
preserves in central China, fought on stubbornly. Once again
Mao had contrived that the initial battle should be the most
damaging. The battle of Huaihai, fought early in January, provided the breakthrough; the destruction of General Pai Hsiung-
hsi's forces in the middle of December by the New Fourth Army
brought the campaign for the conquest of China to a virtual conclusion. At the beginning the Red Army was outnumbered five
to one. For a brief while it fought large-scale guerrilla campaigns,
but after the crossing of the Yangtse positional warfare was engaged in continually. It was not always necessary. A column of
a hundred men entered Chungking and announced that it was
in their hands at the same moment that the rear of the Kuomintang army left the city on its way to Chengtu. It was exactly as
though the annihilation campaigns were being waged in reverse,
not over the frontiers of Kiangsi and Kwangtung, but over the
whole map of China.

Why had the victory come about? The Communists pointed
with pride to their army and to the students who volunteered to

do political work in the rear, to the twenty-year-old traditions of Communism and to the military genius of Mao Tse-tung.

It is conceivable that the reasons were much simpler. The destinies of nations are not determined by military forces; they are determined by those undefined psychological forces which we know as legends: and now quite suddenly there arose the legend of Mao Tse-tung, the savior of China. "Do not suppose that Mao Tse-tung could be the 'savior' of China." wrote Edgar Snow shortly after his first meeting. "Nonsense. There will never be any one 'savior' of China." Edgar Snow's remark was perfectly understandable, and based on wide experience of the Chinese scene, but by 1949 it had lost its relevance. Suddenly there were portraits of Mao everywhere, even deep within Kuomintang territory. Sometimes the portrait stood together with a similar one of Chu Teh, but generally it stood alone. Soldiers went into battle with paintings of Mao on their red flags. Trains were provided with paintings of Mao thrown over the boilers like saddlecloths. In Shanghai there were portraits five stories high. Not all of them were prepared by the propaganda corps. They answered a psychological need of the people. Mao was shown with his head uplifted toward the rising sun, youthful and smiling. There had never been portraits of Chiang Kai-shek like this. Hitler scowled and accused from a million German walls; Chiang Kai-shek glared frostily; Stalin looked stern and demanding; only the portraits of Mao suggested a twenty-year-old youth awakening from a long dream, the new man, the savior.

In 1927 the playwright Tsao Yu produced a drama called Peking Man. It described the life of a decadent mandarin family caught up in interminable delicate quarrels in Peking. Suddenly, bursting through the window, there comes the terrible, avenging image of the original owner of the Peking skull, a triumphant youth who is not in the least concerned with the problems of a declining mandarinate. He seizes the young daughter of the mandarin and disappears with her into the hills. The play, later banned by Chiang Kai-shek, achieved considerable success. It spoke of the new youthful China which had suffered sufficiently under the rule of senile warlords, and possessed an unappeased desire to escape from the ancient traditions. So it was now. With the arrival of Mao, there occurred an almost religious fervor, a recognition of religious resources, even a new religious ritual. The Communists had long employed the phrase *Fang Shen*, which occurs in Mencius and has the meaning of "renewing the body," though it meant more than this, for it included in its meaning a complete transvaluation, a total renewal of all the resurgent forces in China. Chiang Kai-shek had merely paid lip service to the idea of renewal; the Communists deliberately assumed new attitudes, deliberately invented new rituals, refused to make any compromise with the past, and turned their heads defiantly against the most sacrosanct customs. To misunderstand these psychological resources is to misunderstand the whole course of the Chinese revolution.

With the portraits of Mao as savior, there came the songs where he was openly greeted as "the savior." The most celebrated, sung to a lilting dance tune, begins with a line modeled on one of the most famous lines of the Confucian *Book of Songs*:

Tung fang hung t'ai-yang sheng.
Chung-kuo ch'u-lai i-go Mao Tse-tung.

The sun is rising red in the East.
China has brought forth a Mao Tse-tung.
He labors for the welfare of the people.
Aiyayo, he is the people's great savior.

The Communist party shines like the sun,
And wherever it shines there is light,
Wherever there is the Communist party,
Aiyayo, there the people have freedom.

Mao Tse-tung has a great love for the people:
He is the man who guides us along the pathway.
With him, we shall build a new China.
Aiyayo, he leads the people into the future.

Mao Tse-tung is a son of the Chinese earth:
He will lead us to fight the enemy.
There will come a time when we shall have mastery.
Aiyayo, all our enemies shall be beaten.

There were endless verses to this song. Every town or village added its quota of new lines. It was as though Mao was a living presence in places where he had never been, and which he may never have heard of. A wild and dangerous faith had been born: all problems could be solved by Mao. He would have been the first to reject such a claim, but the claim was seriously made by hundreds of thousands of people who saw in him "the people's savior." Such a faith may have conceivably been ill founded, but of its existence there is no doubt. Devotion had become as real as the air men breathed. In another song, nearly as popular as the one already quoted, he becomes the "victorious flag":

> O, you are the bright sun and the flag of victory,
> Long live our highly thought-of Mao Tse-tung.
> We are happy to live in your age and learn from your example.
> We will follow you and enter a new world,
> Where there will be liberty and welfare for all.

Not only the songs but the names he received among the peasants reveal the peculiar quality of veneration in which he was held. Chiang Kai-shek was called Ling Hsiu, "the leader." Mao was called Chiu Hsing, "the saving star," a title which places him immediately among the legends, for three guardian stars protect the peasants from their high vantage point near the roof beams. It was out of such things, legends, the peasants' desire to own his land, "the broad masses of the people"—that phrase which was interminably repeated, acquiring an extraordinary resonance and depth of meaning—that Mao brought about the revolution.

It is important that the logic of the revolutionary process be understood. The tragic failure of the Kuomintang lay in the absence of any point of contact with the people. Like Henry Luce, who demanded that millions of dollars, hundreds of thousands of guns, and thousands of war planes be sent to China to aid the Kuomintang, the Kuomintang itself had come to live among shadows, where huge figures, fantastic dreams of power, took the place of actual power. The momentous figures became the reality, before which the people paled into insignificance.

Mao did not forget the people. He based his strength upon the thousands of social groups in China, and he saw, very early in his career, that power in the modern world is not waged by guns, but by the agreement of the social groups to enforce their demands; *and there is no other ultimate power.* It is conceivable that the immense campaign fought in 1949 could have occurred without the use of a single weapon; and indeed, as it was fought out to its inevitable conclusion, it became a nonviolent resistance on the part of the Kuomintang, who fled in a rout.

The psychological forces which brought the revolution into being have long been known. They were known to Confucius. Asked the three things necessary to a ruler, he answered that there should be a sufficiency of food, a sufficiency of military power, and a sufficiency of faith by the people in their ruler. Asked what should be omitted if only two of these were possible, he answered, "Omit the military power." Asked further what should be omitted if only one of these was possible, he answered, "Let them lose their food, and keep their faith in you."

The faith had been provided. It was almost a personal trust in Mao's intentions. Mao might talk, as he did occasionally, in the strange, unwieldy language of Marxist symbolism; but he could also talk in simple, communicable terms. He explained, in language that a child might understand, that there was absolutely nothing to fear. If the Kuomintang was armed with American weapons, their armaments should be regarded simply as part of a process of "blood transfusion"—the weapons would fall into the hands of the Chinese Communists. He repeated his old adage concerning reactionary rulers: "They are paper tigers, fierce to look at, but they melt in the rain." All through 1949 they kept on melting at a mounting pace, while the rain fell and the storm gathered strength. Sometimes, as victory followed victory, it was as though the Red Army resembled the monkey in one of Mao's favorite books who in one somersault could leap tens of thousands of miles.

But if he could talk simply, Mao could also talk dramatically. On April 21, 1949, when he ordered the crossing of the Yangtse River, the words of the order suggest his own dramatic instinct.

He wrote: "Advance boldly, resolutely, thoroughly, cleanly. Completely annihilate all the Kuomintang reactionaries who dare to resist. Liberate the people of the whole country." On that day a million Red Army troops crossed over to the south bank of the Yangtse.

With the crossing of the Yangtse successfully accomplished, the end of Kuomintang rule was already in sight. The Red field armies swept through the southern and northwestern provinces, and by June 15, Mao could say that in three years the Red armies had destroyed 5,590,000 Kuomintang troops, with comparatively small losses to themselves. In a speech delivered to the People's Consultative Conference in Peking he was understandably jubilant, and once more he spoke of the victory as caused by the broad alliance of the laborers, the peasants, the petty and national bourgeoisie—"an alliance so consolidated that it possesses the powerful will and inexhaustible capacity to vanquish all enemies and conquer all difficulties." He added: "We are now in an era in which the imperialist system is heading toward complete collapse. These imperialists are bogged down in an inescapable crisis, and no matter how they will want to continue to oppose the Chinese people, the Chinese people have the means to win ultimate victory." He concluded his speech with a peroration which subtly repeated the words of the song then sweeping over China. "Once the destiny of the people is in the hands of the people, the Chinese people will see a new China rising like the sun from the East, shining with brilliant rays. They will see her swiftly clearing away the debris left by the reactionary government, healing the scars of war and building a new, strong, prosperous People's Democratic Republic in China, which will be true to its name."

Now there remained little except to form the new republic. On October 1, 1949, in an astonishing ceremony held in the heart of Peking, the new republic was officially brought into being.

Looking out over the immense square from the high balcony of the Tien An Men, or "Gate of Heavenly Peace," the scarlet, brass-studded gate through which the tribute-bearers came in the past to make their way, on their knees, to the yellow-lacquered throne of the emperor, Mao watched the processions of people filing into the square. He was wearing the same drab cloth cap and the same worn clothes in which he had entered Peking in March. He kept nodding vigorously, but he looked tired in the chill wind coming from the Gobi. Chu Teh and Chou En-lai stood beside him, but on an impulse they stepped back—it was Mao's name, not theirs, which echoed thunderously over the square: "Mao Tse-tung wan shui! Mao Tse-tung wan shui!" "May Mao Tse-tung live ten thousand years!" He kept nodding, while the shouting echoed from the red-painted palace walls. And then there came a sudden hush, as the people saw the flag slowly sliding up the immense white flagpole in the square: a flag like a small bundle which cracked open at last to become the largest flag that anyone had ever seen, for it was at least thirty feet broad, blood-red with its five yellow stars, and immediately afterward the guns roared a salute. Then the crowd thundered the words of the anthem which had been sung for fifteen years all over China, by the Kuomintang troops as well as by the Communists, the famous Chi-lai sung by schoolchildren, but also by soldiers entering battle:

> Arise, you who refuse to be slaves.
> Our very flesh and blood will build a new Great Wall.
> A savage indignation fills us now,
> Arise, arise, arise!

At the end of the song, from all over the square, where only recently there were trees and small, yellow-roofed palaces isolated behind high walls, now leveled to provide a parade ground and a meeting place for the people, there came more cries of "Mao Tse-tung wan shui" until at last, over the microphones in the square, there could be heard a low Hunanese voice saying, "The Central Governing Council of the People's Government of China today assumes power in Peking. . . ." There was some significance in the fact that Mao used the imperial name meaning "northern capital" rather than Peiping, meaning "northern peace," the name bestowed upon the city at the end of the Kuomintang northern march in 1927. Shortly after the declaration of the new government, the tanks rumbled across the square with their red-painted stars glittering in the low sun which come through the low clouds. They were followed by the mechanized troops in armored trucks, and after these came the captured cannon, sailors with fixed bayonets, Red Guards with automatic rifles, a detachment of peasant guerrillas, and at the end, in their traditional white costumes, the yang-k'o dancers. It was almost exactly twenty-two years since an armed rabble of a thousand men climbed through the wooded, icecold slopes of Chingkanshan.

Looking down at the people waving madly in the square, calling his name, Mao may have reflected that it had happened much sooner than he had dared to expect. External forces had been at work, making the victory easier. The tanks, the armored trucks, the automatic rifles, even the machine guns in the parade had all been captured; only the red-tasseled spears carried by the guerrillas were made in China. Even the uniforms were captured. "Above all," he had said in *Strategic Problems*, "we must concern ourself with the spoils of war." Now the spoils were paraded in the harsh October sunshine; and soon the fireworks rose over the yellow roofs of the palaces, and red lanterns, shaped to resemble red stars, twined through the city streets with the coming of dusk, and late into the night.

A new dynasty had come into being. There had occurred one of those events which happen only at long intervals in the history of China. Though on this same day it had been agreed that the Christian calendar would be employed "since this is the calendar universally recognized throughout the world," in fact, a new element of time was involved, and people would date events from this strange parade of foreign weapons, and the stranger speech heard in the square: "The Chinese nation will never be insulted again. We have stood up! Let the world tremble!"

The world did tremble. A huge, convulsive movement had been brought into being, breaking through the crusts of feudalism and corruption, exploding in violence across the length and breadth of China. Only a few had foreseen it. Mao himself in 1946 seemed to think that the Communist revolution in China would take twenty or thirty years more to accomplish. Only

Ch'en Tu-hsiu, who founded the movement, saw into the future
with elaborate accuracy. One day in March 1927, before the
Shanghai massacres in April had shown the extent of the cleavage
between the two wings of the Kuomintang, Ch'en Tu-hsiu was
talking to the patriarchal old Kuomintang member, Wu Chih-hui,
who in 1902 had founded one of the many revolutionary societies
which sprang to birth under the monarchy. Wu Chih-hui was
commenting on the long period it had taken for the Kuomintang
to come to power. Had not Sun Yat-sen said it would take
thirty years for the Kuomintang to achieve the conquest of
China? "What about the Communist party?" Wu Chih-hui asked.
"Oh, in twenty years the Communists will completely control the
country," Ch'en Tu-shiu answered. "I suppose that means we
have only got nineteen years to live," the old man said, shivering
a little. There was no answer, only a quiet laugh from the man
who had founded the Communist party, and who, a few months
later, was expelled from it because he had failed to understand
the forces at work.

Ch'en Tu-hsiu's twenty years were very nearly accurate, for
by 1947 the wheel was beginning to turn full circle, and the
defeat of the Kuomintang was certain. It could hardly be otherwise. Chiang Kai-shek had proved his incompetence on the field
and in his knowledge of social affairs. Not he, but Mao, was
being greeted with the traditional acclamation reserved in the
past only for Chinese emperors.

The new republic came into being in October. By December,
Mao was planning a journey to Soviet Russia—an unusual ven-
ture for the head of a new state. There were, however, sufficient
reasons. If Stalin's seventieth birthday was the excuse offered
publicly, there were other excuses closer at hand. For the first
time there existed two large Communist states, and it had become
immediately necessary to form long-range plans for their co-operation. Increasingly after 1939 Mao had read Stalin's works. There
had been waverings in Stalin's attitude toward the Chinese Communists, but some clear principles could be seen; and consciously
or unconsciously Stalin had supported the revolution Mao had
brought into being, without sending more than token aid. Mao

believed that the time had come for a complete understanding between them. There were now two poles to the Communist empire; and Mao himself ranked as the leading theoretician after Stalin, with all the extraordinary powers which theoreticians possess in Communist countries. At Potsdam, Stalin had disavowed the Chinese Communists, saying, as he had said many times before, that the Kuomintang was the only political force capable of ruling China. Mao's visit to Moscow was a demonstration that the Chinese Communist revolution was a complete success.

There were many things to discuss. The treaty signed by Molotov and T. V. Soong in 1945 had something of the appearance of one of the "unequal treaties" which China had been compelled to sign as a result of an inherent weakness. It was necessary to obtain a loan, to bring the Chinese Eastern Railway into Chinese hands, and to revise the treaty. It was also necessary to put Sino-Soviet relations on a firm theoretical basis and to discuss the implications of the inevitable alliance. These matters were presumably discussed during Mao's visit to Stalin on January 8, 1950, the longest of all his visits to the inner sanctuary of the Kremlin—he had been received previously by Stalin immediately after his arrival on December 16. The photographs show him looking worn and tired after the journey, wearing a heavy fur coat and a fur cap. He attended a meeting held at the Bolshoi Theater in celebration of Stalin's seventieth birthday, standing immediately on Stalin's right. He visited factories, attended a performance of Swan Lake, and made a prolonged study of the Soviet Union's economic development; and he laid some Chinese flowers on Lenin's tomb within the Kremlin wall. The long visit, so long indeed that rumors were spread that he had been arrested, could be easily accounted for. He realized that Chinese recovery depended upon a spurt in industrial development, and he had comparatively little knowledge of the technical accomplishments of a modern industrial society. A day-by-day summary of his movements in Russia reveals an endless peregrination among factories in Moscow, Leningrad, and all the surrounding territory.

The minutes of the meetings between Mao and Stalin were

never revealed. The text of the treaty was, however, published, and it contained few surprises. The Soviet Union promised a loan to China—a loan that was strangely small and bore little relation to the vast needs of a country shaken to its roots by a prolonged civil war. But if the $300,000,000 purchasing credit was inadequate to fulfill the immediate needs, the Soviet Union also promised to send large numbers of technical assistants to supplement the financial aid.

The incursion of thousands of Soviet Russian technicians was a calculated risk that had to be taken. The loan of $300,000,000 was considerably larger than the loan of $20,000 which, according to the American White Paper, Chu Teh had asked for in 1942 from the United States. The American loan had been refused. Now, with a three year economic plan, with the promise of Soviet Russian support, and with the knowledge that an entirely new adaptation to world conditions had become necessary, Mao prepared to return to China, having seen more collective farms and aircraft factories than he could conceivably have digested. More important than his survey of Soviet Russian industry was the knowledge that an alliance was on firm grounds. He might view Russian concessions in Sinkiang with alarm, and he shared the Chinese distrust of all foreigners, but the importance he attached to the alliance should not be underestimated. Addressing "the peoples of the East" on June 4, 1920, Lenin had emphasized that "for the time being actual communism can be crowned with success only in the West." In the colonial and semicolonial countries "the bourgeois-democratic movements must play the leading role." The times had changed. Lenin had been proved wrong. The revolution in China had come about as the result of an agrarian peasant revolt, and only in its last phases had there been any reliance on the proletariat.

As he left for China, Mao declared at the Yaroslav station that he was content with his long stay; he praised Stalin; he said that it had been his life's ambition to enter "the country of Lenin"; and as he stepped onto the train he added, "The new alliance between our two nations will inevitably influence not only the development of the great powers, China and the Soviet

Union, but the future of all humanity all over the world." It seemed, at that moment, extremely likely.

There followed a long silence. Living in a palace in Peking, working on administrative affairs, Mao spoke more and more rarely. For a short period after the journey to Moscow he was ill. He had aged considerably during the years of conquest. He had hoped to announce the complete conquest of Chinese territory on his return, but Formosa still held out. It was not until June that he delivered his first report on the state of the nation. As so often before, he spoke cautiously, succinctly, warning against dangers, against dogmatism, against every manner of foolhardy action. He said:

> Since the decisive victory in the campaigns of Liaosi and Mukden, Hsuchow, Pengpu, Peiping, and Tientsin in the winter of 1948, the People's Liberation Army has occupied all the territory of China except Tibet, Formosa, and a few islands. In the thirteen and a half months since the crossing of the Yangtse on April 20, 1949, we have annihilated 1,830,000 Kuomintang troops and 980,000 guerrilla bandits. At the same time the people's security organs have discovered large numbers of secret service organizations and special agents; and we still have the task of rooting out remnants of guerrilla forces in the newly liberated areas.
>
> In the past year, too, we have suffered widespread calamities. Eight million hectares of farm land and forty million people have to a greater or lesser degree been affected by flood and drought. . . . So it is that we must carry forward the work of agricultural reform step by step, and in an orderly manner. The war has been fundamentally ended: the situation is entirely different from that which existed between 1946 and 1948. Now the government is in a position to help the poor peasants through their difficulties by means of loans. There must be a change in our attitude toward the rich peasants. We must no longer requisition surplus land and the property of the rich peasants: we must preserve our rich peasant economy, for nothing matters so much as the restoration of production in the rural areas.

Most of this he had said before; now he stated it with absolute authority. He outlined briefly a three-year plan of agrarian reform, industrial development, and large reductions in expenditure by government organizations. He warned against an excessive bureaucracy. Finally, he developed another "eight-legged essay," calling first for more production, then for an end to "blindness and anarchy" in the economic field, and then for a large-scale demobilization of the Army. He urged reform in education, relief for the unemployed, and once again he denounced those who refuse to allow free speech. "All delegates," he said, "must have the full and entire right to speak what is on their mind: any action which suppresses the people's representatives from speaking is wrong." Finally, he urged the suppression of all bandits and counterrevolutionaries, and the resolute carrying out of the party program in the summer, autumn, and winter of 1950. The peroration was brief. He said, "We must regard bureaucracy and authoritarianism as enemies. At the same time we must train ourselves, by reading certain set books, to understand the revolutionary process. Above all, we must conquer all sentiments of complacency and pride, all that makes us believe that we are heroes."

Pride was the enemy. Caught in pride's toils, the Communists could do incalculable harm if they felt disposed. Mao had spoken in June 1950 about the old problems—the whole speech followed the speech made in December 1944, with comparatively few changes—and the old problems remained. He was still the peasant intellectual, wary, cautious, precise. As he said then, so he said now: "If we are proud, comrades, we shall fall."

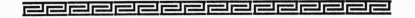

THE YEARS OF STORM

IN OUR OWN day no man has reached power so quickly or so dramatically as Mao Tse-tung. Two years before he achieved supreme power he was hiding among the loess caves of Shensi. Today, he is the master of China, with an effective power greater than that possessed by any of the Chinese emperors. Never in history has any man possessed so much direct power over so many people. For good or evil the power represented by him has come to stay, and from now on the destiny of the world will be intimately, and perhaps violently, affected by the decisions made by him and by the people he leads.

Today, stoop-shouldered and sunburned, looking every day more and more like the portraits of Sun Yat-sen taken in his old age, Mao Tse-tung can look out from the ruined temple near Peking, where he occasionally lives, upon an empire he has conquered almost singlehanded. He knows that without him the Chinese Communists would not have succeeded in capturing China, just as it is inconceivable that the Communists would have captured Russia without Lenin. No one else possessed the peculiar talents he had: the patience, the foresight, the astonishing capacity to learn thoroughly from his mistakes, the knowledge of military science, and the capacity to think in broad, strenuous outlines—all these were predominantly his contributions to the Chinese Communists. He was not simply a political figure: he was the novelist whose novel had become suddenly true, or the poet whose words have suddenly become people.

"Those who do great things have done them because they are in a difficulty, in a *cul de sac*," wrote Henri Michaux. The statement, which is so true of many great leaders, is probably untrue of Mao. It would be unwise to seek the causes of his rise to power in his hatred of his father or his love for his mother, even though rejection by the father plays a peculiarly characteristic role in the rise of nearly all the men who have made a name in history. The chief reason for his rise to power lies almost certainly in the failure of the three Chinese revolutions, beginning with the Taiping Rebellion and ending with the revolution of 1927. Mao was one of the few who realized how and why they had failed. By sheer willpower he made himself the technician of revolt. Carefully, over a long period of years, he prepared himself for the role he desired to play; and from 1924, when he first set eyes on Chiang Kai-shek, he realized that he possessed qualities his adversary could never acquire. In time, the history of China could be summarized as a duel fought to a finish between Mao and Chiang Kai-shek.

No duelists could have been more dissimilar. Chiang Kai-shek admitted to his close friends that he traced his descent directly to Duke Wen, the father of the founder of the Chou dynasty. This incredible claim provides one clue to his downfall. Proud and intolerant, regarding himself as the secret possessor of the imperial mantle, conscious of belonging to a family even more ancient and honorable than that of his brother-in-law, H. H. Kung, who implausibly claimed direct descent from Confucius, Chiang Kai-shek was apt to treat people with a contempt which he took no pains to hide. When Mao flew to Chungking in 1945, Chiang Kai-shek's intolerance and contempt was only too evident. "He treated me like a peasant," Mao complained. It was probably the gravest mistake the Generalissimo ever made. Incapable of understanding his opponent, capable only of hating him, the Generalissimo never fully realized the resources of his enemy, and he continued to underestimate the enemy until it was too late. In a very real sense the pattern of the Chinese civil war followed the pattern of ancient Greek tragedy: overweening pride produced its own Nemesis.

These conceptions of pride and humility must be faced. In China, where personal relations acquire a complexity unknown to the West, the duel between Mao and Chiang was essentially personal, but at the same time it was a duel between two opposed facets of the Chinese mind. Chiang's faith in his own stubborn powers and in his almost divine ancestry were the chief motivating factors in his rise to power. Mao found his resources in Confucianism and in a theory of revolution which derived partly from the Confucian classics and partly from the Marxist belief in the inevitability of the class conflict and the final victory of the proletariat. For the proletariat, in defiance of the *Communist Manifesto*, he substituted the peasants. Chiang never understood the peasants, and never made credible advances to them. Mao did understand them, because he came from them, and he was under no illusions about his ancestry. Yet he was not humble in an ordinary sense, perhaps because no Hunanese is ever humble. He had modeled himself on the Confucian hero, who is scholar and man of action at the same time; and from his youth he had said very simply, and with a full consciousness of what he was about, "I shall overthrow the dynasty."

In *The 18th Brumaire of Louis Bonaparte*, Karl Marx sought for the causes of revolution. He did not find them in economic factors or in the waywardness of despotic rulers; he found them to be part of an inevitable evolution, the same kind of evolution which is present when a serpent sloughs off its skin. A revolution arises, he says, when the dead weight of the past becomes an insufferable torment to the present:

> Men make their own history, but they do not make it just as they please; they do not make it under circumstances chosen by themselves, but under circumstances directly found, and given

and transmitted from the past. The tradition of all the dead generations weighs like a nightmare on the living. And just when they seem engaged in revolutionizing themselves and things, in creating something entirely new, precisely in such epochs of revolutionary crisis they conjure up the spirits of the past to their service and borrow from them names, battle slogans, and costumes in order to present the new scene of world history in time-honored disguise and this borrowed language.

In effect, both Mao and Chiang had summoned up the past in order to help them wage their war in the present; but they had conjured up different pasts. Chiang saw himself as a Chou dynasty prince leading his feudal armies to battle, like any one of the princes described so brilliantly in the *Tso Chuan*. Mao saw himself as one of the heroes of *All Men Are Brothers*. Both employed ancient rituals, Chiang Kai-shek even going so far as to encourage his lieutenants to present him with copies of the ancient bronze tripods traditionally presented to victorious emperors. When the bronzes were already made, he professed to be unworthy of the honor, but even his profession of unworthiness followed a classic pattern. Mao resurrected the ancient peasant brotherhoods who took to the woods and defied the emperor on the grounds that the Mandate of Heaven had lapsed, and he was never so innocent as to believe that the Chinese peasants were powerless.

Having reached the summit of power, Mao walked along a dangerous eminence. Few Chinese rulers have survived intact on these heights. The Empress Dowager went mad, and killed the young Emperor Kuang Hsu on the day before her own death. The leaders of the Taiping Rebellion seem to have gone mad quite early, and when the Manchus closed around Nanking, they set fire to their palaces and murdered one another. There is no reason to believe that Mao will succumb under the inevitable strains. Like many previous rulers of China, he has been moved by what Thomas Hobbes has called "the perpetual and restless desire of Power after Power, which ceaseth only in Death"; but unlike most previous rulers of China he is a peasant who has wandered through most of China and kept close to the earth and to the peasants.

Perhaps the danger lies here. Antaeus lost his strength when he left the earth: Mao loses his whenever he removes himself from the Chinese peasants and the Chinese earth. It is possible that the complexities of the international scene may in the end confound him. He knows well only the peasants of Hunan, Kiangsi, and Shensi. Though he has traveled over the whole length and breadth of China, he still remains remarkably ignorant of the world outside, and he still tends to simplify problems, seeing everything in black and white, whereas most things are shaded between the two extremes. He was convinced, as he wrote in *The New Democracy*, that "without the assistance of the Soviet Union, final victory in China against Japan is impossible." It happened that his prophecy came true, but it might very well have happened otherwise, and indeed there was little ground for the belief, for the Soviet Union appeared to have no intention of entering into the war against Japan. Because Mao tends to simplify, there is always the danger that he may become one of the "Great Simplifiers," whose existence in the twentieth century Jacob Burckhardt prophesied in the nineteenth. Once he told Edgar Snow that he never took any interest in drawing. Asked to draw a picture representing Li Po's famous description of a scene which is "half sun and half rock," he simply drew a straight line with a semicircle over it. The danger point comes when the "Great Simplifiers" draw up innumerable lists of people and then strike lines through them.

When Mao Tse-tung took power in 1949 he was virtually the sole ruler of China. He was the philosopher and strategist who had brought the Communist revolutionaries to power, and swept the remnants of Chiang Kai-shek's broken armies to the island of Formosa. He had all China at his feet, and he could afford to be merciful. But he showed no mercy.

Years before, in the famous essay called "Report of an Investigation into the Peasant Movement in Hunan," he denied that there could be anything gentle in a revolution. "A revolution," he wrote, "is not the same as inviting people to dinner, or writing an essay, or painting a picture, or doing fancy needlework: it cannot be anything so refined, so calm and gentle, or so kind, courteous, restrained, and magnanimous. A revolution is an uprising, an act of violence by which one class overthrows another." More than twenty years had passed since this report was written, but he had not changed. He proceeded to destroy completely the property-owning class in China. The landlords had been rendered powerless: now at his orders they were killed.

The extent of the terror which swept over China during the first year of Communist power will probably never be known. It reached down into the most remote villages, and in one way or another affected the lives of nearly everyone on the mainland. China was not encircled; there were no foreign armies invading the mainland of China; there was no rational reason for the expenditure of so much time and energy on extirpating a class which could no longer defend itself. By its very nature terror is a weapon which can never be satisfied, but must go on and on until it reaches a state of mechanical exhaustion, endlessly and mindlessly repeating itself. Quite deliberately Mao chose the weapon of terror to ensure the permanence of the Communist revolution which had already been ensured by his victories in the field.

In the great purges of the first two years of Communist domination the utmost harm was done to the body politic. The Communist cadres who aroused the villagers against the landlords acted on instructions from the top. They had license to kill whomever they pleased. There are altogether too many reports of villagers whipped into vengeful fury and stoning landlords to death, or summarily executing them, to allow us to believe that these excesses were not deliberately planned, encouraged, and sometimes artificially induced. There were no trials. Anyone who wished to work off an ancient grudge was permitted to do so. Legality was thrown to the winds, and the only law was "revolutionary necessity," which could be interpreted according to the whims of any local Communist commander. Completely innocent people were murdered, and their families were reduced to beggary. Eventually the great purges caused such nation-wide revulsion that Mao Tse-tung was forced to admit that he had gone too far. But there is no evidence that he ever regretted the original impulse to shatter the old society by a prolonged and widespread use of terror. The harm was done, leaving in its wake an all-pervasive atmosphere of fear which has never been dissipated.

There was however a difference between the Chinese purges and the purges ordered by Stalin against the kulaks. In Russia the purges arose as the result of a declared policy, and were carried out by the army in cooperation with the peasant militia. In China they were carried out by local party officials, often singlehanded. The peasants were goaded into action, largely against their will, only too happy to let Communist officials bear the burden of guilt.

A succession of laws and slogans was introduced to bring about these changes in the ownership of land. In June 1950, eight months after the inauguration of the Communist Republic, there came the New Land Reform Law, followed a few months later by a pronouncement called "Decisions concerning Differentiation of Class Status in the Countryside." The peasant class was divided into four groups—rich peasants, middle peasants, poor peasants, hired laborers. The last two groups comprised more than seventy per cent of the total, and the land was accordingly distributed among them and new title deeds were solemnly handed to them. The time of the communes was not far away.

It was a time of upheaval with the government still unsure of itself, seeing enemies where there were none, magnifying the number of Kuomintang soldiers who still fought in the hills, and drastically punishing those who dared to raise their voices against the excesses of the regime. The myth of American imperialism was cultivated to a dangerous extent; and a blind hatred of America was encouraged. In power Mao retained the habits of mind which made him a magnificent guerrilla leader; and sometimes he seemed to be a guerrilla leader waging war against the world.

The terror continued; officially it lasted until the early months of 1954, and according to Mao Tse-tung the number of those who were "liquidated" amounted to eight hundred thousand persons, a figure which is about as meaningful as any estimate compiled by any secret police.* An official Kuomintang estimate that nine million people were killed during the first five years of the Chinese Communist domination of the mainland of China is equally devoid of meaning. No one will ever know how many died. All that is certain is that there was a blood bath of unprecedented proportions; and the guilty suffered equally with the innocent.

The early years of Communist power were the bitterest of all. Relentlessly the Communists were compelled to stamp the Communist image on the country, and this task was made easier, rather than more difficult, by the Korean war, which broke out in June 1950. Within two months of the outbreak of the war, China was placed on a war footing; and the hordes of Chinese "volunteers" who were hurled into the Korean war in November under the command of General P'eng Teh-huai represented the flower of the Red Army. The risks were great, but cheerfully accepted, and there is little reason to believe the widely circulated story that Mao Tse-tung debated with himself for three days before giving the order to send his army into Korea. The logic of the revolution demanded it. A free, independent, anti-Communist Korea on the eastern border of China represented a very real threat to the regime, and the decision to fight the war if the North Korean forces were seriously endangered was unavoidable. Characteristically the Chinese Communists in Korea fought exactly as they had fought during the last stages of their war against the Kuomintang on the mainland of China, throwing ill-equipped soldiers into battle in a human flood, often winning by sheer force of numbers.

* The figure eight hundred thousand, was given by Mao Tse-tung in his 1957 speech "On Contradictions." In the fall of 1950 Chou En-lai reported to the National Committee of the Chinese Communist Party that "about eight hundred thousand out of a million Kuomintang bandits left on the mainland had been liquidated." In the following year Po Yi-po, vice-chairman of the Committee of Financial and Economic Affairs, reported that "in the past three years we have liquidated more than two million bandits." From time to time other figures have been quoted. It has proved impossible to reconcile them.

Originally the Korean war came as an unhappy surprise to the Chinese Communists. They were not prepared for it, nor had they been consulted. The decision to fight the war was made by the Russians and the North Koreans. In June 1950 the Chinese Communists were poised for "a war of liberation" against the island of Formosa, with a massive fleet of junks ready to sail for the island at a moment's notice. The momentum of the revolution demanded a quick settlement with Chiang Kai-shek. Delay—even a moderate delay—would permit the Kuomintang to become entrenched on the island; and the high-pitched quality of the propaganda directed against Chiang Kai-shek testified to a real fear of this man who had led his armies on so many disastrous campaigns.

Two days after the Korean war broke out President Truman ordered the United States Seventh Fleet to "neutralize" the Straits of Formosa. This decision was fatal to the Chinese Communist plans. It was in fact the most serious blow they had yet suffered. Against a massive fleet equipped with heavy guns they were powerless, and the invasion of Formosa was called off.

Years ago in Yenan I asked Mao Tse-tung what the Red Army would do when confronted with modern tanks. He answered, "We shall tear them to pieces with our bare hands." But one cannot tear battleships and dive-bombing airplanes to pieces with one's bare hands. Mao Tse-tung was to learn the realities of modern war as conducted by the great powers. In Peking the threat of American power was very real. The Inchon landing proved, if any proof were needed, that the Americans were not "paper tigers."

In power Mao Tse-tung remained the prisoner of his own history. He still thought of war in terms of guerrilla war. He had not changed remarkably since 1927 when he wrote the "Investigation into the Peasant Movement in Hunan," and the directives issued from his office during the early years of power often repeated verbatim whole sentences and paragraphs from early speeches. The man who had lived for ten years in a cave in Yenan, quietly raising his own tobacco and spending his nights poring over books and writing long essays on the theory of Communism as it applied to China, seemed to change very little when he became the undisputed master of China. Yet inevitably power corrupted him, for no head of state is ever immune from its poisons.

He had always dressed well when he could afford it; now he dressed a little better, but his uniform was still the workman's cap and the Sun Yat-sen coat tightly buttoned at the collar, with no insignia of rank. Chu Teh blossomed out in a marshal's uniform with gold braid and epaulettes, perhaps in emulation of the Russian generals who flocked to Peking, but these small vanities were pardonable in a man who had waged so many wars, and won them all. Deliberately Mao avoided the outward vanities. He was still the scholar, working at night, endlessly reading and studying. His desk at Yenan was untidy; his desk in Peking was, if possible, untidier. He no longer lived in a cave, but in the small palace of the Fragrant Concubine, the unhappy and exquisitely beautiful Turki princess who was the favorite of the Emperor Ch'ien Lung and who was strangled to death by the Emperor's mother. The small palace lies on the shores of the South Lake, and can be reached through the heavily guarded Hsin Hua Men, or New China Gate, a name given to the gate more than two hundred years ago. There was nothing remarkable in Mao's choice: ever since the Chinese Republic came into existence in 1911 the cluster of small palaces beside this gate have been the official residences of the president and his closest advisers. On summer days he abandons the palace and works in a tent set up on the shores of the lake. He has a villa in the Western Hills near the Jade Temple and a summer house at Peitaho. His only known extravagance is a swimming pool, which was built for him by his associates; when he learned the cost he insisted on paying for it himself out of the royalties of his books. From these royalties he has become a rich man, but he shows no interest in his riches, and indeed it would be surprising if he did, for all his expenses are paid for by the government. His official salary is six hundred yuan a month—about $200.

In old age Mao is beginning to look his years. Most of his life he looked younger than his age. His body is growing heavier, his hair is receding, and there are deep wrinkles around the eyes. In recent years he has often been ill. The first severe illness was in the spring of 1951, followed by another bout of illness in the winter of 1954. Any doubts about his recovery were dispelled in May 1956 when he swam the flooded Yangtse river from Wuchang to Hankow, repeating the experiment twice in the summer. He still smoked too much, but he has smoked ever since he was a student in Changsha and seems to be immune from nicotine poisoning. He traveled tirelessly. He especially enjoyed his journeys among the peasants, and he had a peasant's abiding respect for the ancient arts of Chinese medicine. Sometimes he calls himself "Lao Tai-tai," the traditional Chinese term for the old and respected woman, grandmother or wife, who looks after the family. He lives quietly with his third wife and his two daughters, who were both born in Yenan and aspire to be ballet dancers. No one has ever suggested there was any scandal in his private life.

Mao has the peasant virtues, and many of the peasant vices —intolerance, sudden rages, a harsh joy in his triumphs. There is perhaps more of his peasant father in him than he suspects. He can be warm and friendly toward individuals he has known for a long time, but strangers are often treated coldly, warily, with a kind of detached tolerance. He has never succeeded in learning a foreign language, and the evidence of his writings suggests a vast ignorance of foreign ways. More often than he realizes he has been trapped by his own slogans.

Many of the slogans he introduced have been curiously negative. The "Three Anti" Campaign (anti-waste, anti-corruption, anti-bureaucratism) was followed by the "Five Anti" Campaign (anti-bribery, anti-tax evasion, anti-theft of state property, anti-cheating on government contracts, anti-leakage of government economic secrets). The campaigns effectively reduced corruption, but accomplished relatively little in reducing the widespread nuisance of bureaucracy. The rage for negative slogans continued. There were "Anti-America" weeks. "Anti-Rightist" campaigns were revived at intervals. There was even a nation-wide campaign directed against a single man, the critic Hu Feng, a veteran Communist whose influence on journalism and literary circles dated back to the early 1920's. Hu Feng's crime was that he publicly opposed the official Communist attitude to literature as an off-shoot of propaganda. Accordingly a venomous "Anti-Hu Feng" campaign came into existence, and continued long after Hu Feng offered a humiliating apology for his "errors." Before the "Anti-Hu Feng" campaign was over scores of writers found themselves exiled to remote provinces, among them the poet Ai Ching and the woman novelist Ting Ling, the two greatest writers to emerge out of Communist China.

On the whole these wholly negative slogans did more harm than good. They pointed to widespread corruption within the Communist party. Waste, bribery, tax evasion, theft, and cheating had become endemic. To call a halt to them the government mounted costly propaganda campaigns which had the effect of proclaiming the inadequacies of Chinese Communism to the whole world.

The Communists speak often of the irreconcilable contra-dictions of capitalism; they speak less frequently of the irrecon-cilable contradictions in their own system. As a realist, Mao would seem to be perfectly aware that the theory of communism is often in contraction to its practice. The theory is almost painfully simple, but by the nature of things the practice must always be arduous, complex, and curiously illusory. The five-year plans, the fixed norms, the constant appeal to statistics give an air of preci-sion to problems which are often unmeasurable, and sometimes insoluble. Mao was attempting to rule a vast continental empire by the same methods he employed in the small valley of Yenan. Contradictions lay all around him. In time he was to learn that these contradictions were inherent in the very nature of human existence and would have to be reckoned with.

In two lectures delivered in February and March 1957 he addressed himself to the problem of contradictions as he saw them. He had been shocked by the sudden collapse of the Hun-garian Communist party a few weeks earlier, with the result that he spoke with unusual emotion. He admitted that the Chinese Communist system was "not yet fully established." He foresaw a long period of hardship for the Chinese people, and he was in no mood to exaggerate the successes of the Chinese Communists. Of all his recent speeches this is the one which most usefully repays attention.

Mao's speech seems to have owed its origin to a profound uneasiness with the developing structure of the Communist state. Communist China was strong, and growing stronger each year; the people were reasonably content, or at least in no mood for open rebellion; the internal enemies of the regime had been executed, or in other ways silenced; and no wars were being fought. Then why was it that the state showed so many signs of cracking at the seams? Why was there so much incomprehension and doubt about the future of the state? Why were people murmuring about the curious inability of the Communists to give them a better and fuller life?

Mao answered these questions with characteristic ingenuity. He reviewed briefly the history of China under the Communists, pointing out that it was in the nature of a very large, heavily populated, agricultural country with small industrial resources to suffer dislocations and setbacks. There were no simple pathways to the millennium. The Communist state itself suffered from many ambiguities. There existed contradictions in nearly all the fields of communist endeavour. Instead of a clearcut, simple, easily comprehended formula there were many conflicting formulas. Various offices in the state were rivaling other offices. The interests of the government conflicted with the interests of individuals. The monolithic dictatorship of the few was in conflict with the democracy of the many. There were conflicts between the working classes and the national bourgeoisie, between the intellectuals who desired the utmost freedom for their work and the Communist commissars who demanded that they follow Communist guidance. Wherever one looked, there were conflicts, ambiguities, rivalries, contradictions so extreme that they must be reckoned with. It was not enough to say that these conflicts must be abolished. On the contrary they must be harnessed to the welfare of the state.

In admitting that there were conflicts within the internal organization of the state, Mao was flying in the face of established

Communist doctrine. Khrushchev hotly denied the existence of any contradictions between the Communist rulers and the people of the Soviet Union. Stalin, on the contrary, accepted the fact that there were contradictory elements and sought to crush them completely; he believed that the closer the country came to socialism, the more desperate became the internal enemies of the state, and by this thesis he justified the use of mass terror. Mao arrived at an exactly contrary thesis. He contended that the closer China came to socialism, the fewer were the real enemies of the state, and the more reason there was to tolerate them. The state in its majesty and power could afford to be lenient. Surprisingly, he went on to say that the state needed enemies capable of challenging it, otherwise it would become a hothouse plant, suffering from the sterile weaknesses of such plants. Criticism was necessary. It was a fact of growth. For this reason the government in Peking once decided to publish the complete works of Chiang Kai-shek and a selection of Voice of America broadcasts.

"These contradictions among our people are the very forces which make society move," he wrote. "Many people refuse to admit that contradictions still exist in a socialist society, with the result that when they are confronted with social contradictions they become timid and helpless. Contradictions arise continually and are continually resolved; this is the dialectical law of the arrangement of things."

But to admit to the existence of contradictions is one thing: to encourage them is another. Mao proceeded to encourage them with the famous slogan: "Let a hundred flowers blossom! Let a hundred schools of thought contend!" At the time he seems to have meant exactly what he said. The argument is carefully buttressed, and his purposes are carefully explained:

> The policy of letting a hundred flowers blossom and a hundred schools of thought contend is designed to promote the flourishing of the arts and the progress of science; it is designed to enable a socialist culture to thrive in our land. Different forms and styles in art can develop freely, and different schools in science can contend freely. We think that it is harmful to the growth of art and science if administrative measures are used to impose

one particular style of art or school of thought and to ban the other.

Questions of right and wrong in the arts and sciences should be settled through free discussion in artistic and scientific circles, and in the course of practical work in the arts and sciences. They should not be settled in summary fashion. A period of trial is often needed to determine whether something is right or wrong. In the past new and correct things often failed at the outset to win recognition from the majority of people and had to develop by twists and turns in struggle.

Correct and good things have often at first been looked upon not as fragrant flowers, but as poisonous weeds. The Copernican theory of the solar system and Darwin's theory of evolution were once dismissed as erroneous, and had to win through over bitter opposition. In a socialist society conditions for the growth of new things are radically different from and far superior to those in the old society. Nevertheless it still often happens that new rising forces are held back and reasonable suggestions smothered.

The growth of new things can also be hindered, not because of deliberate suppression, but because of lack of discernment. That is why we should take a cautious attitude in regard to questions of right and wrong in the arts and sciences, encourage free discussion, and avoid hasty conclusions. We believe that this attitude will facilitate the growth of the arts and sciences.

What Mao was here suggesting was a radical alteration in the accepted party dogma that Heaven has bequeathed to the Communists alone the knowledge of the secret workings of the universe. He was saying cautiously that dogma was itself in contradiction with facts and that human experience demanded the widest possible use of all the talents, whatever the source. Communism was not enough.

Mao's preoccupation with "a hundred flowers" was relatively new. There is no hint of it in the works he wrote before he came to power. On the contrary, his writings up to this time were filled with petulant dogmas on the supremacy of Communist art and science over all other arts and sciences. No quarter was to be given to those who did not share these absolute convictions. Again and again he emphasized that art and science were weapons to be used against the enemy; all were to be placed at the service of the party.

There is evidence that for some months before the speech Mao was privately discussing the need for relaxing controls. According to Professor Chow Ching-wen, who served for eight years in high-ranking positions in the Communist party until he escaped to Hong Kong in 1957, Mao called a meeting of senior officials in the winter of 1956 and discussed with them the need for peaceful coexistence between all parties. Professor Chow appears to have been present at the meeting. He records that Mao was in high good humor, waving a cigarette above his head as he spoke, and beaming at his audience. He said:

> "The masses and cadres have had a hard time of it these past years with our movements, and we ought to give them a chance to take a breath. They ought to have a chance to express their views about the conduct of the Government and the Party. I think we will all benefit from hearing their opinions." Then he puffed at his cigarette and continued, "I know that there is friction between Party and non-Party members, and in all the Party organizations as well. I hope that everybody will express his opinions openly. It's no crime to talk, and nobody will be punished for it." Everyone responded agreeably to this, and Mao Tse-tung became more and more lively.
>
> "We must let a hundred flowers bloom and a hundred schools of thought contend," he said, "and see which flowers are the best and which school of thought is best expressed, and we shall applaud the best blooms and the best thoughts." Everyone was extremely pleased. "With us today are leaders of the democratic parties and groups. We have gone through a great deal together. We struggled together before our success was achieved. From now on, it isn't only 'Long Live the Communist Party' but also 'Long Live All The Parties!' We and the other parties must live in a prolonged period of peaceful coexistence and mutual guidance." Mao was interrupted by applause.*

This was not quite the end of the discussion, for Mao went on to speak ruefully about the Hungarian revolt, which he ascribed

* Chow Ching-wen, Ten Years of Storm (New York: Holt, Rinehart & Winston, 1960), pp. 162–163.

to "big country chauvinism," placing the blame squarely on the Russians, saying that "Soviet Russia is a socialist country, and yet she is trying to grab territory from brother nations. This is contrary to the principles of socialism." He returned to these ideas in his speech "On Contradictions," where it is quite evident that the fate of Hungary weighed heavily on him. The Communist party in Hungary had disappeared "in the matter of a few days" and the whole state apparatus threatened to disintegrate. The revolt in Hungary suggested either that the Communist party had no deep roots among the people, or else that it was hopelessly inefficient; in either case it showed itself to be contemptible. These strictures against the Hungarian Communists were not included in the revised version of the speech published in Peking.

Mao's speech was regarded with grave displeasure in the Soviet Union. The call for "a hundred flowers to bloom" was found especially incomprehensible in a country where monolithic rigidity had become the commonplace of political life. It was pointed out that differences in political expression were permitted during the early years of Communism in Russia, but the time had long passed when the government could officially tolerate disagreement. The "correct" path was known. How could anyone be permitted to stray from it?

In China the speech was greeted with jubilation by non-Communist students and intellectuals, and by members of the splinter parties which had identified themselves with Communist aims while disapproving of Communist methods. From March to June the hundred flowers bloomed wildly. Criticism became rampant. One after another, intellectuals delivered scathing attacks on the Communists under the delusion that full liberty of expression was now permitted. They attacked the monolithic party power, the sham of coalition government, the incompetence of party officials. They complained bitterly about party interference in research, scholarship and the arts. They questioned the infallible laws of Marx-Leninism, and even more courageously they questioned Mao's competence as a logician, as the leader of his country, and as the deified successor of the ancient sages. Professor Keh Peh-yi, a teacher in the People's University, went so far as to say that every single Communist in the country deserved to be hanged, or otherwise reduced to impotence, for all the harm they had brought upon the country. The Chinese share with the Russians a passion for excess. With characteristic and dangerous abandon the critics proceeded to attack the Communists where they were most vulnerable. On June 8, 1957, the Communists had had enough. They replied in the only way open to them—by force, by terror, by depriving the critics of the power of speech. The hundred flowers withered on their stems.

There were many among the high echelons of the Communist party who disapproved of Mao's theory and openly expressed their disapproval. Among these was Liu Shao-ch'i, whose narrow and puritanical mind found the most exquisite pleasure in dogma. Accordingly, he was accused of being responsible for the sudden *volte-face*. Alternatively Mao was accused of being the author of a diabolical trap designed to catch the unwary and to discover the extent of opposition in the country. It is more likely that Mao meant exactly what he said, and called a halt only because the Communist revolution was being endangered by criticism which amounted in an authoritarian state to the purest license.

Inevitably those who had spoken too freely were punished, but just as inevitably the "hundred flower" theme has come to stay. Mao knows perfectly well that the arts and sciences, including the science of government, cannot progress indefinitely in strait jackets. Until the Red guards entered the scene, the idea would continue to be revived at intervals, never completely forgotten. Significantly, on March 1, 1961, the Central Committee of the Chinese Communist Party recommended that the "hundren flower" theme be applied to academic research, and once more there was proclaimed Mao's favorite adage: "Marxists ought not to fear any criticism."

In fact, of course, Marxists do fear criticism. The antiquated theories of Marx rest on such insecure foundations that Marx's followers have an almost pathological fear of even the gentlest criticism. In June 1957, when Mao ordered an end to the brief period of permissive criticism which had lasted barely a hundred days, the inevitable reaction set in, and a prolonged campaign of "rectification" was announced. The critics of the regime were denounced as "rightists," compelled to attend self-examination meetings, and publicly attacked. Some lost their jobs and others were exiled to distant provinces. But not even the most violent of the critics was executed. The days of bloodletting were not yet over—local revolts were put down mercilessly, and the secret police continued to employ secret murder as the most powerful of their weapons—but it is significant that the Chinese Communists are still more tolerant of ideas than their Russian counterparts. Rigidity has set in, but not to the extent that abrupt changes of direction can no longer take place.

From the beginning, the tempo of Chinese Communism has been amazingly fast. Victory in the civil war came much earlier than they expected. Within five years of the establishment of the new government in Peking Mao had consolidated his power over an empire which extended from Tibet to the China Sea, an empire nearly as great as that of the Emperor K'ang Hsi. He had spoken in Yenan of bringing communism to China in perhaps two generations. In fact he was able to impose communism on China in less than ten years.

By October 1959, on the tenth anniversary of Mao's rise to power, China was more communist than Russia and becoming progressively more egalitarian every day. The communes, begun tentatively in 1954, now reached from one end of China to another, and the collectivization of all the means of production was already established. The communes with their quasi-military discipline enabled the state to control the lives of the peasants to a degree which even Khrushchev thought inadvisable. The peasants were swallowed up into the state machine. In exchange for their labor everything was provided for them except the freedom to live their own lives. These communes were closer to the Fourierist "phalansteries" envisaged by socialists at the beginning of the last century than anything envisaged by Marx or Lenin. Members of the communes were given the choice of accepting the "free tens," the "free sevens," or the "small dividend." The "free tens" consisted of free food, free clothing, free housing, free child care and education, free medical care, free heating, free entertainment, free haircuts, free weddings, and free funerals. Under certain circumstances it was possible to modify the arrangement and accept money instead of the gifts offered by the state—hence the "free sevens" and the "small dividend." Nothing was said about free automobiles or free television sets. Meal tickets and clothing tickets largely took the place of money, and in the communes people live very much as they lived under the Communists in Yenan, where a single store catered to the needs of the whole population, with tickets signed by government officials as the only means of currency.

With the introduction of the communes the government achieved what it had long desired—total economic control of agriculture. The experiment went much further than the *kolkhozes* established by Stalin in the Soviet Union, for the peasants were not permitted to cultivate private plots, keep livestock, or possess their own implements. In theory life was to be lived in perfect community; in fact such a system was very nearly unworkable, and in 1958 a man could possess a small plot of his own. It was only a partial reversal of the established principle. Peasants were ordered to spend their free time in working for the community, not in working their own plots.

It was the year of the Great Leap Forward, the sudden emergence of backyard iron furnaces, small-scale industries invading the villages, and fantastic efforts to improvise industrial progress from the grass roots. All over China eager young students with insufficient technical education were busy building factories and improvising water conservation projects. The government was calling upon everyone to become an industrialist, a builder of dams, an iron smelter, a canal digger. They were to learn later that enthusiasm alone cannot generate industrial progress, and engineers do not rise out of the ground at government orders.

During the following years China suffered disaster upon disaster. Flood, drought, typhoons ravaged the land; the Yellow River became a trickle; the dams which had been especially designed to bring water to the parched earth were dry. No one could remember a time when so many disasters were visited upon China. Suddenly in July 1960 the Soviet Union recalled the technicians sent to assist the Chinese industries, and the cup of bitterness spilt over.

For a long time the Chinese and the Russians had been at odds. It was not only that they interpreted Marxism in different ways, each believing that they alone had inherited the true doctrine; but they were profoundly suspicious of each other's motives and contemptuous of each other's claims. The Soviet Union had reached a stage in its development when it could afford to relax its revolutionary fervor; the Chinese Communists, masters of a poor land, lived in a state of chronic excitement, at the mercy of their revolutionary beliefs. They had always despised the Russians, and they despised them all the more when they came bearing messages of peaceful coexistence.

At the end of September 1959 Nikita Khrushchev arrived in Peking to celebrate the tenth anniversary of the Chinese Communist regime. He had recently visited President Eisenhower at Camp David. The President, who had spoken of the need to relax international tensions, had found a willing listener in Khrushchev, who proceeded to share his opinions with Mao Tse-tung. At a banquet given in his honor Khrushchev warned Mao Tse-tung against embarking on wars of revolutionary conquest. He said:

> When I spoke with President Eisenhower—and I have just returned from the United States of America—I got the impression that the President of the United States—and not a few people support him—understands the need to relax international tensions.
>
> Perhaps not every bourgeois leader can pronounce the words "peaceful coexistence" well, but they cannot deny that two systems exist in the world—the socialist and the capitalist. The recognition of this fact ran like a red thread through all the talks. This was repeatedly spoken about by the President and other leaders. Therefore we on our part must do all we can to exclude war as a means of settling disputed questions and settle these questions by negotiation.

If Khrushchev thought he would please Mao Tse-tung by describing his conversations with the American president, he was mistaken. In the eyes of the Chinese Communists there was nothing to gain by coexistence and everything to lose. The theory of coexistence demonstrated only that the Soviet Union had gone over to the enemy, was no longer ruled by true Marxists, and was not worthy of its Communist past. Since capitalism was the historical enemy of communism, Mao Tse-tung could see no reason why there should be a détente. On the contrary the capitalist camp should be hit hard and without respite. Khrushchev's declaration was merely an admission of weakness, an abandonment of revolutionary purpose. "Revisionism" had set in, and the Communists in Moscow no longer deserved to be called the leaders of the world proletariat.

Khrushchev was to say later in a CBS television interview that Mao Tse-tung was completely uncompromising in his demand that the Soviet Union make war with the United States. It was necessary to unleash a world war to destroy the capitalist system once and for all. "You have only to provoke the Americans into military action," Mao Tse-tung told Khrushchev, "and I will give you as many divisions as you wish—a hundred, a thousand divisions, as many as you please." According to Khrushchev, Mao Tse-tung spoke with complete conviction and the offer was meant seriously. When Khrushchev replied that he had not the least intention of provoking the Americans and had absolutely no desire to unleash a world war, Mao Tse-tung bluntly accused him of cowardice. Khrushchev believed that by refusing to accept Mao Tse-tung's offer, he preserved the peace of the world.

Khrushchev is not an impeccable witness of the truth; nevertheless his account of his meeting with Mao Tse-tung rings true. The Chinese Communists had never abandoned the hope of a world revolution, a cataclysmic confrontation between communism and capitalism; they had no fear of the atomic bomb; and they saw Communist China emerging triumphant from the holocaust because it could afford to lose three or four hundred million men and no other country could afford a similar loss. By outnumbering all other nations including the Soviet Union, they were assured of victory.

The argument was specious, as Khrushchev well knew, and he was in no mood to sacrifice the Soviet Union to Chinese ambitions. The Russian Communists felt an overwhelming need to relax international tensions in the nuclear age; the Chinese Communists felt there was only one overwhelming need—to increase the tempo of the world-wide revolution. In their own eyes they were the inheritors of the revolutionary tradition, and the Russians had fallen by the wayside.

The dispute between Moscow and Peking grew astonishingly bitter, at times achieving an almost unbelievable degree of hysteria. The charges and countercharges were couched in the abstruse algebraic language of Marxist dogmatism, but the inflexible terminology did not conceal the naked passions involved. Mao Tse-tung wrote to the Russians with something of the same spirit as a Chinese emperor writing to the chieftain of a rebellious tribe on the frontier of China; and while the letters were signed by the Central Committee of the Chinese Communist party, no one doubted that he was the author. The Chinese Communists called for a world congress of Communists to decide the issue, but the Russians refused to take part, apparently on the ground that it would be a waste of time to examine a wound which could no longer be healed. For four years the debate continued. Then, as though they had grown weary of it, the Chinese Communists sent a long and impassioned letter accusing the Russians of twenty-six ideological errors and representing themselves as being free from any such errors whatsoever; it was the last attack, and thereafter they merely contented themselves with occasional references to the Soviet Union as a nation treacherously following the capitalist road.

The withdrawal of the Russian technicians and the abrupt halt in Russian aid hurt the Chinese deeply. The Chinese air force consisted of Russian aircraft, which were now deprived of spare parts. The Russian technicians who had been building factories left them unfinished and took the blueprints with them when they departed. From 1959 to 1962 China suffered unprecedented tribulations, but in the eyes of Mao Tse-tung the greatest tribulation was the knowledge that the Soviet Union was no longer an ally but an implacable enemy.

Since the Korean war the Chinese Communists have shown little disposition for military adventures. No serious or prolonged effort had been made to take Formosa by force; there had been occasional brief skirmishes with Russian frontier guards; arms had been sent to Africa in the hope of stirring up "wars of liberation";

but there were no massive attacks on China's neighbors. Suddenly, on November 19, 1962, the Red Army went into action. Some twenty thousand Chinese troops attacked the Se-La Pass through the mountains guarding Assam. The Indian troops stationed on the pass were thrown back in confusion and the Red Army found itself on the banks of the Brahmaputra River; before them lay the rich, flat, undefended plains of Assam. India was within their reach, and the statesmen of the world held their breaths. There were many who felt that Mao Tse-tung had begun a long-threatened war of conquest. On December 7, eighteen days later, Peking radio announced that the troops were being withdrawn behind the Chinese frontier.

The reasons behind the attack on the Se-La Pass were not hard to find. There was above all the hope of being able to join with the Indian Communists to bring about a war of revolutionary liberation, while at the same time paralyzing the Indian government by a show of overwhelming force. Chinese intelligence, notoriously inaccurate, had informed the Communist leaders that India was ripe for the plucking. Jawaharlal Nehru, the Indian prime minister, had appointed a pro-Communist to the Indian embassy in Peking, and his defense minister was also pro-Communist. Mao Tse-tung reasoned that he had nothing to lose and much to gain by a sudden attack, and he could always withdraw in the classic Chinese manner if the adventure proved to be too dangerous. Russian influence had been increasing in India, and it especially pleased him to challenge the Russians. He despised Nehru, who was aging rapidly. Nehru, on the other hand, had the greatest admiration for Mao.

The withdrawal of the Red Army was accomplished without incident. The Chinese Communists did not regard it as a retreat but as a tactical maneuver. Mao Tse-tung took some comfort from the knowledge that he had acted heroically, for a few days later, on December 26, he wrote a poem in which he celebrated his invincible virtue and described his enemies as "flies frozen to death."

The winter clouds are weighed down by fluttering snow;
The myriad blossoms have faded and are rarely seen.
High in the heavens the frozen currents are whirling,

While only a faint warmth stirs from the earth.
Only the hero drives away tigers and leopards,
And the brave have no fear of bears.
The plum tree rejoices in the snowy sky,
Paying no attention to the flies frozen to death.

The poem, which was written on his birthday, was too clearly
a self-portrait for anyone to mistake his intention; nor was there
any doubt what he meant by tigers, leopards, and bears. That he
was the plum tree rejoicing in the depths of winter and that the
whirling currents in the heavens derived from ancient Chinese
cosmology were also self-evident. What was less understandable
was why he should have chosen that tragic month to write a poem
of such towering self-adulation.

Two weeks later, receiving a congratulatory ode from the poet
Kuo Mo-jo, in which he was described as "pure gold never to be
consumed by the flames" and "the unfurler of the flags which will
turn the world scarlet," Mao Tse-tung remembered the flies and
his own burning ambitions, and wrote:

On our small earth
A few flies are dashed against the walls,
And the sound of their buzzing
Is like a lamentation,
Like the sound of sobbing.

Ants climbing a locust tree boast of their country,
But they cannot shake the roots of a strong tree.
In Ch'angan the west wind is dropping its leaves,
And the signal for the march is being given.

There are so many urgent deeds
Crying out to be done.
Heaven and earth revolve,
But there is little time left.
Ten thousand years are too long.
Every day, every hour must be put to use.
The four seas are tempest-ridden, clouds and waters rage.
The five continents are shaken as thunder roars in the wind.
Harmful insects must be stamped out:
In this way we become invincible.

Official commentaries were written on the poem, and no attempt was made to disguise the poet's rage and impatience. But few commentators observed that the world and his enemies had suddenly grown small, as though they were scarcely worth conquering. The "flies frozen to death" had come to life again. Simultaneously he was speaking of a universe in a state of upheaval and of insects which must be stamped out. Lear on the blasted heath was busily catching flies.

Because he is sometimes a brilliant poet Mao Tse-tung's poems are always worth studying. They tell us more about the man than he sometimes cared to admit, and this poem written in reply to Kuo Mo-jo's fulsome praise reveals him in a mood of contemptuous anger as much against his enemies as against his own advancing years. He was seventy, and already suffering from an obscure illness. He was appearing less and less in public. On the rare occasions when he appeared on the balcony of the Gate of Heavenly Peace to review the processions of soldiers, peasants, and workers, he would look down at the huge white marble cenotaph in honor of the fallen heroes. The cenotaph bore the words, "The people's heroes will be remembered eternally." They were his own words, and he confidently expected to be counted among those who will be eternally remembered.

As he grew older, he became more impatient, more demanding, more tyrannical. Wherever he turned, he was met with adulation, as though he were a god walking the earth. In his earlier days he had succeeded in regarding himself with detachment, indifferent to his own growing fame, amused by the portraits of himself and by his own triumphs. But as he grew older he came to believe in his own legend, and the mood hardened. The break with the Soviet Union was a shock from which he never completely recovered, and the naked rage spilled over in his poems, in his rare speeches, and in his acts. Those who believed he was a spent force gradually retiring into the obscurity reserved for aging revolutionaries were proved to be mistaken. In his own time he would launch a second revolution and shake China to her foundations.

THE CULTURAL REVOLUTION

IN FEBRUARY 1966 an elderly woman who had played no previous role in politics and was completely unknown to the Chinese people held a series of seminars in art and literature with some army officers in Shanghai, and set in motion a chain of events which led to a second Communist revolution.

The elderly woman was Chiang Ch'ing, a former film actress who played minor roles in films produced in Shanghai during the early thirties. In her film roles she took the name of Lan P'ing, meaning "Blue Apple." She married a young actor, divorced him, became a Communist, and in 1938 she set out for Yenan, where she joined the Lu Hsün Academy and directed plays for the peasants and Red Army men, being especially successful in producing operas which were staged in Yenan's small theater. She attracted the attention of Mao Tse-tung, who married her the following year, although his second wife, who had given him five children and accompanied him during the Long March, was still living. There was some opposition to the marriage from the Central Committee, but he overcame it. His second wife had become mentally deranged and was living in a sanatorium in Moscow.

In Yenan the third wife of Mao Tse-tung shunned the limelight. She lived quietly with him in a small cave, gave birth to two daughters, and continued to teach at the Lu Hsün Academy. A correspondent who visited Yenan in the summer of 1946 was impressed by her quiet beauty, her delicate skin and graceful gestures. In a town where the women dressed like men, she retained her femininity. When the Chinese Communists entered Peking in triumph, she retired into obscurity, and no one expected to hear anything more of her. She became one more of the anonymous wives of the Communist leaders, their names never mentioned in the newspapers, their presence in the capital unknown except to a small circle of acquaintances.

In February 1966, when she began to emerge into the limelight, she was no longer a beautiful woman. She was about fifty-seven years old, with a gaunt, thin face ravaged by illness. She had spent many months in bed during the previous year, recovering from tuberculosis.

According to a published account, the decision to send her to Shanghai was made by Lin Piao, who was impressed by her wide knowledge of literature and art. The military authorities in Shanghai were ordered to give her all possible assistance in formulating precise codes for the "artistic and literary work" of the Red Army, by which was meant the propaganda conducted by the armed forces. All relevant documents were to be shown to her, and she was given extraordinary powers to change, revise, and make decisions on all matters connected with propaganda. Nothing was said about her relationship to Mao Tse-tung, although this was well-known to the officers she met in Shanghai. She was simply "Comrade Chiang Ch'ing," sent on a special mission on the orders of Marshal Lin Piao, the minister of national defense.

The seminars lasted for nearly three weeks and began, predictably, with readings of Mao Tse-tung's writings on literature, art, and the theater. Private discussions were followed by group discussions and the presentation of films and operas. Altogether thirteen films were shown, and there were three special theatrical performances for the benefit of the "cultural committee." Chiang Ch'ing pronounced her verdict on the films, and it soon became clear that she found many of them unsatisfactory, because they did not conform to Mao Tse-tung's writings, "On the Correct Handling of Contradictions Among the People" and "Speech at the Chinese Communist Party's National Conference on Propaganda Work." In particular, she objected to films and plays which described the sufferings and tribulations of "middle characters," who were defined as people caught in the no-man's-land between Communism and the fascism of the Kuomintang. In these dramas the "middle characters" were usually shown making their final peace with Communism. Chiang Ch'ing felt that this was scarcely a subject worth discussing.

Since Chiang Ch'ing's knowledge of the arts was limited to films and the theater, very little attention was paid to poetry or the novel. What concerned her above everything else was the production of films and plays which would hew faithfully to the line announced by her husband in Yenan, and with few exceptions she found most of the current plays and films wanting. The term "cultural revolution" was invented to describe the new orientation in the arts, which henceforth must never be permitted to deviate from the strict party line. Film-makers, writers, and playwrights had for too long enjoyed the license to describe the world as they saw it; now they must describe the world as Mao Tse-tung saw it. Only those films and dramas which showed the toiling workers, peasants, and soldiers marching under the banner of Mao Tse-tung were to be tolerated. Mao Tse-tung had complained that for fifteen years the writers and artists of China had failed to carry out the policies of the party. According to Chiang Ch'ing, the time had come for a massive re-examination of past practices and a sudden change of direction.

The implications of the "cultural revolution" extended over a vast area. There was the implication that the arts, including the art of propaganda, had fallen into the hands of reactionaries, who must be smoked out and destroyed. Extreme measures had become necessary, and an entirely new machinery must come into existence to enforce the new code. Chiang Ch'ing's task was to see whether the army might not possess some hitherto unknown machinery for this purpose. Mao Tse-tung had come to the conclusion that the army must take the lead.

A report on the February seminars was published in March. That it was far more than a mere report on some obscure meetings in Shanghai became clear when it was learned that Mao Tse-tung studied the document at length, rewrote and revised it three times, and discussed it with his chief advisers. Chiang Ch'ing had been his mouthpiece, faithfully reflecting his prejudices and opinions. The "cultural revolution" was to be the work of Mao Tse-tung, and it was to bear the imprint of his mind throughout.

The report, as it finally appeared, described a "cultural revolution" which was essentially reactionary and had little enough to do with culture. All art was to be propaganda, every artist must obey the party, all bourgeois elements must be extirpated. The literature of the Soviet Union was to be critically examined in the light of "revisionism"; since the crowning sin of the Soviet Union was its revisionist policy, and its literature for many years had reflected this policy, the Chinese Communists must be especially on guard when reading Russian works. "We should catch the big ones, catch Sholokhov and dare to tackle him, because he is the father of revisionist literature and art," wrote Mao Tse-tung, who particularly objected to the "revisionist tendencies" in *And Quiet Flows the Don* and *Virgin Soil Upturned*, although they were written in the twenties and thirties and could not conceivably have reflected the prevalent Soviet ideology. Stalin, though praised as "a great Marxist-Leninist," sharply critical of bourgeois literature, was blamed for having permitted the publication of European and Russian classics without sufficiently criticizing them.

In 1957 Mao Tse-tung had bitterly attacked the persistence of bourgeois ideas in revolutionary China. "We still have to wage a protracted struggle against bourgeois and petty bourgeois ideology," he wrote. "It is wrong not to understand this and to give up the ideological struggle. All erroneous ideas, all poisonous weeds, all ghosts and monsters, must be subjected to criticism; in no circumstance should they be allowed to spread unchecked." Now, nine years later, he returned to the attack. Unfortunately, there existed no suitable machinery for destroying weeds, ghosts, and monsters.

In the weeks following the publication of the report on the seminars Chiang Ch'ing became the unofficial "commissar for the arts," while Mao Tse-tung turned his attention to a revolutionary concept which had hitherto escaped the attention of Chinese revolutionaries. The machinery for enforcing the new discipline lay at hand in the awakened youth of the country. With their help the last surviving elements of bourgeois ideology would be utterly destroyed. One of the conclusions reached at the Shanghai seminars was, "There must be both destruction and construction." The youth would be the agents of the destructive process.

By early May the pattern of the "cultural revolution" had already formed in Mao Tse-tung's mind. The task of revitalizing the revolution would be given to the students. They would act as the policemen of culture, the enforcers of revolutionary morality, the heralds of the revolutionary storm. They would be given power and authority to destroy what needed to be destroyed. If necessary, the period of their schooling would be shortened and the entire system of education would be revised in order to permit them the freedom to act as standard-bearers of the revolution. What had begun as an attempt to censor films and plays had broadened to include the censorship of the whole of existing society. Students from the colleges and high schools were to be let loose on China; their task was "to purify the revolution."

In June the first of many waves of Red Guards descended upon Peking without warning. Sent by their local party cells on railroad passes, they wore red armbands, carried the little red books,* and let it be known that they had been appointed by Mao Tse-tung to direct the proletarian revolution. They marched in procession and sang Communist songs, but they had been given

---

* The Sayings of Mao Tse-tung, compiled by Lin Piao in 1960 for use in the Red Army, was a small handbook containing brief passages from Mao Tse-tung's writings gathered together under thirty-three headings. It was intended as an easy guide to Mao's thought, but was not intended to replace the voluminous four-volume edition of his works. None of the passages was written after 1957, and the first edition, which was later withdrawn, includes an approving reference to Liu Shao-ch'i. It was bound in red plastic. Chiang Ch'ing is credited with the idea of distributing it to the Red Guards.

sterner tasks. They took over large sections of the city, conducted house-by-house inspections, and when they found evidence of bourgeois tendencies they held drumhead courts-martial and punished their victims. They invaded government offices and cross-questioned government officers, taking voluminous depositions. Everyone was on trial, and the judges were youths from fifteen to twenty years old who had come from all over China to take part in the revolution. A few shops were set on fire, some beauty parlors were wrecked, a church was desecrated, foreigners were sometimes attacked, and there were some ugly incidents involving public trials in which the victims were condemned to death. But on the whole the Red Guards acted with revolutionary discipline under the control of older and more experienced men. They exulted in their newfound strength, and sometimes a group of Red Guards would argue with another group as to which showed the more revolutionary fervor, and there were street battles between them. Teachers and professors inevitably incurred their wrath. "The domination of our schools by bourgeois intellectuals should by no means be allowed to continue," Mao Tse-tung had written in May. In the eyes of the Red Guards most teachers and professors were bourgeois intellectuals and deserved to be punished.

Mao Tse-tung had unleashed a powerful and potentially dangerous weapon which served to strengthen his own domination over the country, but otherwise served little useful purpose. The students added nothing to the productive wealth of the nation; they were interfering with the government, clogging the railroads, conducting trials, and driving nearly everybody to the edge of hysteria. A vast army of vigilantes had come into existence, and could not easily be disbanded. The economy of the country suffered, for they lived at government expense. In some manner still undiscovered, it was necessary to harness them to a creative purpose.

All over China bands of Red Guards, armed only with the authority granted them by Mao Tse-tung, swept into the cities and took charge, acting as though they were appointed officials. Wherever they appeared, they threatened established authority. They formed a second government. China was being ruled simul-

taneously by a bureaucracy and by bands of youths in red armbands who decided all questions by consulting the appropriate
page in the little red book.

In the midst of the upheaval Mao Tse-tung left Peking and
made an extensive tour of central China. On July 18, 1966, he
went swimming in the Yangtse River at Wuhan. Ten years before
he had swum three times across the river, but this time he contented himself with a leisurely swim downstream; according to the
reports published at the time, he covered some fifteen kilometers,
from the Wuchang dikes to the Wuhan Iron and Steel Works,
in sixty-five minutes. Although the photographs showing him in
the water are so retouched that they look as though his head had
simply been pasted over a photograph of a stretch of water, there
is little doubt that he did swim for some minutes in the Yangtse.

An official account of the swim was broadcast all over China
and published in all the newspapers. Thousands of people lined
the shores, watching the launch with Mao Tse-tung standing on
the bows as it made its way to midstream. At last, at eleven o'clock
in the morning, under a blazing sky, he climbed down the gangway
and slipped into the water. Although the photographs show him
swimming in calm water, the official account was inclined to suggest the ferocity of the waves and the turbulence of the river:

> The Yangtse was in spate; its current was swift, and the rolling
> waves pounded the shores. Swimming in the vast river, Chair-
> man Mao sometimes made his way through the turbulent waters
> by sidestroking and sometimes floated on his back, looking at
> the azure sky. As he swam through the waves, he chatted ani-
> matedly with the comrades around him. A young woman told
> him, "This is the second time I have swum in the Yangtse."
> Smiling, Chairman Mao said, "The Yangtse is wide and deep.
> It is a good place to swim." When Chairman Mao discovered that
> another young woman accompanying him could only swim in one
> style, he amiably taught her the backstroke. He said, "The
> Yangtse is deep and its current is swift. This can help you
> train your body and strengthen your willpower."
>
> While swimming, Chairman Mao also chatted with Com-
> rade Wang Jen-chung, the first secretary of the Hupeh Provincial
> Party Committee. "How are the young people in Wuhan taking

to swimming?" he asked. "More and more of them are taking
to the water," replied Wang Jen-chung. "They have shown
themselves to be bold, brave, and quick in learning. In general
they can swim by themselves after only five or six days." Then
Chairman Mao asked, "Can one in every three swim?" Comrade
Wang Jen-chung replied, "Yes." Very much pleased, Chairman
Mao said, "That is very good."

Newspaper correspondents may be excused if they fail to
hear all the words spoken by a man swimming in the Yangtse,
and it is not necessary to believe that all these conversations
took place. Like the young swimmers of Wuhan, the Red Guards
had proved to be "bold, brave, and quick in learning." When he
returned to Peking, Mao Tse-tung was determined to give the
Red Guards an important assignment.

The Red Guards possessed the authority to interfere with
the lives of ordinary people, to act as judges and sometimes as
executioners, to censor films and plays, and to bully the lower
ranks of the bureaucracy, but they were forbidden to use guns, to
broadcast from the radio stations, or to publish newspapers. Their
powers, at least at the beginning of the new revolution, were
severely limited. They were storm troopers whose tasks were to
clean up the streets and to be the advance guard for some un-
named and even more dangerous revolutionary experiment, but
they were not to take over power or to exercise any real power.
Theirs was to be a bloodless revolution, and their voices were not
to be heard above the voices of high government officials, whose
instruments they were.

By creating the Red Guards, Mao Tse-tung solved one pressing problem. For many years the youth of China had felt that
they were powerless. By 1966 a whole generation had arisen which
had never known a time when the Chinese Communist party was
not in total command of the country. But within the party power
was being wielded by a small group of elderly men, who were
usually described as "the close comrades in arms of Mao Tse-tung."
They were the survivors of the Long March, men in their late
sixties and early seventies, resourceful, dogmatic, insular, determined to retain their privileged positions. No youthful revolu-

tionary leader had come to prominence. Now, quite suddenly, thousands of students felt that they were acquiring power as leaders of the Red Guard movement. In the excitement of the times it rarely occurred to them that they were being given, not real power, but the simulacrum of power.

Their instruments were their voices and their proclamations written in large Chinese characters. The first of these "big-character posters" was said to have been written in June by a woman professor of philosophy at Peking University and posted up on the east wall of the university refectory. She attacked the administration of the university, accused it of "revisionist tendencies" and "antagonism to our beloved leader, Mao Tse-tung." Soon "big-character posters" began to appear everywhere, especially on the walls of universities and high schools. There was nothing intrinsically novel in these posters, for in China dissident groups had always used posters to proclaim their grievances, and we hear of posters being used for this purpose as far back as the Han dynasty. Professor Nieh Yuan-tzu's poster was simply the first of an interminable series of posters attacking "revisionism" and proclaiming loyalty to Mao Tse-tung.

The posters which began to appear on the walls of Peking were remarkable for their ferocity and virulence. Every dissident group was proclaiming its independence; the hundred flowers were blooming again. The Red Guards, armed with the powers of censorship, tore down any posters with which they disagreed. Posters went up at night, and every dawn there would be crowds patiently reading them. Many assumed that these inflammatory posters would die a natural death, forgetting that they filled a need and represented a human response in a world where little real news was being distributed. These wall newspapers were not written in the stylized manner of the official newspapers, heavy with Marxist jargon. They were fresh and vigorous and flamboyant, with bold brushstrokes in bright-colored paint. Because they dealt with internal problems and seemed to reflect only the views of the students, the government paid little attention to them and seems to have regarded the writing of posters as a method of letting off steam. It was thought that they would never reach the attention of people abroad. Japanese correspondents who attempted to copy the posters were sometimes attacked, and the Chinese complained that the Japanese did not always know Chinese sufficiently well to understand what was said on the posters. In fact, the Japanese understood Chinese perfectly.

On August 5, 1966, there appeared the most surprising of all the "big-character posters" written up to this time. In bold, vivid characters Mao Tse-tung announced that the time had come for an attack on the government. The poster read:

BOMBARD THE HEADQUARTERS
My Big-Character Poster
MAO TSE-TUNG

China's first Marxist-Leninist big-character poster and the commentator's article on it in *People's Daily* are indeed superbly written! Comrades, please read them again.

Meanwhile, during the last fifty days or so some leading comrades from the central down to the local levels have acted in a diametrically opposite way. Adopting the reactionary stand of the bourgeoisie, they have enforced a bourgeois dictatorship and struck down the surging movement of the great cultural revolution of the proletariat.

They have stood facts on their heads and juggled black and white, encircled and suppressed revolutionaries, stifled opinions differing from their own, imposed a white terror, and felt very pleased with themselves. They have puffed up the arrogance of the bourgeoisie and deflated the morale of the proletariat. How poisonous! Viewed in connection with the Right deviation of 1962 and the wrong tendency of 1964 which was Left in form but Right in essence, shouldn't this make one wide awake?

At first it was thought that this revolutionary proclamation —for it was nothing less—was an elaborate hoax. Although Mao Tse-tung was no longer the acting head of the government, he was still head of the Chinese Communist party. The proclamation calling upon the Red Guards to bombard the headquarters was an invitation to them to destroy the government appointed by the party. In Mao Tse-tung's view there was no longer a Communist government, only a bourgeois dictatorship imposing a white terror on an acquiescent people.

Mao Tse-tung was an old man, suffering from throat cancer, who had been living for a long time in semi-isolation. He had partially recovered his health, but until the beginning of the year he had had very little contact with the outside world except through the newspapers. For a long time he had cherished a growing hatred for Liu Shao-ch'i and for the entire bureaucracy. The "cultural revolution," which had begun as an attempt to change the arts and literature, had grown step by step until it encompassed a revolution which would inevitably affect the lives of everyone in China. A new kind of society would come into existence, and once more he would assert his personal domination. By setting the youth against the bureaucracy, he hoped to tear down the existing superstructure. With his "big-character poster," composed in white-hot fury, he announced that the battle was about to be joined.

Many factors contributed to this strange proclamation. Old age, his physical sufferings, the feeling of impotence which overcomes everyone suffering from cancer, and wounded vanity all played their part. He knew—he must have known—that there were statements in the proclamation which had no basis in fact. The government was far from being a bourgeois dictatorship; there was no white terror; the "great cultural revolution of the proletariat" had not been struck down. Some Red Guards had been arrested, and there had been some ineffective attempts to dissuade him from organizing his own paramilitary troops, but he had been treated with respect and deference by the government. What he wanted was more than respect and deference; he wanted to be the government.

Two weeks after Mao Tse-tung wrote the "big-character poster" there was held the first of ten Red Guard parades which were to dominate the life of Peking for the rest of the summer and autumn. The parades marked the emergence of the Red Guards as an active and powerful force in the country. More than a million Red Guards took part in the processions of August 18. Mao Tse-tung, standing on the balcony of the Gate of Heavenly Peace, took the salute. Beside him stood Lin Piao, the minister of national defense, who delivered the speech of the day, calling upon the Red Guards "to destroy, utterly confound, and discredit the counter-revolutionary revisionists, bourgeois rightists, and bourgeois reactionary authorities, who must never be permitted to rise again." Mao Tse-tung said nothing. He looked puffy and very old, unlike the youthful portraits of him carried by the Red Guards.

Throughout August, September, and October the Red Guards virtually controlled Peking. Their powers were still vaguely defined, but the tempo of their activities increased. They invaded homes and shops seeking any vestige of foreign or bourgeois influence, smashed Buddhist statues, consigned ancestral tablets to the flames, hurled down the tombstones in Peking's only foreign cemetery, which was henceforth to be known as "the anti-imperialist antirevisionist orchard," and changed the names of streets. They sacked a Roman Catholic convent, assaulted the nuns, and expelled them from the country. But these were merely peripheral activities. The real work of the Red Guards consisted of a minute examination of the lives, histories, and political beliefs of everyone living in the city. Street by street, house by house, room by room, they pursued their victims and ensured their conversion to the principles of Mao Tse-tung. The police were ordered to assist them in their inquiries; the army, although under the direct control of Lin Piao, who was also in command of the Red Guards, appeared to be indifferent to them and kept its distance.

Denunciations and public trials increased; people suspected of "revisionism" were paraded through the streets in dunce's caps and made to confess their errors in public; the nation-wide witch-hunt continued unabated. Since the schools remained closed, the students could devote their whole time to their new tasks, but the teachers did not enjoy a holiday, for the "cultural revolution" involved a direct attack against their authority. In May Mao Tse-tung had described them as "scholar-tyrants" indistinguishable from the reigning bureaucrats, who "have usurped the name of the party, do not read books, do not read the daily press, have no contact with the masses, have no learning at all, and rely solely on 'acting arbitrarily and trying to overwhelm people with their power.'" Schools, colleges, and the bureaucracy were all expendable.

Toward the end of the year Mao Tse-tung turned his attention to Liu Shao-ch'i, the president of the People's Republic, the author of a well-known treatise entitled *How To Be a Good Communist*, originally written in Yenan and often rewritten to conform to the changing nature of Chinese Communism. The book was dull and prolix, written without fire and perhaps without conviction. It was easy to find fault with it. Mao Tse-tung found many faults in it and characterized the author as "the top party man in authority taking the capitalist road." Suddenly Liu Shao-ch'i was singled out as the enemy of the "cultural revolution," the archenemy of Communism, a man who for seventeen years had been waiting patiently for the moment when he could destroy the revolution and impose a bourgeois dictatorship. The Red Guards, informed that their greatest enemy was the president of China, howled for his blood, arrested his wife, put her on trial, humiliated her, and then let her free. Liu Shao-ch'i himself remained in seclusion, protected by the dignity of his office. There was a widespread belief that in Yenan the Communist leaders had agreed among themselves never to indulge in the luxury of killing one another after they achieved power; the examples of the French and Russian revolutionaries were to be avoided.

A revolution feeds on its enemies, real or imagined, and the "cultural revolution" had found its victims in the surviving remnants of the middle classes. During the winter it turned against the bureaucracy and the local administrations; the Red Guards were given authority to remove or replace officials who were not sufficiently imbued with the concepts of the "cultural revolution," and as the months passed the administration became increasingly erratic, with rival factions of Red Guards battling among themselves and with local administrations, while the army reserved its right to interfere whenever one or other of the contenders for power got the upper hand. China appeared to be splitting at the seams, returning to a state of primitive anarchy. The Red Guards were drunk with power, untrained, inexperienced; and the party officials, who had grown up with the regime and were experienced in all the subtle ways in which power can be enforced, were sometimes able to cope with them. The beleaguered officials organized the first major mass opposition to the "cultural revolu-

tion." They encouraged industrial strikes, dislocated transporta-
tion, connived at raids on the state granaries, and showed themselves to be masters of sabotage. By purging the bureaucracy Mao
Tse-tung was sowing the dragons' teeth. Communists were at war
with Communists, and the rest of the world was left wondering
why an aging dictator had decided to inflict so much punishment
on China.

From one end of China to the other the young were reading
the *Sayings of Mao Tse-tung*, chanting them, debating them, waving the little red books, as though caught up in a religious frenzy.
All wisdom reposed in the sayings; nothing written in China had
ever been so widely read. Yet the sayings, divorced from their context, were often curiously elliptic and contradictory. "Political
powers grows out of the barrel of a gun," he wrote in what was
perhaps the most famous of all his pronouncements, but he also
wrote that "military and economic power is necessarily wielded
by the people," implying that the masses, rather than guns, were
the final arbiters. The Red Guards were intended to assume the
role of a mass movement spontaneously generated at a critical
moment in revolutionary history. Logically they could have only
one purpose—to sieze power. Deprived of guns, too lawless to
administer the laws, at war among themselves, they could neither
seize power nor impose their will upon the country's leaders.
Power remained in the hands of old and dying men.

THE SHADOW OF A COMING DEATH

WHILE THE "cultural revolution" was at its height, three short essays written by Mao Tse-tung more than twenty years before were reprinted in millions of copies and offered to the Red Guards as the quintessence of his thought. They became known as "the three good old essays," and it was claimed for them that they were "powerful ideological weapons for the establishment of a spirit of perfect devotion to the country by changing people to the very depths of their beings." Still more powerful claims were made for the essays, and it was said that the mere recital of them would help to overcome all problems, from combatting drought to designing machine tools and marketing watermelons profitably. Some mysterious power lay in them. In these essays was revealed the fundamental purity of Communist belief.

The essays were "Serve the People," "In Memory of Norman Bethune," and "The Foolish Old Man Who Removed the Mountains." They were written in Yenan between 1939 and 1945, and together they formed a booklet of about ten pages.

In none of the essays was there the slightest reference to

Marxist-Leninist doctrine, and they were mercifully free from polemics. Two were obituary notices written in devotional tones and pointing a moral. In the third Mao recounts the story of a foolish old man whose view was obstructed by two enormous mountains and who became so angered by their presence that he decided to dig them away until God in his mercy sent two angels to do the work for him. It transpires that the names of the mountains are Feudalism and Imperialism, but Mao Tse-tung evidently enjoyed telling the story of the foolish old man for its own sake, as though he were talking to children by a fireside, happy to be among them and amused by their laughter. There is no violence in the three essays. They are calm, reflective, gentle. Throughout them runs a note of unappeasable longing and lamentation. Mao Tse-tung evidently chose them because, although written in middle age, they reflected his mood on the threshold of old age.

"Serve the People" was originally delivered on September 8, 1944, as a funeral oration for a Red Army soldier who had been one of Mao Tse-tung's personal guards and had taken part in the Long March. He had not died in battle but was killed by the sudden collapse of a kiln while he was making charcoal in the mountains near Yenan. Although his death was the result of a stupid accident caused by his own carelessness, Mao Tse-tung felt that he deserved a hero's funeral. The oration was a testimony to a long friendship and to the soldier's loyalty to the party. The soldier, Chang Szu-teh, had joined the Communists in 1932, and it was proper that his twelve years of service be suitably celebrated.

For the first time Mao Tse-tung presented himself as a man who felt keenly about death; he was no longer the hardened revolutionary accustomed to regarding death coldly and impersonally:

> Death awaits all men, but its significance varies with various persons. The ancient Chinese writer Ssu-ma Ch'ien said, "Although death befalls all men alike, in significance it may be weightier than Mount Tai or lighter than swan's down." In significance, to die for the interests of the people is weightier than Mount Tai, but to work hard and die for the fascists, for those who exploit and oppress the people, is lighter than swan's down.

Comrade Chang Szu-teh died for the interests of the people, and his death is indeed weightier in significance than Mount Tai.

There followed a brief dissertation on the necessity of self-examination and of accepting advice from people who are not party members; these words appear to have strayed into the text from another speech. He went on:

In times of difficulty our comrades must be able to see our achievements and the bright side of things and screw up their courage. Since the Chinese people are suffering and we have the duty to save them, we must exert ourselves in struggle. Struggle necessarily entails sacrifice, and death is a common occurrence. But if we keep in mind the interests of the people and the sufferings of the great majority, then we see that to die for the people's sake is to die a worthy death. Nevertheless, we ought to avoid as much as possible all unnecessary sacrifices. Our cadres should be concerned about every soldier, and all people in the revolutionary ranks should care for each other and love and help one another.

From now on, if anyone in our ranks who has done some good work passes away, there should be a funeral procession and a memorial meeting to render him honor, whether he is a cook or a soldier. This should become a regular practice. And it should also be introduced among the common people. When someone dies in a village, hold a memorial meeting for him. This will serve to express our mourning for the deceased and to unite all the people.

The last words were perhaps the most significant, for never before had he maintained that the people could be united by grief. It was as though at long last he had come to the conclusion that death was important, that it must be reckoned with, and that it should have a place of honor in public ceremonies of mourning. "When someone dies in a village, hold a memorial meeting for him. . . ."

The funeral oration for Norman Bethune, the Canadian surgeon who served in Republican Spain and set up a field hospital in Communist China early in 1938, disclosed no private emotion.

Mao Tse-tung had known the soldier Chang Szu-teh well, but he had met Norman Bethune only once, and only very briefly, during the doctor's brief passage through Yenan. Nevertheless, he appears to have read reports of the doctor's activities and to have been deeply impressed. Norman Bethune contracted blood poisoning while operating on wounded soldiers and died on November 12, 1939. Six weeks later, when the news finally reached Yenan, Mao Tse-tung wrote:

> Comrade Bethune's spirit of doing everything for others' benefit and nothing for his own was shown in his extreme sense of responsibility in his work and his extreme warmheartedness toward his comrades and the people. Every Communist must learn from him. Quite a number of people are irresponsible in their work, "picking up the light and shirking the heavy," i.e., shoving the heavy loads onto others and choosing the light ones for themselves. When anything comes up, they think of themselves first and of others only afterward. When they have exerted themselves a little, they swell with pride and brag about it in case others should not know. Toward their comrades and the people they are not full of enthusiasm but cold and reserved, indifferent and apathetic. Such people are really not Communists, or at least cannot be counted as pure Communists. None who returned from the front failed to express their admiration for Bethune whenever his name was mentioned, and none remained unmoved by his spirit. . . .
>
> I saw Comrade Bethune only once. Afterward he wrote me many letters. But as I was busy, I wrote back only one letter and do not know if he ever received it. I feel deeply grieved over his death. Now all of us commemorate him; thus we can see how profoundly people are moved by his spirit. We must all learn from him the spirit that is so completely free from selfishness. Starting from that point, one can become a person of great use to the people. A man's ability may be great or small, but if only he has this spirit, he is already a nobleminded man, a pure man, a moral man, a man who has left vulgar taste behind, a man who is useful to the people.

Mao Tse-tung appears to have written this sermon out of an obscure sense of guilt, remembering that he had failed to answer the doctor's letters and perhaps taken him too much for granted. It was a sermon in praise of a man's devotion to his fellow men, and of the three esssays it was the one most calculated to have some effect on the Red Guards, who needed to be reminded that devotion was virtuous and that it was criminal to act irresponsibly.

"The Foolish Old Man Who Removed the Mountains" was taken with some slight modifications from the works of Lieh Tzu, the Taoist philosopher who probably lived about A.D. 300 and therefore belonged to the period when Taoism was in full decadence. Lieh Tzu borrowed his symbolic stories from earlier philosophers, but the origin of the story about the man who wanted to remove a mountain is unknown. Mao Tse-tung simplifies the story, omitting an argumentative wife and some snake spirits, but otherwise keeping close to the original:

> There is a story told about an old man living in north China in ancient times, called the Foolish Old Man of the North Mountain. His house faced south, and its doorway was obstructed by two big mountains, Taihang and Wangwu. With great determination he led his sons to dig up the mountains with pickaxes. Another old man, called the Old Wiseacre, witnessed their attempts and laughed, saying, "What fools you are to attempt this! To dig up the two huge mountains is utterly beyond your capacity."
>
> The Foolish Old Man replied, "When I die, there are my sons; when they die, there will be their own sons, and so on to infinity. As to these two mountains, high as they are, they cannot become higher but, on the contrary, with every bit we dig, they will become much lower. Why can't we clear them away?"
>
> In this way the Foolish Old Man refuted the erroneous view of the Old Wiseacre and went on digging day after day uninterruptedly. God's heart was touched by such perseverence and he sent two angels down to earth to carry the mountains away on their backs.
>
> Today two big mountains lie like a dead weight on the Chinese people: Feudalism and Imperialism. The Chinese Communist party has long ago made up its mind to dig them out. We must persevere and work unceasingly, and we too may be able to touch God's heart. This God is no other than the masses

of the people throughout China. And if they rise up and dig
together with us, why can't we dig these two mountains up?

The choice of this story as propaganda for the Red Guards
is somewhat puzzling. By 1966 the last vestiges of feudalism and
imperialism had been removed from the Chinese mainland, and
there was no longer any need to dig up the mountains. The point
of the story appears to be that everything, even the most improb-
able things, are possible to determined men. In the original story
composed by Lieh Tzu, the mountains are seven hundred miles
square and seven hundred thousand miles high.

It was a theme which had long dominated Mao Tse-tung's
thoughts. Once, talking to Hsiao San, he had asked casually why
there was only one sun in the sky. In his view it was perfectly
possible for men to build another sun, and if necessary a single
man might be able to accomplish it.

Not everyone in China approved the publication of "the three
good old essays." Some felt that the publication on such a massive scale was an act of self-indulgence, for they were essentially
personal documents. Thirty-six million sets of his four-volume
collected works had been published, and the pamphlet was given
a press run of seventy million copies. There were some who
feared that all the forests of China would become paper for the
works of Mao Tse-tung.

Yet the pamphlet served a useful purpose by insisting on
the personal qualities of Mao Tse-tung, who showed himself to
be possessed of compassion and kindliness, a man who urged
reverence for the dead and demanded that "all people in the
revolutionary ranks should care for each other and love and help
one another." That he identified himself with the mountain-
moving Foolish Old Man only made the story more appealing. It
seems never to have occurred to him that this slender pamphlet
derived at a great distance from the devotional Buddhist texts his
mother had read to him in his childhood.

Although the pamphlet became the Bible of the Red Guards,
its teachings were ignored. The unruly, lawless youths who spread
out over China were in no mood to love one another, or to love

other Communist cadres or the people. They were vigilantes armed with increasingly wide powers. From time to time the government issued serious warnings against the practice of subjecting people to summary execution. They were told that their function was to criticize and correct abuses, and to attack only those who were attempting to return to the capitalist road. The government, which had filled them with a wild excitement and offered them free license, could no longer police them. It could only hope that they would eventually learn to police themselves. Orders went out that the basic organization of the country should assume a tripartite form, with the Red Army, the Red bureaucracy, and elected representatives of the masses forming the governing committees ruling in the provinces, the towns, and the *hsiens*. The idea appears to have originated with Chen Po-ta, who had been Mao Tse-tung's political secretary before being given the post of director-general of the Red Guards. He had studied the French communes, and believed that they answered the needs of China. The new form of government left little room for the Red Guards.

By 1968 Mao Tse-tung was already in partial eclipse. The newspapers and magazines still published photographs showing him youthful and ebullient, the thick, black hair brushed smoothly back, the face gleaming, the lips forming a faint smile. Many of these photographs were recognizably doctored photographs from the distant past, and many more bore the telltale marks of the retoucher. What he really looked like, how he really appeared to the small circle of acquaintances who had access to him, was unknown. He began to vanish into his legend.

When a man becomes a legend, strange things happen. The legend assumes a life of its own, obedient to its own laws, formulating its responses according to its own needs, which are not the needs of a flesh-and-blood human being. The legendary Mao Tse-tung came to resemble an enormous red balloon flying high over China, growing larger with every passing day until everyone in the country lived in its shadow. To some extent the movement of the balloon could be manipulated by the unknown people who held the strings, but it was at the mercy of incalculable winds.

A strange air of unreality dominated the Chinese scene. The

few foreign observers who were permitted to remain in Peking were
struck by the disparity between the members of the government
and the acts performed in their name. Too many high officials
were acting out of character, and the real power seemed to be
in the hands of a shadow cabinet composed of curiously erratic
functionaries. Moreover, the members of the shadow cabinet
seemed to be constantly changing. There was no focus, no con-
sistent policy, no effective planning organization. The more ve-
hemently the official newspapers proclaimed that Mao Tse-tung
alone was guiding the destiny of China, the more evident it
became that China was being governed by a small group of
anonymous men who hid in the shadows.

What had happened was something that had rarely happened
before in China, except during an interregnum or when an emperor was dying. Power was being wielded in an emperor's name,
but the emperor himself had no control over events, remained
silent, withdrawn, and inscrutable behind the screen of his own
infallibility, and sometimes the words he had uttered in the distant
past were broadcast as though they had special relevance to the
present time. Speeches delivered in Yenan thirty years ago were
dusted off, edited and emended, and presented as contributions to
the understanding of present problems. For five years Mao Tse-
tung had delivered no new speeches. The silence was filled by the
old speeches, which were reprinted and rebroadcast continually.
Obviously the recital of the old speeches was intended to give the
impression that his ideas had not changed and that his intellectual
authority remained unchallenged, but there were many who
wondered why he never spoke in public about the affairs of the
day.

He had withdrawn into the shadows, appearing rarely at
public functions, remote from the world as in a grave. On the
few occasions when he appeared at the theater or at ceremonial
functions, he would remain silent, though it was observed that he
smiled broadly when greeted with applause. His silence was deafening. Never before had a dictator so little to say during a period
of permanent crisis. He was ungainly in his walk, shambling hesi-
tantly with the assistance of nurses, and usually wore a uniform

which was two sizes too large for him. Old and ill and suffering, he took only an intermittent interest in affairs of state. Like the dying Lenin, he had divorced himself from the world, spending his days in complete isolation, reading the newspapers and on the basis of his reading sometimes bestirring himself sufficiently to give orders which were not necessarily obeyed.

The struggle for the succession had begun and was being fought in deadly earnest. There were contenders for the throne in the government offices in Peking, while all over China there were dissident revolutionary groups, determined to oust the reigning Communist faction from power, though none of them possessed a coherent revolutionary program or a charismatic leader who would lead them to victory. It was not enough to be totally disenchanted by the policies announced in Mao Tse-tung's name. What was needed was a new revolutionary philosophy, a clearly stated alternative to the existing party program, a set of revolutionary principles and symbols. In addition the revolutionaries needed control of a propaganda machine and a well-trained army. Most of the sporadic uprisings began in the army.

The most serious and threatening of many unco-ordinated uprisings took place in the summer of 1967 in Wuhan, where the revolution which toppled the Manchus from power had begun fifty-five years earlier.

The leader of the Wuhan uprising was Chen Tsai-tao, the military commander of Hupeh province, who was in communication with revolutionaries in Kwangsi in the south and Manchuria in the north. It was hoped that there would be simultaneous uprisings in Nanning in Kwangsi and the Manchurian province of Kirin, and that other provincial armies would join the revolt. The Peking authorities got wind of the affair and sent urgent messages to Wuhan to forestall the uprising. Vice-Premier Hsieh Fu-chih and Wang Li, one of the leading members of the cultural revolution, who was later purged, were sent to Wuhan to take command of the situation and were promptly kidnapped by the revolutionaries. The Peking radio went into action with a steady stream of appeals and threats to the people of Wuhan, promising that the rebellion would be crushed with overwhelming force. Chen Tsai-tao and Chung Han-hua, the political commissar of Hupeh, had already captured Wuhan, arrested thousands of Red Guards, and proclaimed an independent revolutionary government. Following the traditional custom they gave a special name to their revolutionary army, which became known as the "Million Heroic Troops."

For five weeks there was street-fighting, with Mao Tse-tung's Red Guards battling against the more disciplined soldiers of the Red Army. Only confused reports of the battles became available, but it soon became evident that the Red Guards were no match for the Red army, for Peking radio complained about the "inhuman butcheries" suffered by the Red Guards. It was reported that on a single day, June 17, the Red Guards lost more than two hundred and fifty dead and a thousand wounded. Chen Tsai-tao had given orders that no Red Guards should be left alive in the city. From Peking there came a strangely worded announcement that the "Million Heroic Troops" were no more than bandits "wearing steel helmets or safety caps, wielding iron spears and daggers and armed to the teeth, going over to the attack day and night, using fire-fighting engines, gasoline, and gas shells." The newspapers published what purported to be eyewitness accounts of the fighting, with axes, spears, and pitchforks as the principal weapons. One such account described how trucks manned by peasants converged on a Red Guard stronghold in Hankow, one of the three cities which form the Wuhan complex. A truck belonging to the Red Guards was isolated, and everyone in it was massacred. According to an eyewitness report published from Peking and evidently written by a Red Guard, a "bandit" was seen to jump into the driver's seat and split open the skull of the driver with his ax; other "bandits" crowded around the truck and dispatched the Red Guards with spears, pitchforks, and axes. A week later, in another engagement, we learn that the "bandits" fought against Red Guards who had barricaded themselves behind the walls of an engineering college. The "bandits" brought up "searchlights and fire-fighting engines, water hoses, poison gas, smoke, and fire." The engineering college was burned down, and Red Guards were seen falling into the flames from the roof.

There is no doubt that savage street fighting took place in Wuhan, but there is some doubt about the nature of the contending forces. Rifles and machine guns are never mentioned; and it is unlikely that axes, spears, and pitchforks were the customary weapons of the Red Army in Wuhan. It would seem likely that Chen Tsai-tao encouraged the peasants to fight the Red Guards, reserving the "Million Heroic Troops" for the inevitable confrontation with the troops of Mao Tse-tung. In this way he could claim that he was not responsible for the destruction of the Red Guards, who had perished in a peasant uprising.

It was a strange war, and except for the fact that there was heavy fighting in June and July very little definite information came out of China. A brief and bloody uprising occurred in Kirin, but there appears to have been no co-ordination between the commanders of the two revolts. There was widespread looting in Kirin, the military headquarters were successfully attacked, and the leaders of the revolt professed to be Red Guards obeying the orders of Mao Tse-tung.

In the early summer of 1968 the *Cultural Revolution Bulletin,* published in Canton, reported that Mao Tse-tung, Lin Piao, and Chou En-lai were actually in Wuhan during the uprising and had narrowly escaped arrest. They were said to have arrived in Wuhan on July 19, two days after the "black day" which saw the massacre of the Red Guards, and to have set up their headquarters in the local military command post. When soldiers belonging to the "Million Heroic Troops" attacked the post in the early hours of July 21, they learned that Mao Tse-tung had left only twenty minutes before the building was captured. They failed to find his hiding place, and he returned safely to Peking.

Such was the story published by the *Cultural Revolution Bulletin,* and there are good reasons for believing that it was at least partially true. Vague references to Mao Tse-tung's presence in Wuhan had appeared in the Peking wall newspapers, and it was generally believed that Chen Tsai-tao's "Million Heroic Troops," not yet possessing a revolutionary program of their own and not yet organized into a well-trained army, had acted too precipitately. According to the *Cultural Revolution Bulletin* Mao Tse-tung, with his accustomed brilliance, had devised a strategic plan for bringing the enemy to heel. The East China Fleet, carefully trained and organized under his instructions, steamed up the Yangtse and trained its guns on Wuhan, while paratroopers dropped on the city, fanning out in all directions and taking control of key installations. Ten ships and five hundred paratroopers were involved. Wuhan immediately surrendered, peace was restored to the city, and the "Million Heroic Troops" were disbanded, while Chen Tsai-tao was flown off to Peking to receive an appropriate punishment.

One may doubt that it happened exactly in this way; a vast city like Wuhan is not likely to be intimidated by ten small gunboats. What is much more likely is that there was a negotiated peace, with the "Million Heroic Troops" once more integrated into the Red Army and the Red Guards ordered to be more circumspect. If Mao Tse-tung had conquered Wuhan, the victory would have been trumpeted in all the newspapers. That nothing at all was said officially about the conquest suggests that there was no conquest.

The uprisings in Wuhan and Kirin came as a deep shock to the party leaders in Peking. For the first time it became apparent that clashes between the Red Guards and the Red Army might lead to civil war. All over the country there had been sporadic fighting, with some notably bloody conflicts in Shanghai and Canton. The monolithic structure of the Chinese Communist party had collapsed; the Red Guards, the Red Army, and the Red bureaucracy were pulling in different ways. The processes of disintegration were setting in, and only the appearance of a powerful and challenging new revolutionary leader could put an end to the disintegration. While Mao Tse-tung remained alive, it was unlikely that such a leader would be permitted to arise.

For a little while longer Mao Tse-tung would remain the heroic leader, worshiped by the faithful and adored by the multitudes who waved their little red books and solemnly believed that the *Sayings of Mao Tse-tung* offered suitable answers to all the problems of life and revolution; but time was running out. Mao had launched the Red Guards in order to perpetuate his rule, but they had failed to produce the revolution he desired. Sooner or later he would be forced to the conclusion that he was too old to lead and that his judgment was failing. He could speak only in hoarse whispers and walk only with the assistance of a nurse; his appearances in public were rare, and would become rarer; he was entering a shadowy world where there were no clear demarcations between power and powerlessness. Old age, which is always a heavy burden, falls especially heavily on dictators.

Meanwhile, like a man who is so accustomed to wielding power that he cannot tolerate the thought of losing it, he continued to exert his influence from the shadows. From time to time new tablets of the law would be handed down, there would be further embellishments of the doctrine, and new strategies for dealing with the ever present contradictions of Communism would be invented. His task was to print his doctrines so firmly on the country that they would never be erased, yet he sometimes seemed to realize that his influence would not survive him. His infallibility would end with his death, and though some of his doctrines would survive him, many would be changed. Over China there lay the shadow of a coming death.

During the 1950's we could see the gradual decline of a mind which was once keen and malleable, uncompromising only in essentials, capable of sudden compromise and vivid improvisations. By the beginning of the 1960's the mind had become closed to all outside ideas, and Mao was incapable of being influenced by any of his followers, or even by the course of events. He had become deified, and suffered the fate of all those who permit themselves to be regarded as gods. He was that remote and solitary figure who lived somewhere in the Western Hills outside Peking, and who appeared irregularly and infrequently to receive foreign dignitaries. He had lost contact with his own people, and seemed to be uninterested in their fate. All he demanded of them was that they devote their whole lives to obeying his precepts.

It was a strange and terrifying decline, for it involved the fate of hundreds of millions of people who could not escape, even if they wanted to, from the machine he had brought into being. The Chinese Communist party reached down into the remotest village, the furthest outpost of the Communist empire, and every day, week after week and year after year, Chinese of all ages were commanded to read, study, and explore the writings of Mao Tse-tung. No other Chinese authority need be read; salvation could be obtained only by reading the works of the Master, which were published in millions of copies and continually revised, with the result that speeches made twenty years ago would find themselves suddenly ornamented with ideas which had come into being long after he had assumed power. History was falsified in a manner which was breathtakingly simple; but these continual revisions, far from simplifying history, only made it more complicated.

Mao's decline probably dated from the moment he took power. He had none of the talents of an executive; paperwork bothered him; new faces troubled him; and he regarded the young with impatience, dislike, and indifference. The men who had taken part in the Long March continued to be his closest associates, and in his eyes they alone were reliable and trustworthy. He made friendships with difficulty, not so much because he distrusted people as because he demanded implicit obedience to his own arguments and the give-and-take of ordinary conversation had no pleasures for him. Long before he became the unchallenged ruler of Red China, he spoke as an emperor; and the habit continued.

After he took power he was faced with problems which were not always susceptible to his commands. His relations with Russia, however friendly they appeared to be in the early days after he had assumed power, were never close. Though the official communiqués spoke of an absolute identity of interests, their interests even in 1949 were conflicting. From the beginning Mao Tse-tung was wary of Stalin, who treated him with good-natured casualness, as an elderly uncle treats a promising nephew. It was not a role which Mao Tse-tung was inclined to play with any zest. They had little enough in common: the jovial Georgian, fond of his liquor, collapsing into the last stages of paranoia, and the scholarly and abstemious Hunanese, who was not yet hardened by power. Moreover, Mao Tse-tung was scarcely in a position to forget that Stalin had more than once attempted to remove him from the leadership of the Chinese Communist party. The recent blasts of the Chinese Communists against the leaders of the Soviet Union have a naked urgency which can only be explained by a sense of frustration so great that it can scarcely be borne. The raw hate rises from a xenophobic base, and is propelled with psychotic force. But it is important to observe that this hatred of Russia has its roots in the nineteenth century, and that Mao Tse-tung's scorn of Stalin, and still greater scorn for Stalin's successors, has its roots in the distant past.

Fundamentally lazy, Mao Tse-tung never made any attempt to come to grips with the histories of other countries, and knows very little about the forces that move them. In his office there were never any maps of the world; there was only China. He saw few foreigners, and with rare exceptions they were dedicated Communists who shared his belief in his own mission. Determined on world revolution, he sent his agents into South America, Africa, Cuba, and Indonesia; at vast expense the revolutionary seeds were planted on fertile ground; and there was so small a harvest that a man less ridden by dogma might have pulled up stakes and announced that "Chinese Communism in one country" was more than enough. The habits of conspiracy were enduring ones, and led him to form a China-Indonesia axis, with President Sukarno acting as the obliging servant of a greater power. It was expected that all of southeast Asia would be caught in a vise, with China and Indonesia acting together as the crunching levers. But neither Mao Tse-tung nor Sukarno had any close understanding of the temper of the Indonesian people; and the last months of 1965 saw a massacre of Communists on a scale which history has never previously recorded. There, on the tropical islands which he had never visited, Mao Tse-tung suffered his greatest defeat.

There were other defeats—so many that they were past counting. As he grew older Mao Tse-tung became uncomfortably aware that the bright promises were not being fulfilled, that the age of Communist peace was receding further and further into the future, and that all the great forward leaps were no more than hesitant footsteps over uncertain ground. Yet there was no New Economic Policy, no blueprint for a more tolerable society. The dogma remained, and the law continued to be handed down. He seemed content that it should be so. As long as he lived, he would insist on the rightness of the course he had mapped out, and until his last breath he would not let power slip from his hands.

Now old and obviously ill, walking with shuffling steps, sometimes losing the train of his thought and falling into prolonged silences, he still rules China with an iron hand. In spite of reverses he has raised China to its greatest power, and he still envisages a time when all the nations of the earth will follow the path he has opened out for them. It is unlikely that they will listen to him, for the tide is turning.

For many more years China will present a threat to the world. The Chinese people possess formidable talents, and they are never more dangerous than when harnessed to a pitiless dictatorship. But when Mao Tse-tung dies, the dictatorship must necessarily die with him, for he alone among the Chinese Communists possessed the charismatic power to induce the entire population to follow him blindly. No doubt another dictatorship will be formed, but it will lack the authority which is vested in his person and in his name, for he was the sole ruler, the single emperor, and there is no one who can replace him.

Chronological Table

1850–65 Taiping Rebellion.

1853 Yen Fu born.

1858 K'ang Yu-wei born.

1866 Sun Yat-sen born.

1893 Mao Tse-tung born.

1894 Sino-Japanese war begins.

1895 Sun Yat-sen organizes his first insurrection.

1900 Boxer uprising. Sun Yat-sen's second insurrection.

1906 Hwang Hsing's second uprising in Hunan.

1910 Ninth unsuccessful revolt organized by Kuomintang at Canton.

1911 October 10. The revolution breaks out at Wuchang.

1915 Yuan Shih-k'ai accepts the Twenty-One Demands presented by Japan.

1917 Sun Yat-sen elected generalissimo of military junta in Canton.

1919 May 4. Student revolt breaks out.

1920 Civil war in Kwangtung between the armies of Sun Yat-sen and Ch'en Chiung-ming.
September. Congress of Oriental Nations held at Baku.

1921 June 30. The First Congress of the Chinese Communist party held in Shanghai.

1922 May 6. Sun Yat-sen resumes northern punitive expedition. The first All-China Labor Congress, and the First Congress of the China Socialist Youth League held in Canton in May.
The Second Congress of the Chinese Communist party held at Hangchow, in July.

1923   February Seventh Incident—39 workmen in Wuchan,
Chengchow, and Changshintien killed, by orders of
Marshal Wu P'ei-fu, while on strike. Third Congress
of the Chinese Communist party held in Canton, in
June, authorizing co-operation between the
Communists and the Kuomintang. During the summer
Chiang Kai-shek sent to Moscow by Sun Yat-sen.
November. Reorganization of the Kuomintang.

1924   January 20–30. First National Congress of the
Kuomintang. Complete reorganization of party, the
Communists being permitted to become members.
June 16. Whampoa Military Academy opened near
Canton.
In September civil war breaks out between Chekiang
and Kiangsu, to be followed in October by another civil
war between the Fengtien and Chihli factions.
October 15. Revolt of the Merchant Volunteers in
Canton suppressed.
October 18. Sun Yat-sen launches unsuccessful northern
expedition.
November. Chinese Communist party, in *The Fourth
Statement on the Present Position*, urges convocation
of a National Assembly in Peking, in agreement with
Sun Yat-sen.

1925   January 22. The Fourth Congress of the Chinese
Communist party meets in Shanghai; speedy
convocation of a National Assembly is urged.
March 12. Sun Yat-sen dies.
May 30. Workers in Shanghai fired upon by Sikhs
under British command, causing a wave of strikes and
protests against foreign influence.

1926   July 9. Beginning of the northern expedition against
warlords. Hunan, Hupeh, Kiangsi, Anhwei and Kiangsu
occupied within three months.
November 10. Formation of the Wuhan government.

1927   March 22. Capture of Shanghai by workers led by
Communists in three separate uprisings.
April 12. Formation of Nanking government. Massacre
in Shanghai.
May. Fifth Congress of the Chinese Communist party
meets in Wuhan.
May 21. Hsü K'o-hsiang orders massacre at Changsha.

Chiang Kai-shek orders destruction of peasant and workers unions.

July. Borodin leaves for Moscow.

August 1. Nanchang uprising, following the "split" between the Chinese Communists and the Kuomintang.

August 7. Chen Tu-hsiu deposed at a secret meeting of the Central Committee of the Chinese Communist party.

August 17. First Chinese soviet organized at Hailofeng.

September 12. Autumn Harvest Uprising organized by Mao Tse-tung in Hunan.

October. Mao leads three regiments to Chingkanshan, and holes in for the winter.

December 11. Canton commune. Canton held by the Communists for three days.

1928   January 1. Uprising in southern Hunan led by Chu Teh.

February 29. Hailofeng Soviet destroyed.

May. Arrival of Chu Teh at Chingkanshan.

July. P'eng Teh-huai leads a revolt in Pingkiang, joins Mao at Chingkanshan.

July-August. Sixth Congress of the Chinese Communist party, held in a suburb of Moscow.

1929   April. Chiang Kai-shek finally wins the struggle for power between himself and the Kwangsi militarists.

August. Kian uprising led by Lo Ping-hui.

December. Military conference at Kutien; Mao formulates the basic principles of guerrilla warfare.

1930   July 27. P'eng Teh-huai captures Changsha.

June. Li Li-san advocates attacks on Wuhan and Changsha.

December-January. First Annihilation Campaign.

1931   May-June. Second Annihilation Campaign.

July-October. Third Annilation Campaign.

November 7. First All-China Soviet Congress held at Juichin. Mao Tse-tung elected party chairman.

September 18. Mukden Incident.

December 14. Uprising in Ningtu.

1933   April-October. Fourth Annihilation Campaign.

May. Formation of Tungkiang-Nanchang-Pachou Soviet.

October. Beginning of Fifth Annihilation Campaign.

1934   January 22. Second All-China Soviet Congress held at Juichin.
October 16. First Front Red Army begins the Long March.

1935   January 4. Conference held in Tsunyi, Kweichow, leading to new developments in strategy.
May 30. Crossing of Tatu River.
June. The First Front Red Army contacts the Fourth Front Red Army under Hsu Hsiang-ch'ien at Tawei, Szechuan.

1936   July-October. The various Red armies drive through Sikang and Kansu to northern Shensi.
December 12. Chiang Kai-shek arrested by Chang Hsueh-liang.

1937   February. Battle between the Mohammedans and the Fourth Front Red Army.
July 7. Japan invades North China.
July-October. Elections in Soviet territory, followed by establishment of the Shensi-Kansu-Ningsia Border government.
August. Communist armies invade Shansi.
September 22. End of the ten-year-old civil war, establishment of the united front, and reorganization of the Red armies as the Eighth Route Army.
September 24. Lin Piao's victory at Pinghsinkuan.

1938   February. Red Army guerrillas in Central China reorganized as Fourth Route Army.
Mao Tse-tung's *On a Prolonged War* and *The New Stage* published.
March. Wang Ching-wei forms puppet government in Nanking.

1939   December 15. Mao Tse-tung's *The Chinese Revolution and the Communist Party of China* published.

1940   January 19. Mao Tse-tung's *The New Democracy* published.
August 20-December 5. Hundred-Regiment Campaign launched against the Japanese.

1941   January 7. New Fourth Army Incident.
February. Publication of Mao Tse-tung's *The Strategic Problems of China's Revolutionary Wars*.
December 7. Attack on Singapore and Pearl Harbor.

1945 April 24. Mao Tse-tung delivers a report "On Coalition Government" before the Seventh Congress of the Chinese Communist party.
August 10. Japanese government accepts terms of surrender.
August 28. Mao Tse-tung flies to Chungking.

1946 January 10. Truce orders issued by the Military Executive Headquarters based on Peiping.
July. Assassination of Wen Yi-tuo and Li Kung-po.
December 28. Denunciation by the Chinese Communist party of the Kuomintang constitution.

1947 March 19. Kuomintang troops occupy Yenan.

July. The Eighth Route Army crosses the Yellow River.
October 10. Chinese Communist party issues the Basic Program of Chinese Agrarian Law.
December 25. Mao Tse-tung reports that the revolutionary war has changed from defensive to offensive.

1948 April 1. Mao Tse-tung delivers a speech on agrarian policy before a meeting of party members of the Shansi-Suiyuan Liberated Area.
April 21. Yenan recaptured.
November. Winter offensive in Manchuria comes to an end.

1949 January 10. Hsuchow-Pengpu campaign comes to an end.
January 31. Peiping occupied by Chinese Communists.
March 25. Mao Tse-tung enters Peiping.
April 21. Mao Tse-tung and Chu Teh issue orders to Communist troops to cross the Yangtse.
April 23. Nanking and Taiyuan captured.
May 3. Hangchow captured.
May 22. Nanchang captured.
May 27. Shanghai captured.
June 2. Tsingtao captured.
August 7. Fuchow captured.
August 26. Lanchow captured.
September 30. Mao elected chairman of the Central People's government.
October 1. Proclamation of the People's Republic of China by Mao Tse-tung in Peking.
November 15. Kweiyang captured.

November 22. Kweilin captured.
November 30. Chungking captured.
December 16. Mao visits Moscow.
December 27. Chengtu captured.

1950   February. Mao returns from Moscow.
June 6. Mao issues a general report on the Chinese situation.
June 24. Outbreak of Korean war.
October. U.N. troops cross 38th Parallel.
Autumn. Big drive against counter-revolutionaries.
November. Chinese troops enter Korea.

1951   March. Mao Tse-tung ill. Government temporarily handed over to Liu Shao-ch'i.
May. Chinese troops enter Tibet.

1952   January. Mao Tse-tung launches "Three Anti Campaign."
December. First Five Year Plan.

1954-5 Mao Tse-tung ill for six months.
Summer. "Anti-Hu Feng" campaign.
July. Mao Tse-tung orders collectivization of farms.
September. Ten new Marshals appointed.

1956   May. Mao Tse-tung swims the Yangtse river from Hanyang to Wuchang.
Summer. Mao Tse-tung swims the river twice.

1957   May. Rectification Campaign begins.
June. Mao Tse-tung delivers speech "On the Correct Handling of Contradictions Among the People."
November. Mao Tse-tung pays a second visit to Moscow.

1958   April. First model commune, called "Sputnik."
July. Khrushchev visits Peking.
August. Peoples' Communes ordered on nation-wide scale.

1959   March. Flight of Dalai Lama from Tibet.
April. Liu Shao-ch'i succeeds Mao Tse-tung as Chief of State. Mao retains his position as Chairman of the Chinese Communist party.

1960   Crop failures. Chinese Communism losing ground.

1960   Break with Soviet Union becomes more open.
Between May and September thousands of Russian technicians withdrawn from China.

1962   November. Chinese attack India, and withdraw suddenly.

1964   October. First Chinese A-bomb tested in Sinkiang.

1965   Lin Piao emerges as Mao's heir apparent. Autumn. Destruction of the Communist Party in Indonesia.

1966   February. Chiang Ching sent to Shanghai on propaganda mission.
       July. Mao swims in the Yangtse.
       August. Mao writes his "big-character" poster. The Red Guard movement is formed.

1967   Mao takes part in May Day procession for the first time in eight years.
       June. First hydrogen bomb exploded.
       July. Revolt of Chen Tsai-tao in Wuhan, followed by brief revolt in Kirin.
       August. British embassy burned down.

1968   Sporadic revolts. The Red Guards in eclipse.

Bibliography

CLAIRE and WILLIAM BAND. *Two Years with the Chinese Communists*. New Haven: Yale University Press, 1948.

A. DOAK BARNETT. *Communist China and Asia*. New York: Harper, 1949.

JACK BELDEN. *China Shakes the World*. New York: Harper, 1949.

CONRAD BRANDT, (editor). *A Documentary History of Chinese Communism*. London: George Allen & Unwin, 1952.

JEROME CH'EN. *Mao and the Chinese Revolution*. New York: Oxford University Press, 1965.

CHIANG WEN-HAN. *The Chinese Student Movement*. New York: King's Cross Press, 1948.

China Digest. (All issues.) Hongkong-Peking, 1947–1950.

China Handbook 1937–1945. New York, Macmillan, 1947.

CHOW CHING-WEN. *Ten Years of Storm*. New York: Holt, Rinehart & Winston, 1960.

DAVID J. DALLIN. *Soviet Russia and the Far East*. New Haven: Yale University Press, 1948.

TYLER DENNETT. *American in Eastern Asia*. New York: Barnes and Noble, 1941.

STUART GELDER. *The Chinese Communists*. London: Victor Gollancz, 1946.

HALDORE HANSON. *Humane Endeavor*. New York: Farrar & Rinehart, 1939.

EMI SIAO. *Khuananskaya Fleita (The Hunanese Flute)*. Moscow: Government Printing Press, 1940.

K. H. FAN (editor). *The Chinese Cultural Revolution: Selected Documents*. New York: Grove Press, 1968.

333

DAVID FLOYD. Mao against Krushchev. New York: Frederick A. Praeger, 1962.

HANS GRANQVIST. The Red Guard: A Report on Mao's Revolution. New York: Frederick A. Praeger, 1967.

E. R. HUGHES. The Invasion of China by the Western World. New York: Macmillan, 1938.

ARTHUR W. HUMMEL. Eminent Chinese of the Ch'ing Period. Washington, D.C.: U.S. Government Printing Office, 1943.

HAROLD ISAACS. The Tragedy of the Chinese Revolution. S. J. R. Saunders, 1938.

ELIZABETH KENDALL. A Wayfarer in China. Boston: Atlantic Monthly Press, 1913.

T. E. LAWRENCE. Seven Pillars of Wisdom. New York: Doubleday, 1938.

HENRY MCALEAVY. The Modern History of China. New York: Frederick A. Praeger, 1967.

CHARLES B. MCLANE. Soviet Policy and the Chinese Communists. New York: Columbia University Press, 1958.

KLAUS MEHNERT. Peking and Moscow. New York: G. P. Putnam's Sons, 1963.

ROBERT C. NORTH. Moscow and Chinese Communists. Stanford, Stanford University Press, 1963.

EDGAR O'BALLANCE. The Red Army of China. New York: Frederick A. Praeger, 1963.

GEORGE PALOCZI-HORVATH. Mao Tse-tung: Emperor of the Blue Ants. New York: Doubleday, 1963.

P'ENG TEH-HUAI. Unity and Defense in North China. Chungking: New China Information Committee, 1940.

M. N. ROY. My Experience in China. Calcutta: Privately printed, 1945.

JOHN E. RUE. Mao Tse-tung in Opposition 1927–1935. Stanford, Stanford University Press, 1966.

STUART SCHRAM. Mao Tse-tung. Harmondsworth: Penguin Books, 1966.

SIAO YU. Mao Tse-tung and I Were Beggars. Syracuse: Syracuse University Press, 1959.

VERA SIMONE (editor). *China in Revolution: History, Documents, and Analyses*. Greenwich: Fawcett Publications, 1968.

AGNES SMEDLEY. *Red China Marches*. New York: Vanguard Press, 1934.

————. *The Great Road: The Life and Times of Chu Teh*. New York: Monthly Review Press, 1956.

EDGAR SNOW. *Red Star over China*. New York: Random House, 1937.

GUNTHER STEIN. *The Challenge of Red China*. New York: McGraw-Hill, 1945.

PETER S. H. TANG. *Communist China Today*. New York: Frederick A. Praeger, 1957.

TENG SSU-YU. *New Light on the History of the Taiping Rebellion*. Cambridge: Institute of Pacific Affairs, 1950.

TSOU LOU. *Reminiscences*. Chungking: Government Printing Office, 1943.

NYM WALES. *Inside Red China*. New York: Doubleday, 1939.

————. *Red Dust: Autobiographies of Chinese Communists*. Stanford: Stanford University Press, 1952.

TSI C. WANG. *The Youth Movement in China*. New York: New Republic, 1927.

VICTOR A. YAKHONTOFF. *The Chinese Soviets*. New York: Coward-McCann, 1934.

The sources of the translations of the more important documents by Mao Tse-tung are:

The speeches delivered during the Kiangsi period are based on translations from Victor A. Yakhontoff, *The Chinese Soviets*, who obtained the documents from Miss Agnes Smedley.

The translation from *On a Prolonged War* I owe to the great kindness of Mr. L. A. Rossinger, of the Institute of Pacific Relations.

The translations from *Coalition Government* are based on the English mimeographed version published in Yenan, checked against the version given by Stuart Gelder, *The Chinese Communists*.

Complete translations of *The Strategic Problems of China's Revolutionary Wars* and *The Chinese Revolutions and the Communist Party of China* are given in *China Digest*.

The translations from *The New Democracy* are based on the official version published by the U.S. State Department.

Our Task in 1945 is taken from the mimeographed version published in Yenan in 1945.

Index

337